THE SOCIAL CONTEXT
OF MODERN
ENGLISH LITERATURE

————————

MALCOLM BRADBURY

OXFORD · BASIL BLACKWELL

Printed in Great Britain by
Western Printing Services Ltd., Bristol
and bound by the Kemp Hall Bindery, Oxford

Yet a culture survives principally, I think, by the power of its institutions to bind and loose men in the conduct of their affairs with reasons which sink so deep into the self that they become commonly and implicitly understood—with that understanding of which explicit belief and precise knowledge of externals would show outwardly like the tip of an iceberg. Spiritualizers of religion (and precisians of science) failed to take into account the degree of intimacy with which this comprehensive interior understanding was cognate with historic institutions, binding even the ignorants of a culture to a great chain of meaning.

Philip Rieff, *The Triumph of the Therapeutic* (1966)

Contents

CONTENTS

Acknowledgements

In writing this book I have acquired many debts. The first and greatest is to Bryan Wilson, who not only proposed the venture but has stimulated it by working with me on several articles and a more general book-in-progress on the topic of *Literature and Sociology*. I am also very much indebted to Professor Richard Hoggart, whose kindness, and whose Centre for Contemporary Cultural Studies at the University of Birmingham, did a great deal to develop my interest in this area. Since then I have acquired other debts at the University of East Anglia, both generally, to its inter-disciplinary climate, and specifically, to my fellow-teachers and students in the Joint History/Literature course in the period 1874–1914 and in the course on 'Literature and Sociology'. I have benefited very much from conversations with Jonathan Raban, Dr Geoffrey Searle, Professor John Jackson, Dr R. Shannon, R. B. Woodings and Professor J. W. MacFarlane. Professor Elting E. Morison and Professor Lawrence W. Levine read parts of the book and commented very valuably on them; so did Peter Conradi. I am also grateful to the University of East Anglia for secretarial assistance from Miss Frances Austin and for the sabbatical term in which this book was finished. Especially I am grateful to All Souls College, Oxford, who awarded me a Visiting Fellowship and enabled its completion not only in the most stimulating, but in the most happy, circumstances.

Some of these themes I have explored previously in articles and broadcast talks, on which I have drawn from time to time: 'The Idea of a Literary Elite', *Critical Quarterly*, II, 3 (Autumn 1960), 233–8; 'The Intellectual Review in England', *Texas Quarterly*, IV, 3 (Winter, 1962); 'The Taste for Anarchy' and 'Literary Culture in England Today', *Listener*, LXVII, 1717

(February 22, 1962) and LXVIII, 1741 (August 9, 1962); 'Uncertainties of the British Intellectual' ('Intellectuals of the World', No. 1), *New Society*, 117 (December 24, 1964); and 'The Writer's Profession Today', *New Society*, 135 (April 29, 1965). I have also drawn on my 'Sociology and Literary Studies II: Romance and Reality in *Maggie*', *Journal of American Studies*, III, 1 (July 1969), pp. 111–21, and 'Literature and Sociology', *Essays and Studies 1970* (London, 1970). My interest in modernism is also extended into two recent essays, 'The Novel in the 1920s' in *The Sphere History of Literature in the English Language, Vol. VII, The Twentieth Century* (ed. Bernard Bergonzi) (London and New York, 1970) and 'The Novel Since 1945' in *The Twentieth-Century Mind*, Vol. III (ed. C. B. Cox and A. E. Dyson) (London, forthcoming).

MALCOLM BRADBURY
University of East Anglia

Preface

This book exists in the middle ground between literary study, sociology, and intellectual history, in an area that has come to be called 'cultural studies'. The area requires a word of explanation. Literature does not normally play an important part in the sociological interpretation of society; and, likewise, one of the familiar tenets of modern literary study is that the business of criciticism is not with context but text—the text of this poem, this novel, this play, looked at in and for itself. But literature *is* a social product, and can properly be studied as such. And literary study, sociology and history do have a common meeting-place; they are all centrally concerned with the study of culture—even though, as we shall see, the word 'culture' often means very different things to them. This interest is not a new one; indeed it is only as a result of the increasing specialization of the different subjects in schools and universities that the topic has today to be recreated by a conscious and deliberate effort. It is, for instance, a fairly recent thing to think of literature as a distinct and special human activity, or to suppose that the techniques of reading are so difficult that they need to be taught at university level. Most literature in the past has been considered as an essential part of the experience of a society—a way of dramatizing its myths, ordering its insights and sensibility, celebrating its values. But equally, from the very beginnings of formal literary criticism in Plato and Aristotle, there has been an awareness of literature's fictiveness, its numinous or universalizing power, its strange ways of transcending the environment from which it derives. As a result those concerned with illuminating and exploring literature, both as writers and as critics, have tended to see it not only as a socially explicable matter but also as something autonomous and integral in itself, potentially violated if the wrong sort of approach, the wrong sort of knowledge, is applied to it. Hence a long-term critical quarrel has grown up between those who have put stress upon the autonomy of art, and those who have sought to see it as social expression. That quarrel is there in modern literary criticism. Twentieth-century critical writing, deeply influenced by modernist or neo-symbolist aesthetics, has had much to say about the 'intrinsic' existence of a work of literature, its purity as a once-and-for-all order and as an integrated whole. But, inevitably in an age as politicized as our own, there has been a wealth of enquiry about the kind of social existence literature, in its sophisticated modern forms, can be said to have. And then again there has been, among creative writers themselves, a similar quarrel about the nature of a literary devotion—is it a devotion to art as such, or a devotion (often vulgarized as 'commitment') to the moral and social power of literature to form culture and affect human awareness, and to speak both for and to the body politic?

We ought, then, to begin by reminding ourselves that a concern with the context of literature is not new; it has always, in its different ways, been a matter of concern to the creators themselves, and has played an important part in that discussion of literature which today we formalize as 'literary criticism'. The modern critic is a very specialized variant of that more general phenomenon we used to call 'the man of letters'; so is the sociologist a specialized version of the social thinkers of the past. The 'balkanization' of knowledge and culture is one of the concerns of this book, and it is as apparent in men's ways of viewing things as it is in the things that they view. But the important point is that our modern specialism has made much more difficult contacts and assumptions that were once very much alive in past thought about literature. Today we have to think in terms not only of the relations between literature and society but in terms of those between literary study and sociology. And this has made certain basic and familiar truths—for instance, that literature is incomprehensible without some real sense of society, whether of our own time or that in which it was written;

or, more daringly, that 'without the literary witness the student of
society will be blind to the fullness of a society's life'[1]—more
difficult to comprehend and to develop. To that we need to add the
fact that modern literature is particularly sophisticated and complex, and at least part of its complexity derives from the difficult
and oblique relationship its authors and its works have formed
with modern society. All of these things make the fairly direct
associations that might have been assumed in the past between
literature and social life—for instance, that literature is an
expression and a structuring of social beliefs; or that (as some
realist writers have assumed) it is a direct imitation of the social
life of the times—into difficult and doubtful ideas.

None the less, the inescapable fact remains: literature is an
aspect of society. It coheres, structures and illuminates many of
its most profound meanings. It is, in a particular sense, an institution of society, an inheritance of artistic practices and values, a
point of formal interaction where writers and audiences meet,
a means of social communication and involvement, and a manifest expression of our curiosity and our imagination.[2] As we read
it, we are inescapably directed towards the life it deals with and
illuminates, to the characters and their social experience that it
evokes, to the sense of lived and felt experience on which it
deeply depends. Of course we are aware of the profound importance of its formal or aesthetic satisfactions; yet even these
things involve satisfactions more than formal, as we recognize
in these structures of metaphor and plot, of symbol and design,
an intense ordering of meaningful sequences in the human
consciousness. Likewise, while literary creativity is in one respect
a highly personal and individual enterprise, a bringing to light of
illuminations that are inwardly and deeply felt by a writer whose
separate, self-dramatized existence is something we appreciate

---

[1] Richard Hoggart, 'Literature and Society', in *Speaking to Each Other*, Vol. II
(London, 1970).
[2] An institution not in the strict sociological sense. It lacks the firm structuring of institutions like family, law, religion, education. But it is a formalized
feature of society, drawing on such social arrangements as magazines, books
and theatres; and it contains strong elements of myth and ritual. But if it is an
institution, it typically rejects routine institutionalization.

and regard, it is also a forming outward, an act of communication through an instrument—language—itself socially created and used. The result is that literary discussion by necessity gets pressed beyond consideration of the text or the writer into matters that are intrinsically social ones. Moreover, as I have said, the social existence of literature is remarkably complex, and its analysis involves a wide variety of different topics and emphases. Writing is the dramatic enactment of characters in social situations. The writer's tone and evaluation in his work is an ordering that bears close relation to contemporary ideas, attitudes and mental casts, and to the copied tones and gestures of the society. Language is a changing social usage. Writers too are social beings, both as men and as members of their profession; they are influenced by the social meaning we grant them, the opportunities they are permitted, the kinds of relationship they can create with particular groups of their fellows, whether these are small coteries or large and general audiences. And books and theatres are social institutions, media of communication and ritual in the society. And, altogether, these matters—the way literature engages with the common experience of life, the way it reflects and affects values, the way it structures, mythicizes and dramatizes, the way it explores internally, through language and structure, its own place in the changing community—all constitute an important part of our critical sense of what constitutes a literary medium, and literary merit.

But, as I have said, it is one thing for us to understand this, and another for us to be good at talking about it. In one way or another our writers and critics always have talked about it. But they have done so in very varied ways. There are, indeed, two main traditions which are worth disentangling. The first of these derives from those writers and critics who, assuming that the literary imagination has a singular power to intervene in society, to call it to its best ends, to express its finest values and concerns, to offer a 'criticism of life', have stressed the power of great art to know and interpret the world and also to act as an humane influence in it. This view runs deep in the tradition of the English 'cultural debate' that Raymond Williams has explored

and described so well in *Culture and Society* (London, 1958), a
tradition in England that derives largely from the romantic poets,
and notably Coleridge, and runs through Matthew Arnold and
William Morris to modern-day critics like T. S. Eliot, F. R.
Leavis and more latterly Richard Hoggart and Raymond Williams
himself. It has had echoes in other literary traditions too,[1]
though it clearly has something to do with the striking fact that
the English writer in the nineteenth century was uniquely able
to function somewhere near the centre of society and felt capable
of intervening in the direction it took. Broadly this tradition of
cultural thought asserts, if in various ways, that culture is a
creative achievement, and that literature consciously and con-
tinuously keeps alive the best values, preserves essential standards
of clarity and worth. The second of my two traditions derives
from a rather more objective view of literature, and is less
associated with practising writers than intellectuals and scholars.
It is concerned less with the causative and active force literature
has in society, and more with its nature as a social manifestation,
an expression *of* the society. Hence literature tends to be seen
as a conditioned thing shaped from particular resources, ideas
and materials in a specified society at a specified time, the powers
of great writing lying in their response to the essential forces at
work in the age and the social structure. This tradition has been
more American and European than English; the classic examples
would be writers like Madame de Staël, in her *De la littérature
considerée dans ses rapports avec les institutions sociales* (1800), or
de Tocqueville in his comments on the social situation of the
American writer in *Democracy in America* (2 vols, 1835: 1840),
or Hippolyte Taine, with his view that literature is the product
of race, milieu and moment, or V. L. Parrington's *Main Currents
in American Thought* (3 vols, 1927–30), which puts literary ideas
into the same context as religious, economic and political ones.
Its bias has been much more historicist and determinist, often
seeking to offer a scientific account of the character of a particular work, style, author or national tradition. It passes through

[1] For example, it undoubtedly influenced many of the American 'New
Critics' of the 1930s like Cleanth Brooks, Allen Tate and John Crowe Ransom.

B

into much Marxist and 'structuralist' critical discussion, and into the view that literature has an important part to play in the historical evolution of consciousness towards a more emancipated state, and that it both reflects and creates 'history' or 'reality'.[1] And it tends to regard 'culture' not so much as a great creative achievement as a particular body of social and economic arrangements, themselves classifiable according to some larger sociological, political or historical scheme. Indeed this tradition reaches towards being a sociology of literature.

Today it would be hard to profess oneself a critic with social interests without assimilating something from both traditions. Yet in some respects they are incompatible, and have different *a priori* assumptions about the nature of literature itself. The former tends to take literature's existence for granted, and look at its witness about society—its imaginative insight, its living representation of those things which sociology, psychology and other modes of learning themselves may seek to organize and and explore, but in more systematic, less imaginative and humanly whole terms. Obviously it is an oblique witness, not an imitation in the photographic sense, but itself life organized, with certain structures in it laid bare, social and moral worlds shown in their complex interaction, in terms determined, however, by the needs and logics internal to art. The latter tends to look at and analyse literature's very existence, and to find congruities between its mode of knowledge and the general structure of the total community. And if, for both viewpoints, a key-word is 'culture', then again the meanings diverge: the positive view of culture as a force of social illumination, cohesion and transformation that marks the work of Arnold, Eliot or Leavis has very different associations from the work of critics of more objectively socio-

---

[1] For examples of this type of criticism, the works of Georg Lukács (e.g. *The Historical Novel* (1937) or *Studies in European Realism* (1950)); of Jean-Paul Sartre (e.g. *What Is Literature?* (1948)); Christopher Caudwell, *Illusion and Reality* (1937); and more recently works by French 'structuralist' writers like Roland Barthes, *Writing Degree Zero* (1953) and Lucien Goldmann, *The Hidden God* (1955) and *Pour une sociologie du roman* (1964). (Dates here are those of first publication.) There is an excellent discussion of the 'sociological' tradition as applied to the novel in Harry Levin, *The Gates of Horn* (New York and London, 1963).

logical orientation, who tend to allow to literature a less causal
or influential role, and are apt to regard culture as a phenomenon
rather than an inward investment. The 'English' tradition—if
one may categorize it in this way—has never quite attained the
theoretical systematization of some of the European versions;
but its virtue has been a deeper involvement both with the individual vigour of particular works of literature, and with the idea
of culture as an elaborate complex of communal experience. It is
the living complex through which society lives best and best
knows itself; and it is known through an appreciation of the
individual and felt life of a society, from which and by which the
literature itself is fed. The 'European' tradition has taken a much
more phenomenological view both of culture and literature. It
has been a good deal less humanistic, and particularly in modern
times has involved itself deeply with theory and abstract comparative analysis, frequently offering a rational, detached view of
a society as the causative environment into which literature must
then be fitted. It thus has a different assessment of the power and
influence of the literary work and the literary intellectual; it
usually has different critical preferences, when it functions as
criticism; and it is often weak on empirical analysis and sympathy, qualities normally closely associated with good literary
criticism.

There can be no doubt that, if the critic today is to take the
social existence of literature as a matter for serious interest, he
must come to terms in some way with the theoretical, systematic
and objective study of society which has grown up over the last
two centuries, and become so crucial in our own. His own
profession of criticism has grown much more a profession and
a discipline. The same thing has happened to the study of society;
indeed sociology has undoubtedly acquired today something of
the same intellectual-synthetic function that the literary and
historical imaginations claimed in the last century. Hence the
critic interested in literature's social dimension will almost
inevitably reach to insights from other disciplines, and especially
to sociology.

Literature as a study has long been eclectic in its nature.

Scholars and critics have always found themselves to some extent dependent on insights from other subjects, and so in turning to sociology they are doing nothing strikingly unusual. Where the problems begin to show, however, is at the point where it becomes apparent that the essentially scientific emphasis and the relatively value-free approach of sociology prove a challenge to their own methods and perceptions. It is impossible for literary study to proceed as if the insights of sociology did not exist; it is also impossible for it to proceed as if these insights did not put severe pressure on some of the central assumptions of literary criticism, and above all on its commitment to value. The internally sympathetic and the externally objective forms of cultural analysis can never be totally compatible; the reasoning observer may reach towards being, but can never quite become, the sympathetic member of the culture he observes, for his rational-comparative method detaches him. The difficulties of marrying the two traditions of cultural study I have already mentioned become greatly increased when sociology is brought into the picture. In short, what often seem to be common interests frequently prove to be very different ones. The matter is complicated further by the fact that sociology has not on the whole shown a great interest in the study of literature, and has regarded it as little more than a reflective phenomenon. There has only been a small contribution from theoretical sociology, though it has been a significant one; and a rather larger one from that kind of intermediate study represented by political analysis of literature. If, as I suggested earlier, the literary approach to sociological or social matters can be roughly divided into two traditions, so can the sociological approach to literary matters. Apart from that kind of general 'cultured' reference of more urbane sociologists, particularly sociologists of knowledge like Karl Mannheim or more latterly Erving Goffman,[1] the two main lines of discussion have derived from those sociologists interested in

[1] See, for instance, Karl Mannheim, *Ideology and Utopia: An Introduction to the Sociology of Knowledge* (London, 1936), plus other works cited *passim* in my text; and Erving Goffman, *The Presentation of Self in Everyday Life* (New York, 1959; London, 1969).

literature as an effective source for examining the ideas and
actual lived life of a time—best exemplified in a book like Leo
Lowenthal's *Literature and the Image of Man* (Boston, 1957)—and
those interested in social communication, which normally means
the description and analysis of the various forms of mass-culture
or folk-culture as species of social expression and value-transmission.[1] But, despite the small part that literature has in most
sociological versions of society, the current state of discussion
and debate is lively, and a variety of approaches to the general
topic of 'literature and society' have grown up, particularly over
the last few years, and with the growing academic interest in
what are called 'inter-disciplinary studies' or 'area studies'.

Since there is a wide variety of approach, not only from
discipline to discipline but within each discipline, we can hardly
hope for a unified method of study. Not only is the meeting
ground between literary critics and sociologists often somewhat
treacherous—the similarity is more likely to lie in the raising
of like questions rather than in the provision of like answers—
but there is always a danger that, as the common ground gets
defined, the methods of study will be very loose indeed. A
further and more subtle danger is that the instrument of synthesis
becomes an overview derived from a third source—for instance,
from politics, and particularly the politics of the left. As we
have already seen, there has been an abundant contribution from
Marxist criticism—partly because Marxist thought has tended to
grant literature and ideas a larger place in society than has most
formal sociology.[2] What is more, the polemics and urgencies of
political thought can always unite easily with the polemicism of
literary criticism. The tendency for the cultural debate to move
leftward has in fact produced many profitable methods and

---

[1] This area of discussion is best seen in the collection of essays made by
Bernard Rosenberg and David Manning White, *Mass Culture: The Popular Arts
in America* (Glencoe, Ill., 1957).

[2] There is a fairly obvious reason for this; Marxism, as a political and revolutionary movement, is dependent on men changing their ideas, on the elimination of 'false consciousness' and the movement of thought towards 'reality'. The
intelligentsia, and those who carry the thought of the society, therefore have an
important part to play.

illuminations, but there is the obvious danger that the synthesis of the subject becomes one based on a reductive and advantage-seeking view of society, or on a 'committed' view of literature. But the most obvious danger of all such affiliations is that litera-ture comes to be regarded in too deterministic a way. Both sociological theory in general and Marxism in particular are, broadly speaking, 'determinist' in the sense that they account for attitudes and ideas in relation to deeper and abstract social processes; literature is a derivation from conditions over which the writer has little control and of which he has possibly only a nominal understanding. The sociological account of the impersonal forces involved is usually more complex, and sometimes more fragmentary, than in Marxism, which sees the 'substratum' as founded firmly on economic forces and conditions of production. But the broad effect is the same. And in the present climate, where in a rationalizing age literature has forgone some of its self-conscious humanism and literary study some of its positivism, it is easy for writers and critics to go too far in assent, to regard literature simply as a social manifestation or phenomenon, or else as an area inviting political polemics.

In summary: what we might say is this. Literature can be regarded as primarily an activity of mind, a creative and self-conscious enterprise—though one that is socially formed in the sense that the writer is part of the current of human thought, shares the language, attitudes and tones of voice of his fellows, and expresses values that come from a discernible context in a society, a nation, a period. And that is how literary critics tend first to regard it. But it is also possible to regard literature as being subject to much larger forces—as the iceberg top of deep mythologies archetypally present in man or at least in men in such a society at such a time. Perhaps what a sociological view-point will most invite is for us to see literature as an 'institution' —an institution around which traditions, customs and patterns of behaviour have clustered. Some of these traditions and patterns will be intrinsic to literature because it is literature and hence has enshrined its own methods, practices and species of experience, handed on as a stock from writer to writer and age to age. Other practices and styles belong to particular literary communities forming at particular times. About literature, we can ask questions to do with the social significance of works of art, by considering what sort of people read them, and what effect they have on them, not simply as individuals but as groups. We can consider how works of art focus prevailing values in society or sectors of society, or for that matter produce variant values derived from small specialized intelligentsias and bohemias. We can consider the way in which a society in a particular place at a particular time regards its writers, and what function it seems to ascribe to literary activity, and what practical consequences such things have in terms of the actual working conditions of writers, their sense of participating with others in a common end, the way in which they make, or have made for them, their channels of communication, and so on. In fact literature is used in society in a very complex variety of ways— some of it we employ humanistically, primarily for educational purposes or some more personally construed notion of betterment; some for dream and escape; some because it informs us about our world, or because it celebrates our cherished values. Not only do we as individuals use it for many different things, but its functions alter considerably from age to age or society to society. Literature does not remain the same thing in all periods and social orders, and the degree of variation is such as to arouse an inevitable interest in the shaping forces involved. But this need not be to say that it is totally belittled by its context; there is plentiful evidence to show that it frequently acquires forms of permanence transcending particular uses, particular aesthetics and environments. To see literature in this way raises all kinds of practical questions about the 'context' of literature, and helps make clearer the complex nature of the literary environment. It helps us therefore understand some of the various forces that impinge on the literary tradition, the nature of language, and the creative act itself.

In these terms, then, sociology becomes an enabling discipline allowing new insights and means to develop in literary study;

and that is how I have used it in this book. There is in these
matters a great danger in assuming that there is a social reality,
which is what the sociologist defines, and then a response to it in
literature. This is to mistake the fact that literature and sociology
are themselves both ways in which we shape and structure our
sense of what reality is. And though I have drawn upon sociological
concepts in this study, I have not thought of it as a sociological
work. Rather I have assumed that sociology and literature are
different ways of seeing the world. *Sociology* is a conceptual discipline devoted to the study of society with particular reference
to the institutions and structures in it. It studies not absolute
reality, but a delimited point of reference which it defines as its
subject-matter. *Literature* is a body usually of written (but also
orally or dramatically transmitted) works linked into a tradition
of practices and forms, which itself 'interprets' society. Of
course it may be studied by sociology; but in a sense it also
competes with it. It is of course a much more personal, subjective and imaginative way of knowing and it inwardly contains
its own methods and ends. Its language does not denote and
describe, as sociology's seeks to, but evokes and values, strategic-
ally using its inbuilt ambiguities not to give a neutral denotation
of the extant universe but to persuade men into a fictive or
verbally created universe. We would be mistaken to suppose
that we could transliterate the insights of literature into sociological terms; we would also be mistaken if we were to assume that
literature was in the position of gesturing towards realities which
the sociologist can state authoritatively. My basic assumption is
that there are certain things lettrists, historians and sociologists
can illuminate in common; and one of them is the idea of change
in sensibility or consciousness, that sort of change that comes to
men's lives, feelings, and ideas when society goes through a
phase of alteration. In history there are periods of marked shake-
up, when conscious ideas and unconscious ideologies, styles,
manners and social structures change under pressure. We can
give deterministic accounts of such turmoil, pointing out changes
in social or economic organization, pattern of life or national
fortune which affect human consciousness. But what this means

for human consciousness, what the quality of this experience is, is
not always something we are good at pursuing; and here literature
might help. Not because it is 'representative' of general feeling;
not because it gives accurate reports of historical events; but
because the complex intuitions of writers do (with whatever
idiosyncracy) involve them at such times in making new relationships with the language they use, the literary structures they
create, the readership they can secure, and their own sense of
function. It is no use going to literature for a report of the kind
of changes we can analyse with other disciplines. On the other
hand, we can draw on the illuminations and explorations of
particular creative experiences of the writer to enlarge our own
more formal modes of knowledge.

The 'shake-up', the change in consciousness, that this book
is concerned with is that that lies behind our own times. There
two important words, from two different disciplines, which we
associate with our age: one is modernization, which is a sociological notion, and the other is modernism, which is a literary
and artistic notion. This book seeks to put them into relation. It
will be recognized that the task is not easy. Modern western
literature is as complex and varied in methods, aesthetic assumptions and general human perspectives as any that has existed. It
is divided in complicated ways among different audiences, views
of art (from humanist to *avant garde* to pop), kinds of artist.
The great writers of the century, especially the literary revolu-
tionaries at its beginning (Lawrence, Joyce, Forster, Yeats,
Pound, Eliot, Conrad *et al.*), clearly responded to an infinitely
complex cultural and emotional situation, reacting in ways we
still find difficult to understand. In this they were part of a
broader movement that spread beyond England and affected
much of western literature; this book, though largely confined to
the English case, attempts throughout to keep it in that broader
perspective. Equally, the character of modern social change,
national and international, is of a similar order of sophistication.
The complexity both of the art and the social development means
that a 'contextual' approach raises greater problems than for
earlier periods, and this must impose a great sense of caution on

any analysis of the present kind. If we are to see the artistic complexity with a due sense that it *is* complex, then we need to recognize that this was a period of singular artistic and intellectual strain; indeed it is precisely the sense of strain and change that so much modern art makes manifest. In art, in thought, in society we can see the strain, the sense of cultural and historical watershed. 'Nearly all the students of the last years of the nineteenth century have sensed in some form or other a profound psychological change', notes H. Stuart Hughes in his book *Consciousness and Society*; and in the broader term we talk of the rise of 'modern consciousness'. The evidence everywhere is strong; and in the arts it is so strong that we postulate the emergence, somewhere at the end of the last century or the beginning of this, of a new era in the arts. We could of course take it as a development primarily appropriate *to* the arts, as Graham Hough does in his book *Image and Experience*: 'Literature, by a fortunate dispensation,' he says, 'does not reflect very accurately the convulsions of the social order.' This is true; accounts of social change and tension will not themselves explain the literature and they will certainly not, as Hough rightly stresses, explain the remarkable *quality* of the arts in this period. It is finally because writers of the power and greatness of Joyce, Conrad, James, Yeats and Eliot wrote in the turn-of-the-century climate that the matter is interesting. But they did not write in a cultural void; and though they made unique and great use of the opportunities, to some extent the opportunities and pressures were themselves the products of contemporary ferment of culture and consciousness. This, and the later developments through to the present, is my theme in this book.

This is then an exercise in the study of cultural change; an exploration of the coming of the modern as it affects literature and its environment. My particular concern is with the serious literature of the period, that we regard as richest and most individual; and my aim to grant the complexity of experience involved in any important, fully realized work of art. But I do assume that literature derives from society—from a tradition, a stock of language, a social frame, an offered sense of the realities

of life which is part of the meaning, literary *and* sociological, of
the word 'culture'—as well as being a structure of language or
the creative act of a single man. Hence the design of this book.
I have begun it by looking—perhaps, for the literary reader, a
bit abstractly—at the nature of modern social change: at how
modernization has changed (or not changed) our world, thought
and consciousness. My second section is about the impact of
change on the arts; and also art's own modes of *internal* change.
Here in particular I have looked at the rise of 'modernism', and
raised the question of whether we should regard it, as many
critics have, as *the* representative modern movement. The third
part is concerned with the contemporary situation of the writer
—his role and function, the nature of his profession, his training,
recruitment, and finance. My fourth, under the general title of
'Communications', considers cultural interaction in society
and cultural institutions: to be more precise, it is about the
changing literary audience and the changing media, with special
attention to the book. Section five discusses high and mass
culture; my conclusion then follows, suggesting the difficulties
of the contemporary writer and the arts he represents in an
egalitarian and inflationary environment. I have concentrated
on book-centred literature, which is to say basically fiction and
poetry; theatre has different social circumstances and requires a
different kind of analysis. My overall approach is both theoretical *and* documentary, and my overall hope to produce a
genuinely 'cultural' study.

Lockington, 1969

Introduction

Every so often, there occur in the arts certain severe upheavals which seem to affect all their products and radically change their temper. For some reason these are often closely associated with centuries: we can sense one such change that belongs to the eighteenth century, which we call 'Neo-Classicism'; another associated with the nineteenth, 'Romanticism'; and another associated with our own century for which we have no clear name but which we often regard as the most radical of all. There are, then, certain phases, often taking place over a relatively short period of time, when 'style' shifts and the structure of perception among artists significantly alters, and when the environment and prevailing assumptions of art are so radically recreated that it seems no longer to be witnessing to the same kind of world, or employing structure, material or language in the same way as before.

What is it that brings about such a change—a change so sharp as to be analogous to revolution in the social sphere? Is it, indeed, social change that produces it; or does it, perhaps, portend social change? Clearly it is in fact something that can happen without *any* corresponding change in the social structure, simply as a result of the internal and natural momentum of the arts, the inward dialectics of the medium and the debates of artists about their function, practice and aims. But actually it *is* something that is usually associated with significant alteration in the social sphere, though we are not likely to find provable causal connections between the two things. None the less, a change in the temper of the arts is usually associated with a change in the temper of society or some significant part of society, and in turn with a shifting in the pattern of social organization. This, in its turn, may well have consequences directly impinging on the artist—bringing in new sources of patronage, new stratifications in the audience, new methods of production, new social origins for those who are recognized as artists, new intellectual stimuli, or simply new ideas with which to see the world. And normally the broader and the narrower and more immediate changes will both affect the arts—not in the form of conditioned reflexes, necessary responses to external pressures, but as part of their sensitive role in the flowing and making of human thought and feeling itself.

Romanticism is a convenient illustration. Romanticism is to some extent a temper or a mood which we can see as a matter of general sensibility—a sensibility which began to emphasize certain attitudes and views of man over others. It is associated with libertarianism, a stress on feeling, a desire to emanicipate the emotions. But it also coincides with certain shifts in the working situation of the artist in many countries, the point of his full emergence from the patronage system to a liberal dependence on the open market. It is also associated with changing patterns of audience, and with the breakdown of a relatively unified reading public that shared a common literary language. The making of a new language, and the reassessment of man's place in the universe and the social system that both preceded and followed on from the French and American revolutions, are all part of its significance. So, in England and in some other countries, is the clear advent of industrialism and the new social dispositions and choices that were created by that. As a term of literary or artistic analysis, Romanticism in fact means an enormous number of different things. But it does suggest a certain broad change of style and feeling and a movement toward a new stylistic community deriving from a new artistic temper. There is an unmistakable upheaval behind it, and it is not only an aesthetic upheaval. Certainly it involves the making of a whole new field of aesthetic norms—which, of course, were very variously interpreted by different artists and different cultural communities (Romanticism is hardly quite the same thing in France, Germany, England and America)—with certain assumptions and styles in common that are markedly of their age and their environment. With a fair expertise in literature, we can date and attribute works to the period from stylistic evidence alone. And we recognize that somewhere in the late eighteenth century (though, again, dates will vary for different nations) the horizons did change. Within them great variety is possible, but they are not the same horizons, and form and language are no longer being used in the same way, as they were in the preceding period of neo-classical or Augustan art.[1]

At the end of the nineteenth century, in the literatures of the west, a somewhat similar change occurs. There is, as I have said, no convenient single word to describe the character of this modern style and consciousness in the arts, in the way that romanticism does suggest these things for the nineteenth century, particularly the earlier nineteenth century. But there is most certainly a similar phenomenon: and anyone who reads in modern literature must be aware of a radical qualitative difference between it and the literature of the mid-nineteenth century. Time, of course, changes everything, but there is more to it than that. For, once more, there is a marked upheaval, when the field of artistic action has changed, and the visible signs of this are apparent in the way language, structure and perception are used across the broad range of modern art. There are a number of semi-specialized words that call up the difference: T. S. Eliot and T. E. Hulme, for instance, pressed the word 'classicism', to suggest that the era of romanticism was over and a new era of controlled and impersonal art was at hand. But the convenient word is obviously *modernism*, though it must be used with caution. To use it to define the literature and art of our age broadens the meaning of the term beyond its more specialized sense as a particular tendency —towards *avant-gardism*, anti-representationalism, atonalism—in twentieth-century arts. The very imprecision of the term suggests in fact what is true: that the change of temper in this case is a good deal more varied and a good deal harder to define, both in its character and in its context. Again, there is an unmistakable

---

[1] A good specialized study of the aesthetic change involved is M. H. Abrams, *The Mirror and the Lamp: Romantic Theory and the Critical Tradition* (New York and London, 1953).

upheaval, but it took more varied forms, produced more varied results, and has seemed much more persistent and continuous. Indeed, a degree of continuous upheaval may well be one of the essential definitions of the 'modern' situation in the arts. In the case of England, the pattern has been somewhat different from that in other countries. None the less, there is, in the English writing of the close of the last century and the early years of this, a marked atmosphere of change, which will be a central topic of this book.

The upheaval takes many shapes, but at the centre of it is a fresh instinct towards literary radicalism, a considerable sense among artists of finding themselves in a context of aesthetic revolution. Many of the passions involved in this are very specifically aesthetic ones. They involve, in literature, a new phase of self-conscious analysis of theory and procedure, when the structural content and the linguistic nature of the work of literature were analysed afresh. At the same time, this involves a wealth of new 'content' in literature, a concern for the introduction of all kinds of new experience, social and psychological. To some extent, then, we might say that the developments are the result of the explosion of knowledge and the broader shifts in ideas which fairly obviously occur at about the same time, for instance in philosophy and psychology.[1] But there is also a manifest change going on in the whole area of human experience, with which the literary change is involved; the frame of social life, the nature of personal relations, are conspicuously altering and their alteration is becoming manifest in art. What is more, the artist himself is evidently finding himself in a new situation; his role and his audience are changing. All of this is apparent in a good deal of the literature of the late nineteenth and early twentieth-century years; and it goes on being apparent through literature up to the present day. And if it were not immediately apparent from the texts, we have plenty of supporting evidence from artists and writers themselves: in the form of a barrage

---

[1] Significantly the change coincides with the emergence of William James and Bergson in philosophy, Freud and Jung in psychology, and Pareto and Durkheim in sociology, as influential forces in thought.

of manifestos, movements and aesthetic assertions. From the Pre-Raphaelites through the Aesthetes and Decadents to the Georgians and Imagists in poetry; from the Naturalists and the Jamesian realists through to 'stream-of-consciousness' writers like James Joyce and Virginia Woolf in fiction, there runs a conscious sequence of assertions that claim new literary and artistic purposes. Of course not all writers belong to movements and not all writers are conspicuously experimental. But the implications of what the conspicuous experimenters are doing are likely to have importance for them, too; and in fact it is apparent enough that they too have the sense of working, necessarily, and by no means less *significantly*, within new structural frames and new modes of knowledge.

So signals of an important change in writing do become apparent in the literature of England from about 1880 forward. It seems different in tone and assumption from what went before—even though there are certain evident continuities. It seems, too, very recognizably associated with ways of perceiving and structuring experience that we ourselves regard as 'modern'. The note of modernity is clearer in some works than in others, in some writers more than others. But what is apparent is that writers start to find themselves differently placed from their predecessors, and a new spirit comes through—one that, in many respects, is part of the temper of writing from then until the present time. The question which follows is whether the upheaval has, in fact, any real social origin. It coincides, after all, with no marked social revolution in England; and many of the writers involved were so aesthetically self-conscious that it would be possible to argue that the main pressures on writers were primarily internal, part of the evolutionary development of literature as such. Literary critical discussion of modern writing has tended to emphasize this aspect, and there is much truth to it. But, as I have said, this sense of change runs through many writers who are not conspicuously experimentalist—writers like Hardy, Wells, Bennett, Shaw, Galsworthy. It is indeed true that experimentalism came and went; indeed the writers active from about 1930 onward have in fact been a good deal less experimental than their

c

forerunners. Yet the ideological and social bases of writing do change at this time—in ways so complete that it is impossible for even those writers who found experimentalism excessive and protested against it (as Wells and Bennett did) to deny it some significance in relation to their own work and vision.[1]

Indeed, however much we look back on the late Victorian and Edwardian periods as times of relative social stability, we cannot miss the forces for change running through them. For this was, after all, the period of late Victorian expansion when certain processes that had been taking place in English society for a century were becoming much more rapid and overt. We often place the climacteric at the First World War; but there are good reasons for putting it earlier. England had been undergoing urbanization for a long time; but by the late years of the nineteenth century the city was the basic population centre and the most familiar human environment. Industrialization was growing more and more rapid, too, and the factory was both a central place of work and the basic transformer of the human environment, as its products began to fill the landscape. It was now completely clear that industrial capitalism was the dominant, inescapable productive process and the structural base of the society. There was a clear challenge to the class basis of society; equally it was growing clearer that society was becoming more and more 'mass'. The writer could sense the new audiences growing in the community and see the evidence of their interests and their force in the new press and the new education. Nor did one need to write for the new newspapers and magazines to feel that one's alliance with the bourgeoisie was under question; socially, intellectually and imaginatively one was forced to sense the plurality of classes.[2] Roland Barthes in fact seeks to explain

[1] As we shall see, there has been a marked tendency in modern criticism to *underplay* the creative innovation of writers of this type. H. G. Wells, for instance, was consciously concerned with the creation of a new type of novel based on 'life' and 'change', as opposed to 'artifice' and 'omission', a novel of deliberate contingency based on the fluidity of the autobiographical narrator.

[2] Raymond Williams, in *The English Novel from Dickens to Lawrence* (London, 1970), sees many of these features affecting and profoundly changing English fiction in the late 1840s. 'The first industrial civilisation in the history of the

modern literature by proposing that in such a situation the writer
'now falls a prey to ambiguity, since his consciousness no longer
accounts for the whole of his condition', and he is forced either
to extend or to make ironic his ideology. He also suggests that
the modes of writing now begin to multiply as the culture becomes
stratified; and hence literary language ceases to be universal,
for increasing social expression from new classes produces a
plurality of languages.[1]

What is certainly apparent is that art now comes to seem much
more problematic. The new experiences, the new forces, the
new awarenesses in society start to leave past literary accountings
incomplete; they seem based on imperfect or historically dated
world-views. And the evidence of this was not only apparent to
the eye but in the very shifts in the context of the literary culture.
The social situation of the artist was changing in this much more
explicitly urban, industrial and massified society. His audience
was broadening and was coming to include whole new strata in
society, with very different reading-patterns; even the artist's
traditional recourse to the leisured middle-class audience was
disturbed by the influx of new men and new living-patterns in
that social sector. His publishing pattern was undergoing
alteration, his financial relation to his craft changing. His very
way of life was becoming different. He felt himself becoming

---

world had come to a critical and defining stage,' he argues; and this brought a
new creative discovery. 'It brought in new feelings, people, relationships;
rhythms newly known, discovered, articulated; defining the society, rather than
merely reflecting it; defining it in novels, which had each its own significant and
particular life.' But he too argues that in the late 1870s 'the Victorian period
ended', and that a new crisis in literature came about, that much wider issues
became explicit, that it became almost impossible for any one writer to carry
the cultural brunt of change in society, thought and feeling, and that all that was
most creative in the modern novel encountered major difficulties of relationship
and of form.

[1] Roland Barthes, *Writing Degree Zero* (London, 1967). This is an inescapable
(if difficult) book for anyone interested in the social role of literature. Its
argument is founded on the social evolution of literary language, which Barthes
sees as progressively alienated by modern social change; but it also raises
fascinating questions about formal structure in literature as well. Incidentally,
Barthes, like Williams, sees the crisis arising somewhat earlier, focusing here on
French writing.

more marginal and isolated. And so, not surprisingly, there runs
through English writing from about 1880, when the Victorian
synthesis seems to be losing intellectual and social cohesion, a
mood of imaginative unease. From that point on, most of the
literature produced was to respond to the spirit of unease and
transformation in the culture. It was to feel that old artistic
structures were expended; that old myths consorted only in
parodic or ironic relationship to present experience; that the
very language of literature was an incomplete form of expression.
It was to sense that the role of the artist was in the process of
change, and that the situation placed the artist under a unique
obligation to innovate.

One way to look at this change would be to consider in detail
the work of the most important writers of this period of literary
innovation—Hardy, Butler, Shaw, Lawrence, Conrad, Forster,
Joyce, Yeats, Eliot and so on—and to see their evaluation of their
society and their literary context.[1] But it seems useful to begin
with a broader base—to consider what sort of change this was
that is being brought to intellectual and artistic focus over this
period. For these changes, in consciousness, sensibility and
situation, were part of the process of bringing into shape, in the
minds of particular men, a sense of the modern world. Artists
felt the change with special force and under special conditions,
though their feelings about the modern were not confined to them
alone. For elsewhere in society it was being understood that new
theories of society, new accounts of man, new overviews of
experience, were being brought to expression in the face of deep
changes in the structure of men's lives and social order. So I
start my argument from the society and move towards the artist,
beginning with some of the broad processes which brought

---

[1] As a number of critics have. See, for instance, David Daiches, *The Novel and
the Modern World* (rev. ed., Cambridge, 1960) and *Poetry and the Modern World*
(Chicago, 1940); F. R. Leavis, *New Bearings in English Poetry* (red. ed., London,
1950); William York Tundall, *Forces in Modern British Literature, 1885–1946* (New
York, 1947), etc. An excellent collection of essays with a critical *and* a con-
textual approach is *The Pelican Guide to English Literature*, Vol. VII, *The Modern
Age* (ed. Boris Ford) (Harmondsworth, 1961); also see *The Sphere History of
Literature in the English Language*, Vol. VII, *The Twentieth Century* (ed. Bernard
Bergonzi) (London, 1970).

about, at the end of the Victorian period, a sharp awareness of cultural transformation. The changes in question range from changes in the processes and the structure of society—with the decline, for instance, of the liberal bourgeoisie as the confident spokesmen for England's culture—to changes in men's understandings and perceptions—their increased rationalism, their fascination with the processes of social, genetic and psychic evolution that derive from the radical thought of Marx, Darwin and Freud, their growing unease with positivism. The changes that developed so rapidly at this time continued and intensified during the present century, and they still affect our lives and thinking today in fairly close ways. The same is true of the literature that began to be written then; it is still very close to us. Without wanting to presume a close or a causal relation, then, between what happened in society and what happened in literature, I want to follow out here some of the relationships that can, I think, with profit *be* pursued. My own way of analysis does not, of course, presume to be exhaustive, but I have tried to make it broad and multiple—as it always must be, if we are to avoid seeing art as the product of a simple conditioning. There is not, in my view, any purpose in conceiving of an *ultimate* account of the social nature of literature; and in all that follows it is necessary to keep in mind the complexity of experience, the variety of ways of knowing and responding, the intense modes of imagining, that are an aspect of the existence of any major work of art.

PART ONE

Modernization in Society as a Context for the Arts

CHAPTER I

Modernization and Modern Consciousness

I

One of the most important ideas of modern man is his idea of the modern itself. 'Men have always lived in "modern" times, but they have not always been as much impressed by the fact,' says Crane Brinton in his study *The Shaping of the Modern Mind* (New York, 1953); and he adds that 'the awareness of shared newness, of a way of living different from that of one's forebears' is one of the most striking features of modern culture. The word 'modern' has not always been a weighty or an honorific word; but for us it is, and behind it lies a particular version of history and of our relationship to it. Living *now* is not at all like living *then*. *We* live in a world of persistent change, where the past is dead and the present is dying; our pressing imperatives are drawn from a temporal location somewhere between the present and the future. Our problems are persistently novel; and precedent and the past are unpromising guides. And so to be modern is not only to live now, but to live now in a certain way. A *modern* woman, a *modern* work of art, is a someone or a something that has an inbuilt element of relevance and chronicity, contains appropriate evidence that life is something we are constantly re-inventing. You can, in that novel armchair, in this radical painting, in this particular combination of skirt-length and material, distil the historical instant. Yet nothing dates as rapidly as last year's modern; evidently the modern is subject to quick change, and the principle of its own impermanence and variability is part of its nature. The modern may be an overall state of man today, but it is also akin to fashion. The future moves us quickly into the past. Hence we assume that we live in a shifting and relative historical sequence, one that is constantly freeing us from the achieved and exposing us to the unachieved or the future, which constantly demands attention. In other words, we are 'historicist'—obsessed by change and movement in time. Or, as that great analyst of modern utopianism and historicism Karl Mannheim has put it, we are always seeking 'to tell by the cosmic clock of history what the time is'.[1]

Are we new in this? Are we not simply doing what men have always done? Men in the past must obviously have had a sense of their own modernity, an awareness of transition, a feeling of the distinction between the lives of their generation and previous ones. Yet, to some extent, we surely do feel the situation in a very different way, both because the scale of change has historically accelerated, and because we depend on it and use it. Men have always been aware of change and mutability. But that can derive from a knowledge of change brought about by large external catastrophes—war, famine, political struggle, rise or fall in national power—and from internal changes in society which reallocate, by generational change or the exercise of power, the roles men hold.[2] But for us there is a more exaggerated knowledge. We employ change and are employed by it. We are aware of a social process at work which is permanently redistributing wealth, power and prestige differently throughout society, and in which new patterns of production and human work, new types of relationships between people, and new social practices are constantly being adopted and established. Change is not new bodies in old functions; it is new bodies in new functions. And this process we recognize as an established fact of modern life, an essential principle of social development, and a permanent aspect of our consciousness. It involves a continuous movement which gives each generation a different experience from that of the previous one, superannuates that generation itself more

---

[1] Karl Mannheim, *Essays on the Sociology of Knowledge* (London, 1952). And see also his *Ideology and Utopia: An Introduction to the Sociology of Knowledge* (London, 1936).

[2] Generational change and role allocation are strongly emphasized in Talcott Parsons's view of social change in the last chapter of *The Social System* (London, 1952).

quickly, and exposes all of us to the risks and the hopes of an unfixed or an impermanent environment. In such a world it is always better to be a son than a father, and to have a flexible identity rather than a permanent one. For each individual lifetime is relative; the human group to which we belong is no longer a community that includes ancestors and posterity. It is a transient association, already superseded before its members die as a new group with a new culture takes over.

In short, when we speak of the modern world, we do not simply mean a world that is modern only because we live in it. We mean a world that is, we feel, historically unique, evolving to new principles, the principles of what we call *modernization*. And modernization means not simply the unparalleled scale of modern change, but the kind of change it is and the direction in which it is going. For modernization—a process which affected much of the west in the nineteenth century, and has continued there and developed in most of the rest of the world in the twentieth—is the product of science, reason and industrialism. It is a transformation of the functioning base of society, one that works by constantly seeking a more effective manipulation and rationalization of resources, through employing newer and newer techniques of production, methods of invention, and training of men for their roles. The point about the industrial revolution, which distinguishes it from all other revolutions, is that it is one that never stops. It is a sequential process ceaselessly affecting the society and cumulatively affecting more and more individuals within it. The various parts of the general change can be independently named and isolated: industrialization, urbanization, secularization, democratization and massification (the movement towards a mass type of society administered by salaried managers). The weight of these particular changes can occur historically at different times, but on the whole they are not independent but inter-dependent. So, for instance, new kinds of work bring men into the city and change their living patterns; their work puts them into a loose collectivity with other workers engaged in the process, which tends to become large-scale; and as it does they tend to face their problems as workers collectively, so that new forms of political organization and action emerge. And though not all the consequences are planned,[1] and though some are likely rather than inevitable, none the less they are profound attributes of the general tendency. In short, modernization involves all kinds of social consequences and presses an accelerating pace of growth on all parts of society. It tends to enhance the total scale of society for any individual participant, to depersonalize and dehumanize his environment. It changes the relations of men and men, as of men and things; and it leads to new forms of personal experience and conscious-ness, as men form new types of relationship, in new places, with new forms of communication and new kinds of expectation. It is, in short, a pattern of continuous change socially and psychologically as well as in the structure of the social order, involving a sense of a much less necessary and more contingent world. In other words, we may add to the processes described above a general proletarianization; the modernized world is a plural environment possessed by no one and with no locatable individual in command.[2]

In many respects, then, there is a marked distinctiveness in modern culture which we ourselves recognize as individual. I have emphasized what lies behind it in its most general aspects, since there is a tendency in certain familiar versions of discussion and analysis to regard the processes I have been calling moderniz-ation as independent, and to find the worst ones in one particular social system. For instance, in Marxist analysis there is a tendency to regard depersonalization as an attribute of capitalism only: a highly dubious attribution. In fact, all the signs are that the broader

[1] Clearly many are unplanned, in the sense that many institutions are not consciously submitted to change, but are jeopardized by changes in other spheres. No doubt it was no intention of those who industrialized England to make men less religious and more secular. But religious faith and institutions became less tenable as other changes occurred, as Bryan Wilson shows in *Religion in Secular Society* (London, 1966).

[2] A good brief discussion of the accelerating nature of modern social change can be found in Wilbert E. Moore, *Social Change* (Englewood Cliffs, N.J., 1963). Moore's argument is, shortly, that rapid change is now constant and—because it affects a widening range of individual experience and is always expanding its range of material technologies and social strategies—it is also cumulative.

process of modernization now has a universal or global momentum, and is quite as closely linked with 'revolutionary' as with 'bourgeois' societies. This does not mean—as we shall see—that its effects are uniform. It has consorted with many different orders of society, from capitalism to communism; it has consorted with great differences of national character; and it has often co-existed with other forms of social emphasis and organization. None the less, it tends towards uniformity, and it tends to work everywhere in due course in the same kind of way, producing internationally similar human experience. So Russia and America are secretly more alike than they say they are; Rome has the same traffic problems and washing-powders as Bradford; and a society which has assimilated the computer is likely to have a good deal in common with any other society that has done the same. The idea that modernization produces 'convergence', and that all modern societies behave in the same sorts of way, has been challenged; and variations are indeed as important as similarities.[1] The fact remains that, in the absence of conscious action, and perhaps not even then, the developments of modernization tend in due course to change national characters and to impose a one-directional process. They tend to become a feature of most prevailing ideologies, whether these are conservative or radical in bias; the main difference between these is one of employment of the processes within a limited number of alternatives. This means, in fact, that modernization is not simply an abstract historical logic but also something we ourselves create through our actions and our beliefs; indeed in one of its aspects it is a feature of the secularization of our desires, for in essence it represents man cumulatively and collectively operating upon and revolutionizing his own environment with new instruments and ambitions.[2] This secularization of desire manifests itself in the modernized world in the form of politics. Politics institutionalize

[1] For some excellent case-studies of different national responses to the same technological innovation (for instance, the Bessemer steel-mill and the Pasteurization process), see Elting E. Morison, *Men, Machines and Modern Times* (Cambridge, Mass., 1966).

[2] So Edmund Leach, *A Runaway World* (London, 1968), argues that men are now set free and are capable of acting 'like gods' to change the rules of life. The

our participation in the processes of change, making modernization an instrument through which we seek to fulfil our needs
and desires within history, while at the same time recognizing
that history is what modernization says it is.

That is to say that modernization is not simply an abstract
process but a place in our own minds. For we characteristically
acquiesce to change as an environment, since it enables us to
have a radical conception of ourselves, of our natures, powers
and needs. Modernization has loosened a great many old dependencies and enlarged a great many expectations, even though,
for all of us, it has increasingly depersonalized and demythicized
our world. Thought, belief and ideology are therefore themselves essential instruments of modernization, whether these
take the form of abstract intellectual or scientific innovation or
in the expressed reasons, prejudices and presumptions of the
social dialogue generally. Modernization can thus be represented
as a logical culmination of scientific, rationalistic and humanistic
views of man, these views themselves being part of the means
by which all men are implicated in the process of change and so
cause it to be an element in our primary social reality. Hence our
conscious and unconscious enactments in the world, our styles
and our structures, become themselves subjected to tests of
historical relevance. We tend to bind ourselves to history and
test ourselves against it, characteristically seeking to suppress
certain features of modernization while accepting others. In fact,
an important part of the modernization process is that we further
it by recognizing it. The sense of an intensifying modernity runs
through much of our thought, our art, our life-style, our ways of
repeatedly disinheriting the past and drawing sharp and distinct
lines between the traditional and the contemporary. The modern

---

same Promethean view is suggested by Dr. Olaf Helmer of Rand: 'The future
is no longer viewed as unique, unforeseeable, and inevitable. There are instead,
it is realized, a multitude of possible futures, with associated probabilities that
can be estimated and, to some extent, manipulated.' However, though we may
tamper with destiny, we may only really do so within the scientific-technological
pattern of development. Though Dr. Leach and others have emphasized our
singular freedom, it is a one-directional freedom. Could we, for instance,
effectively decide *not* to change?

thus becomes assessible not only as an aspect of society but as an aspect of consciousness, a manifest feature of thought, art, expression generally; and it is deeply involved in the internal signalling of our culture, so that, whether we act as modernization's beneficiaries or as its victims, we do so in the spirit of modernity.[1]

II

There is a classic sociological distinction between 'pre-modern' and 'modern' types of society which further illuminates the cultural framework in which I wish to see modern literature. This is Ferdinand Tönnies' typification of social structures as *Gemeinschaft* and *Gesellschaft*.[2] Tönnies' types are ideal (i.e. do not precisely fit any given society) but they constitute revealing images of the scale of modern transition. *Gemeinschaft* social order is that of a society—or rather a community—based upon tradition. Relatively homogeneous in its beliefs and values, it is typically rural rather than urban. Here men tend to function through traditional status arrangements, and to live by certain willing renunciations—by ideologies that encourage them to adjust to their lot, restrain excessive aspiration, and fulfil themselves through inherited roles, patterns of conduct, and a cohesive sense of community. They act and know one another through a series of face-to-face contacts, spread through various types of social occasion (work and religion, home and family). They share a more or less common culture or body of values, and have more need of religion than sociology. *Gesellschaft* social order is, effectively, that of a society modernized. It is typically urban or at least city-oriented; it is heterogeneous in its social mixture and secular in its disposition. It is a community only nominally; people appear and disappear in it. It depends on a multiplicity of relationships, and its relationships are made less through face-to-face contact than through written contracts. Its economic

---

[1] And one need hardly add that much modern literature not only responds to, but creates within its fictional worlds, a 'modernized' universe much like the one I have described.

[2] Ferdinand Tönnies, *Gemeinschaft und Gesellschaft* (Leipzig, 1887), trans. Charles P. Loomis as *Community and Association* (London, 1955).

structure is not readily visible, because of its complex patterns of trade; its family structure is also not easily discerned, because its families are split. It encourages social mobility, and it offers its members a variety of roles and status, themselves variable in different circumstances.

It brings freedom from old dependencies, though subjection to new ones. In *Gesellschaft* societies, men are much more exposed socially and psychically. They are much less centred in the family, much more in the institution. Their ascribed roles in the community diminish, and their functional roles as producers and consumers increase. In their human relationships, they explore more sectors of the society, and know more kinds of contact and experience than they did before; they have greater opportunities for 'identity', for independent selfhood. But identity is increasingly *self*-defined, less created by the social web; they are therefore open to increased confusion and anxiety. There are few problems about who and what one is when men's relationships are defined in a small community and are relatively settled: but in a mobile and urbanized society, in which most men are strangers, the problem grows more acute, the world stranger, and individual consciousness seems a lonely location. The patterns of permission and restraint become abstract— legalized, impersonal, 'bureaucratic'. Authority claims a different type of legitimacy: it is technical-bureaucratic rather than mystical or sacred; it exercises authority more as a 'job' and less as a personal attribute. Men must therefore act more rationally. But at the same time they are less willing to make those renunciations which make their culture shareable with other men; the self freed from commands and institutional arrangements becomes a primary good.[1] Men stress ideologies emphasizing opportunity, freedom, liberation, independence, self-completion. They live in a world in which self-definition seems more possible, where because of the separation of the work-order from other social experience there is more choice of involvements and activities. They are encouraged by their social order to create appropriate

[1] This is Philip Rieff's 'therapeutic' man in his excellent study *The Triumph of the Therapeutic* (London and New York, 1966).

personal ideologies, character types and life-styles, appropriate personal and political claims on their environment. *Gemeinschaft* men tell *Gesellschaft* men that they are atomized and impersonal; *Gesellschaft* men tell *Gemeinschaft* men that they are humiliated, unaware and politically uneducated. In *Gemeinschaft* societies the cheese comes unwrapped and the communication process is called gossip; in *Gesellschaft* societies the cheese is wrapped in cellophane and the communications process is called the 'media'.

In Hobhouse's phrase,[1] *Gesellschaft* society is 'self-directing'; men are persistently informed about the changes being made on their behalf. But this individualism and participation is subject to obvious constraint. One condition of the *Gesellschaft* is, after all, the machine—which itself tends to determine the total environment. It requires the increased specialization and rationality of men; and people are increasingly defined by their functional roles in relation to it and the kind of system it requires. It tends to create a familiar political contradiction very evident among some contemporary radicals; they want a society of politically 'advanced' men but not the machine-centred context which creates their existence. For the machine *is* a conditioning environment as well as a liberalizing environment; it tends to produce a greater sense of satisfying men's needs, but the needs and the satisfactions are necessarily defined in terms of a basic acceptance of the modernizing system. Modernizing society implicates all men in its development, and so tends to expose all men to the difficulties and uncertainties of its structure. And since it does seem to move in a single direction, all those elements of experience and human need which are not included in its syntheses are liable to become matters either for unconscious disquiet or conscious dissent—just as tensions are liable to exist between its rationalizing processes and irrational and personal instincts.[2] Indeed it becomes possible for men to feel that

---

[1] L. T. Hobhouse, *Social Development* (London, 1924).

[2] The view that modern civilization may satisfy rational desires but not irrational or unconscious ones has been explored in a good deal of modern sociology and psychology. Freud in *Civilization and Its Discontents* (London, 1930) broadly suggests that the absence of a feeling of increased happiness in modern civilization reveals the difficulty of aligning socialization with all human

D

society's reality is not theirs, and hence the social process can become phantasmagoric, unreal, an impersonal social contract, while satisfaction is sought within terms of personal conscious- ness, personal life, intense and immediate satisfactions. But this in turn leaves men with a weakened sense of objective reality, or a feeling of deep division between their nature and the historical process.[1] Hence, indeed, the familiar form of revolutionary feeling in our time; its primary images are usually those of an alienation from some former community among men, or some state of unrepressed bodily joy, that modern capitalist democracy has suppressed; this often coupled with some post-Marxist or post-Freudian dream of a future in which these things are restored to us and the bourgeois view of men and things is swept away, and when the domination of the things that have created modern society—the Renaissance, Christianity, western civiliza- tion—is cast off.

Men may thus see modernizing society at once as an abstract process, and (because it promotes secular aspirations at the same time as it withdraws posthumous expectations of the next world) the essential field for their hopes of human fulfilment. In the modern world, therefore, man tends to humanize history to the point of seeking his fulfilments within it. But he also tends to impersonalize it by seeing it as an unconditioned and independent force, contingent rather than necessary. Hence the balancing of the relationship between man and process becomes the recurrent

---

needs. This argument has been extended to the view that modern society may suppress or submerge many desires irrelevant to its overall development. These come to express themselves in other ways—not only in the discomforts revealed in crime, illness, mental breakdown, but in the anti-rational and romantic dimensions of—for instance—modern art, which has characteristically fluc- tuated between conservatism and anarchism.

[1] For further exploration of this sense of weakened reality, see William Barrett, *Irrational Man: A Study in Existential Philosophy* (New York, 1958; London, 1961). And more polemically the attack of Herbert Marcuse, *One-Dimensional Man: Studies in the Ideology of Advanced Industrial Society* (Boston and London, 1964). His view that the implicitly rational ideology of a one-directional society suppresses the instinct towards originality, spontaneity and creativity and leads to a self-destructive principle in our social structure is also explored in other terms in Norman O. Brown, *Life Against Death: The Psychoanalytical Meaning of History* (Middletown, Conn., and London, 1959).

intellectual and emotional crux of our era. To put the problem in another way, it becomes increasingly hard to imagine, as Frank Kermode has said,[1] the relation between the time of a life and the time of the world. In particular terms, the world of change may increase our freedom from brute economic necessities, but increase our servitude to complex and often uncontrollable economic processes; it may enlarge our sense of social participation, but lessen the degree of access to those who run society; it may set us free to enjoy a greater selfhood, yet weaken our sense of personal identity; it may enlarge the opportunities for social advancement and mobility, yet reduce the prestige and satisfactions of success. In more general terms, it may give us a sense that there is a reality working independently of man which is random or destructive, and makes the world too great for comprehension; both the processes of development and the physical universe itself seem to operate in ways beyond the world of sense. It is easy from this to understand why it is that we should tend to make our age into one of rare apocalypse, why much of our art should present a universe that is fantastic or dream-like beyond or even within the limits of self—and why the idea of the modern should count with us so much.

Hence that feeling of increased exposure, of being condemned to freedom, which is a familiar feature of the modern psychic type. According to Jung, the 'modern man is a newly formed human being; a modern problem is a question which has just arisen and whose answer lies in the future'; the exemplary modern man is moving towards 'a fuller consciousness of the present' and finds that the ways of life which correspond to earlier levels of consciousness pall on him.[2] We can represent this sort of figure as heroic or tragic, but it is a recurrent image; the idea of the modern as an imperative is one term of this equation, and the other is the idea of a predicament in defining being and existence. Much of modern thought and art testifies, therefore, to the feeling of the modern as an apocalyptic age, or what Sorokin calls

[1] Frank Kermode, *The Sense of an Ending: Studies in the Theory of Fiction* (New York and London, 1967), p. 166.
[2] C. G. Jung, *Modern Man in Search of a Soul* (London, 1933).

'an age of crisis'.[1] The feeling can be much overstated and it hardly represents the evident condition of all men. But the strong feeling that comes through much modern report that connections have gone awry, that anarchy is universal, that man finds it harder than ever to define his nature, his powers and his identity against a confusing and contingent world, is a part of our total understanding of modernity. Indeed in seeking to define the idea of the modern in our culture, these ideas—that the modern is an imperative, a hope and a predicament—run deep; and even if we find the report perverse, we must also find it pervasive.

III

And so, through many of the accounts of itself that, in thought and art, the modern age has given, there has run a strong sense of the uniqueness of modern times. Indeed often in these accounts there is, whether explicitly or implicitly, a basic assumption that our age is not simply an age of change or transition, but, much more ultimately, an age of crisis. In fact one of the ways we recognize modern sensibility in art and thought is to look for the symptoms of shock, disturbance and crisis. This is not, of course, to say that all men in modern times have responded to their age with such intensity and unease: many have felt themselves the beneficiaries of change, and others have doubted whether the change is qualitatively different from change as all of mankind has known it. It would be excessive to identify modern art, modern thought or the modern situation totally with a sense of anarchy, a knowledge of crisis or a positive desire to rescind the past in the interests of living out one's plight to the full—though all of these things have played an important part in modern writing and thinking. But our belief in this pervasive style of modernity, of the need to manifest and live out the world as if it were a crisis, has meant much. Modernity, suggest Richard Ellmann and Charles Feidelson in their introduction to an anthology called *The Modern Tradition*, is a style of

[1] P. A. Sorokin, *Social Philosophies in an Age of Crisis* (Boston, 1950).

extremity: 'One characteristic of the works of literature and ideas we call modern is that they positively insist on a general frame of reference within and beyond themselves. They claim modernity, they profess modernism.'[1] They embody, then, the profession of strain, the style of self-conscious unease; and *that* is the modern tradition. In fact, of course, only a certain small part of our total art fits this description. But what is significant is that we should regard the extreme as the truly representative case; it is these works and these thoughts that are the most *modern*. We seem inclined to assume, then, that these anguished expressions and explorations of consciousness somehow represent an essential experience for all of us. In fact, of course, they are representative in an oblique rather than a total sense. Lionel Trilling has commented on the ease with which we appear able to look upon and accept as a matter of course works of literature that are ridden with profound disturbances of the author, to take the enactment of his darkest imaginings as a natural object for contemplation and discussion.[2] There is, indeed, always a danger of making one man's experience a type of all experience; equally, there is the reverse danger of accepting fictions and myths as precise historical truths. Writers are frequently concerned with their own most disturbing insights; and art is frequently concerned with its own special situation *as* art. Paintings and writings frequently depend, moreover, on shock to procure their initial acceptance; and that acceptance is often first won with an intellectual audience itself undergoing strains as an intelligentsia, and hence themselves disposed to support works which illuminate their own unease. In short, the crises of art are often special rather than universal or representative; and they can often themselves be fictions, only properly to be understood once we have understood what art is and what predicaments its practitioners are in.

I suppose there are two broad alternative explanations of the

[1] Richard Ellmann and Charles Feidelson, Jr. (editors), *The Modern Tradition: Backgrounds of Modern Literature* (New York and London, 1965).
[2] Lionel Trilling, 'On the Teaching of Modern Literature' in *Beyond Culture: Essays on Literature and Learning* (New York and London, 1966).

sense of crisis in certain of our main modern works. One is that such kinds of art and the ideas that underlie them represent the subconscious recognitions and dramatize the sensations of many (or all) of us living in our kind of world. However, the deliberate limitation by many modern artists of their own constituency, and the fact that modern art may nowadays be fairly widely accepted but is hardly fairly widely understood, would be one reason for doubting this to be completely true. The second is that the complexities of the modern world affect particularly sharply those concerned with thought and art, those who may have behind them a certain vision of human need and a desire to dramatize the forms of life in a certain way. It is obviously true that under modern conditions artists and intellectuals suffer special difficulties and are also exposed to onerous responsibilities. The democratic artist or intellectual is an ill-defined creature. He has lost his caste-like status, and the wisdoms and practices of a secure and stable culture. He lives in a climate of continuous scepticism. He is less than ever before a conserver of knowledge or experience. His task is to explore rather than to explain. The climate of knowledge itself, by analogy with science, becomes innovative; it must be heterodox, multiple and allied with all potential future states of affairs. No one position in the culture seems, in a world that is constantly creating new contexts for knowledge, a sufficient standpoint from which to acquire an overview. Synthesis thus becomes available only at the extreme or with reference to a point in the future, envisioned perhaps utopianly or perhaps apocalyptically. In art and philosophy as in science it becomes necessary to maintain a sense of eclecticism, an openness to change. Art, in such a situation, tends to lose many of its powers to assert a coherent wisdom, sustain a coherent myth or assert the veracity of its own perception. The artist, like the thinker, tends therefore to dramatize his own self-scepticism. His work tends to become self-critical, ironic or game-like in disposition. It is also dubiously placed in relation to those forms of modern knowledge which produce change and development— which is to say scientific or technological knowledge. It also tends to lack the impersonality or 'objectivity' of knowledge of this kind, which aspires to fact as opposed to value, and is hence relative or multi-functional. The writer and intellectual therefore tend to enact many of the uncertainties of their own disposition towards overseeing the multiple society in which they live. Their independence becomes onerous; on the other hand, to forgo it makes them guilty. They become then both the agents and the victims of a changing and pluralizing world; they have an increasing sense of their own marginality and isolation, and yet at the same time the feeling that the onus of historical evolution, the emergence of new modes of thought and the elimination of old and false ones, lies upon them. And it is out of the dramatization of both of these things that there derives that engrained sense of intellectual and artistic difficulty we closely associate with the modern.[1]

While there is, then, some reason for doubting the representativeness of these modern sensations for everyone, we can find good reasons why there is a repeated conviction that modern art and writing is under pressure. As I have said, even these sensations are not universal among writers and artists themselves. In the arts, the sense of internal difficulty is particularly manifest in the idea of the *avant garde*, and that itself seems to come and go in waves, today finally risking a kind of total submergence in the contemporary spectacle of a youth culture that, given the benefits of leisure, a certain affluence and a stark cultural deprivation, itself performs in a mini-*avant-garde* way. However, the *avant garde* in the arts is itself a relatively new and modern phenomenon, marked by the instinct to dramatize its own modernity. Its existence derives largely from the fact that the arts have grown socially more marginal and the audience for them more dispersed. And it responds to and recreates a parallel marginality and dispersion in the minds of artists. Its character is

[1] For much more extensive discussion of these matters, especially having to do with the social and historical 'derivation' of knowledge and the changing place of the intelligentsia, see Karl Mannheim's works, and notably the early parts of his *Ideology and Utopia* (London, 1936) and his 'The Problem of the Intelligentsia' in *Essays on the Sociology of Culture* (London, 1956). Also see George B. de Huszar (editor), *The Intellectuals: A Controversial Portrait* (Glencoe, Ill., 1960).

partly aristocratic or dandyish and partly professional and specialized. It marks the winning of a total independence of artists to
be artists unconditionally; it also marks the loss of a social overview. Socially it is the growth of an independent and specialized
community of the arts, clustered in specialized centres like
Montparnasse or Greenwich Village, where independent mores
and life-style can be lived out and where art is both produced and
consumed, largely by other artists. Formally it is marked by the
growth of a manifest strain and difficulty within its works, and
a heightening of technique. In belief, it is marked by a visionary
apocalypticism, a sense that the problems of art are new, terrible
and complete. Frequently it is, while concerned with creating
art for the present, also concerned with decreating the art of the
past. Indeed it tends towards taking the form of a cultural
proletariat.[1] None the less, it is out of such environments that
much of our most interesting art has come. The *avant garde* after
all normally represents a desire for achievement as well as
separation, and many significant figures have found it the freeing
environment for the independent prosecution of their art, and
often finally a place of intense creative satisfaction. More commonly, though, writers and artists have alternated between it and
other much more localized experiences, so that it represents a
polarity of, rather than an absolute centre of, modern artistic
activity.

I am not here trying to suggest that there is a close relationship to be found between modernization and the modern arts.
Perhaps the startling paradox in the situation is that, in an age
often described as one of alienation and crisis, men have still
persistently retained a belief in progress and in secular advance.
There are those who believe in progress through modernization
by the exercise of greater rationality, efficiency and affluence.

---

[1] Or, as Lionel Trilling puts it, we may see in much modern literature a
deep element of the subversive, in the form of disillusion with the very conditions which have made art in the past. He speaks of culture's disillusion with
culture itself: 'Ours is the first cultural epoch in which many men aspire to
high achievement and, in their frustration, form a dispossessed class which cuts
across the conventional class lines, making a proletariat of the spirit.' Trilling,
op. cit.

There are also those radicals who, while opposed to this version of modernization, have none the less seen the process of proletarianization and exposure as one of liberation, allowing greater expression, permission and self-expansion. Both are ideologies of progress, and one of the striking and important features of many of our literary works—of indeed a distinct tradition in modern English writing—is that it has revolted against both. This is part of its complexity as experience and its commitment as transcendent art. If there is one thing above all others interesting about modern or modernist art, it is the way in which it has engaged strangely with the modern world, accepting and revelling in many aspects of it while suppressing, criticizing and seeking to destroy others. It has been a critical art and often explicitly an anti-historicist art, resisting both the desire to serve the age or any given interest in it ideologically, while having very little joy in the utopias of the future which many men of politics have espoused. Art may manifest the thought, philosophical or ideological, of the time; it may speak in or enact some of the politics of the time. But its politics is essentially the politics of culture, tracing out its own difficult path for its own difficult ends. Indeed much of the best of modern art has finally and firmly chosen to speak against the claim of the historical process to decide everything for us, by transfiguring our place in history through its crucial metamorphoses, by allowing us access to what W. B. Yeats called 'the artifice of eternity'. If, as I think, the satisfactions of twentieth-century writing can run very deep indeed, then to have them we must limit, as our greatest artists have tried to do, the outright claims of historical determinism, while understanding the context by which many of the terms of the effort has been decided. I have also suggested that it has, in different traditions, periods and writers, been decided very variously. It now remains to look more closely at how.

CHAPTER II

'Modernity' in England

I

The broad portrait of modernization and the 'modern consciousness' I have so far given is in certain ways a fairly recognizable and
familiar account of the kind of world which we, and several
generations which have gone before us, have found ourselves in.
But (as with most such grand typifications) if it is to fit the experience of any particular nation, or indeed of any particular individual, it requires a fair amount of qualification. It is, first of all,
fairly evident that, while many societies in the last and this
century have 'modernized', they have done so in very different
ways—a fact of which any overall typing of the situation has to
take account. There are societies which, despite modernization,
seem to have changed remarkably little in character as compared
to others: the United States has changed vastly more than France.
There are societies which seem to have changed largely through
the force of an internal momentum, and others which have been
forced to do so by a large degree of outside influence or by some
cataclysmic internal breakdown. In some countries war and
revolution have played an important part, and in others not. What
is more, there are societies which seem on the whole to have
benefited by the broad process, and others which seem to have
lost in power and internal cohesion because of it.[1] And what is
true of societies is also more or less true for individuals within
them; men in some countries have felt a general overall excitement at these broad developments, while in others they have
felt a sense of doubt, despair or disaffiliation.

[1] As Barrington Moore, Jr., suggests in *The Social Origins of Dictatorship and
Democracy* (Boston, 1966; London, 1967).

Recently a number of social scientists have expressed their doubts about the way the broad model of 'modernization' is applied to particular nations.[1] And it has been pointed out, for instance, that England, which first introduced the world to 'modernity' (to, that is, the industrial use of science, to 'protestant' capitalism, to a secular world-view), has also succeeded throughout most of the process in retaining the characteristics of a *Gemeinschaft* writ large—a 'unique synthesis of traditional elements and the forces which transformed them'.[2] This seems true, and it is an important feature of the texture of the culture, the texture of symbols and values out of which literature and art come. Moreover, if we can hardly accept the broad model of modernization as anything more than a general typification involving many different kinds of experience, many different kinds of response, then we must equally question the notion of the inevitable, universal 'predicament' of modern man—or for that matter the idea of an intrinsic 'modernist' style in the arts. The 'marks of modernity' on modern thought and modern literature cannot therefore be narrowly defined. And we must be uneasy about that sort of fashionable literary-critical historicism which chooses to say, for example, that modern English literature has been less 'modern' than French or American literature because it has been less experimental or less anguished, or because its artists have been less alienated.

In many respects English society seems to have undergone social changes into the modern world more gently and less violently than many other countries. That, indeed, is one reason why, to many foreign observers, the English intellectual and literary scene has often seemed comfortable, compact and not particularly intellectual. To some such observers, in the last century and this, the closeness of English intellectuals to power and rank, their manners and style, their relative concentration and their confidence, all offered a model for an effective intellectual

[1] See, for instance, R. Bendix, 'Tradition and Modernity Reconsidered', *Comparative Studies in Society and History*, IX (1957), pp. 292ff.
[2] Stanley Rothman, 'Modernity and Tradition in Britain', repr. in *The Study of Society* (ed. Peter Rose) (New York, 1967).

life. (That, indeed, is one reason why England attracted a number of important American literary and intellectual expatriates.) To other eyes, English writers and thinkers were gentlemanly, amateur, unrigorous, too close to class-position and power to exercise 'real' creativity or independence of mind. It was this aspect of English culture that led Pound to despair of the national vice of artistic amateurism, and D. M. Mirsky to put, from another extreme, the Marxist complaint that the English intelligentsia had never achieved a sufficiently close alliance with the proletariat to be 'objective'.[1] By the end of the nineteenth century the notion of the intellectual in many other countries had grown much more extreme: some sort of alienation was assumed to be inherently 'necessary'.[2] In fact by some definitions of the word, England had no intelligentsia at all; though the thinking sector of the time (as perhaps still) could be seen as an exemplary intelligentsia of the liberal type.[3] It was drawn from various classes and origins, rooted in a variety of interests, and committed to an ideal of disinterested debate, while a dominantly literary rather than a political view formed common ground for many. But it was neither politically doctrinaire nor notably *avant garde* (and it is notable that in periods of greater political sectionalism there was an increase too in the amount of literary experimentalism). So, on the whole, its aestheticism and bohemianism tended to be shadowy, borrowed versions of French or European manners, appearing more as a style than a manifest necessity. When aesthetic revolution did begin, it tended to draw heavily on foreign ideas and even 'foreign' voices, like Henry James, T. S. Eliot, Ezra Pound, Joseph Conrad and W. B. Yeats. Even the expansion of psychology and sociology in England was not only derived from, but largely conducted by, Europeans; what is striking is that the void should open enough to be filled.

[1] D. M. Mirsky, *The Intelligentsia of Great Britain*, trans. Alec Brown (London, 1935).

[2] Cf. Philip Rahv's definition of intellectuals as those who 'preferred alienation from the community to alienation from themselves', in *Literature and the Sixth Sense* (New York and London, 1970).

[3] As Karl Mannheim describes it in *Essays in the Sociology of Knowledge* (London, 1952).

But to this extent we can agree with H. Stuart Hughes's judgment that 'it was the Germans and Austrians and French and Italians— rather than Englishmen or Americans or Russians—who in general provided the fund of ideas that seem characteristic of our own time'.[1]

At least, perhaps, until very recent years, the English intellectual and writer has not been profoundly noted for his alienation or his extremism, however much he has been aware of the transition into the modern era. The general point made by Richard Chase about the overall character of English culture fits much of our own century as well as earlier ones:

By comparison with America, England is an organic and continuous culture . . . At certain periods of its history England has evolved an admirable middle culture, a main body of taste and opinion, into which the *avant garde*, never radically alienated in the first place, could be temporarily absorbed, without detriment to the cultural life of the nation.[2]

This is not to deny the element of unease or of *avant-garde-ism*, but it is fair comment on its place and fortunes. Nonetheless, of course, the culture of England has, over the last and present century, changed vastly, and the intellectual and artist has been very much affected by this and has responded to it. The process of change may have been gradual and unmarked by extreme revolutionary fervour. But even within our own century we can see enormous alterations in the culture and the place of cultural élites in it; and anyone who looks back now on England at the turn of the century will find it as remote in some respects as he finds it familiar in others. The broad features of the social and economic changes that have taken place in Britian over the course

---

[1] H. Stuart Hughes, *Consciousness and Society: The Reorientation of European Social Thought 1890–1930* (New York, 1958; London, 1959). This begs the question of which ideas *are* characteristic of our times, however.

[2] Richard Chase, 'The Fate of the Avant-Garde' in *Partisan Review Anthology* (ed. W. Phillips and P. Rahv) (London, 1963). (Also reprinted in *Literary Modernism* (ed. Irving Howe) (Greenwich, Conn., 1967).) This topic is also excellently discussed in Jacques Barzun, *The House of Intellect* (New York and London, 1959).

of this century are very familiar to us. It has been a democratizing century, a proletarianizing century, and the English process has been much complicated by imperial decline and the enforced, semi-revolutionary changes of two radical world wars. By the beginning of the century, Britain, thriving on its advanced industrial revolution, had come through many of the consequences of it. It had gone through a century of urbanization, a drift from the land to the cities; the cities were effectively the centres of power and London now had outright dominance. So, as part of the same process, had an early form of the corporate state. Britain had developed a production economy, with a large urban proletariat engaged in manufacturing. It had moved into a phase of technological and scientific development that had already deeply influenced the pattern of education and the general ideology. Secularization had become a self-evident process; the church had lost its power to shape and define the meaning of men's lives, even if the society expressed itself frequently in religious terms. The process of social adaptation to the economic conditions of that type of society had gone very deep. In the nineteenth century the living standards of the middle class had risen, and now the transformation was spreading down the social hierarchy; it was already recognized that the twentieth century was to be the 'century of the common man'. But England was still a first-class world power with a large empire, struggling to hold a world industrial lead. It was still eminently a middle-class society and in many respects a markedly contented one. It was still, of course, without universal adult suffrage and was only beginning to realize the implications of total literacy. The forces of progress seemed to be running ahead, but it was a society always much aware of the needs for equivalent forces of control, and in this sense a liberal society, a mediating society. The extreme 'modernizing' features—revolution, breakdown of law and order, power above justice—seemed to have been contained, despite certain threats to and fears for liberalism. Sectional interests and separatist passions only occasionally seemed likely to outrun national interests.

By the 1950s, England was a country without an Empire, one

of many competing industrial and modernized nations, and with far fewer powers of expansion and advance than many of the others. It was emerging as a mass rather than a class society, vastly more centralized and state-run. It had continued to mediate between the forces of continuity and those of change, and in doing so had clearly and apparently willingly sacrificed its world dominance. It was even more urban, even more secular, and even more proletarianized. The pattern of wealth and social power had markedly changed, and many of the old cultural centres had been eroded, an effect achieved as much by inflation and the destruction of the culture of the fixed or inherited income as anything else. It was a society in which education had vastly extended and in which the opportunities for 'meritocratic' social mobility had considerably increased; at the same time it was a society depending on much more specialized skills. The worker was now engaged not only in manufacturing goods but in consuming them; it was a consumer society. Its professionals were much more a salariat than independent agents; it was a managerial society. It was, geographically as well as socially, a much more mobile society. It was a rationalizing society, attempting to systematize its resources moving towards larger groupings in business and in local government. Affluence had increased, but independence through wealth, function or local influence had diminished. It was also, of course, a welfare society, a society of impersonal concern. Its culture, too, had become much more impersonal. Many of the traditional sources of cultural activity had been eliminated; the culture of a society is always differentially carried by different social classes, and when class differences are diminished or eliminated, new agencies need to develop to maintain cultural interests and liveliness. In fact, the main force that emerged in postwar England to do this was the technologized mass-media, which were relatively independently run but created by a paid and changing salariat and economically dependent (if only by virtue of their technical overheads) on large audiences. Both for economic and for social reasons, then, they showed a marked tendency to 'level' the culture, so reinforcing many of the new patterns of internal relationship that seemed to be emerging. In retrospect it must now seem that they helped to destroy certain old stratifications—those between class and class, for instance—while invigorating certain new ones—those between generation and generation, for instance. At any rate, they became an essential medium for internal communication and the dissemination of values, for exposing the different parts of society one to another, and for centralizing taste, as well as for making it impersonal and much more subject to remote administrative decision.[1] The 'mass' media, particularly in their sophisticated and technological form, which gave them wide and immediate distribution, are central agencies that must be considered in any account of the cultural texture of the pattern of modern England.[2] And of course they have competed with many of the traditional forms (notably the book as such, with its more personal and selective audience and its much more independent creator) for an audience itself considerably changing.

Postwar English society still remained more or less a liberal and mediating society. Writers and artists still tended to conceive of themselves as placed in a position of concerned independence, 'disinterestedness' in Matthew Arnold's word, liberally concerned with and for culture as such. But they were, in the postwar period, working in a considerably changed cultural situation. It is to this liberalism or lack of artistic extremism that Edward Shils was undoubtedly referring when, in a famous *Encounter* article, he commented—speaking, it should be recalled, of the 'Angry' generation of the 1950s—that '[n]ever has an intellectual class found its society and its culture so much to its satisfaction' as the postwar generation of English intellectuals and

---

[1] One thing that cultural sociology could profitably devote itself to is the nature of these large-scale cultural institutions. How does such an institution make its decisions, through what machineries and hierarchies and on what basis? How meaningful is the kind of information they have about general taste, and the ways in which they acquire it? These issues, though they lie outside this book, seem essential for contemporary cultural analysis.

[2] Or modern anywhere. See Marshall McLuhan, *Understanding Media: The Extensions of Man* (New York and London, 1964). See also my much more extensive discussion of the topic in Chapter XI following.

writers.[1] In this respect he was reiterating a familiar judgment, the judgment of Mirsky and Pound. But he was making it about a very differently composed intelligentsia, with different social origins, different possible roles, and different kinds of satisfaction (and in fact of doubt and unease) from that intelligentsia of which Pound and Mirsky had spoken. It may be that the situation is changing now in a new climate of intellectual internationalism; but to know that we would have to wait a while longer.

II

The steady process of cultural and social transformation, the shift from a class to a mass society, the increased application of rational functionalism and, the technologization of the media and means of communication, changed and modernized English writing. But only to a point has it made it 'modernist' and experimental. Modernist sensibility, both in the form of a high artistic self-consciousness and a sense of extremism or despera- tion, has been a feature of some literary traditions much more than others. We sometimes appear to suggest that only 'modernist' literature has truly exposed itself to the reality of our days, and that it is only the *avant-garde* that has sensed fully and deeply those forms of consciousness which profoundly signal the present and intuit the future. But our experience of reading literature tends to confound this, since many modern writers have seen deeply into the times without taking their typology of the artist or his work from the *avant-garde*—writers like E. M. Forster or Evelyn Waugh, for example. The remarkable endurance of the social novel in England, and the way in which the English writer has continued to feel that there is a common literary language, and hence a common and shared convention, that he can speak with to his readers, are evidence that the only valid or real art of our time need not be extreme art. What, in fact, marks modern English writing (and the same thing is there in other national

[1] Edward Shils, 'The Intellectuals (1) Great Britain', *Encounter*, IV, 4 (April 1955), pp. 5–16. For a view of a slightly later period, see T. R. Fyvel, *Intellec- tuals Today* (London, 1968) and my essay 'Uncertainties of the British Intellectual' in *New Society*, 117 (Dec. 24, 1964), pp. 7–9.

E

traditions in literature, though often in less marked ways) is the fascinating, continued interplay that has existed between the technical and emotional extremities of modernism and a much more realist, nativist and provincial manner. This is sometimes taken as 'middlebrow', a preference for whoredom over true artistic celibacy; but it has enabled the existence of a vigorous mainstream tradition from which experimentalist movements have at various stages diverged. This is in some contrast to, say, the French situation, where, from Flaubert on, the ideal of a stylistic absolutism has been more stoutly maintained, and where each artist tends to face the crisis of ensuring his own distinctive language, a crisis that can—as in the contemporary French anti-novel, which has a curious air of 'traditional' modernism—become an arcane purism.

The dialogue between the neo-realists and the experimentalists has in fact been a recurrent feature of modern English writing. There are numerous examples—the arguments between H. G. Wells and Henry James after the publication of the former's book called *Boon* (1915), or between Arnold Bennett and Virginia Woolf, or between John Galsworthy and D. H. Lawrence—of the division, and if the advantage often goes to those novelists or poets who are experimental or anti-realist this is not to say that theirs is the only truth in the situation.[1] There was a further period of marked resistance to neo-modernist norms in the English writing of the 1950s, encapsulated in a number of debates of which a comment by William Cooper may serve as an example:

During the last years of the war, a literary comrade-in-arms (C. P. Snow) and I, not prepared to wait for Time's ever-rolling stream to bear Experimental Writing away, made our own private plans to run it out of town as soon as we picked up our pens again—if you look at the work of the next generation of English novelists to come up after us, you'll observe we didn't entirely lack success for our efforts.[2]

[1] Stephen Spender discusses these three 'quarrels' in his book *The Struggle of the Modern* (London, 1963); that between Wells and James is explored and documented in Leon Edel and Gordon N. Ray (eds.), *Henry James and H. G. Wells: A Record of their Friendship* (London, 1958). The matter is discussed further in Chapter IV below.

[2] William Cooper, 'Reflections on Some Aspects of the Experimental Novel',

He went on to say, however, that: 'We had no qualms about incorporating any useful discoveries that had been made in the course of Experimental Writing; we simply refused to restrict ourselves to them'. What is apparent in this continuing dialogue, then, is that the belief of certain modern artists that common social symbols and myths, and shared literary languages, have been lost in the conditions of the modern world has not been universally felt within the English tradition. There is a 'modernist' tradition in English writing, and it has been a very important one; but this is not to say that modernism has somehow been historically 'necessary.' To see and sympathize with the important currents of English literature, we have to recognize the power of continuing cultural forces that have enabled many writers to see themselves as part of a national literary inheritance reaching back into the past, however much they too have been aware of the forces for change in the times.

My purpose here is to qualify the application of sociological theories of 'modernization', or critical theories of 'modernism', to the modern world—and especially to twentieth-century England. What has happened in society and in literature may well be associated with the gradualism of English social change, and to the pragmatic or empirical bias in English thought which has tended to resist a theoretical systematizing of the 'modern situation'. It has indeed been argued that the most radical period of English social change has taken place since the Second World War, and that only over this period have the English felt the brunt of the struggle into the modern alienating society. There is, I think, some truth in this; and it may have significant consequences for the future of our literature. But in these days when alienation is a fashionable and well-explored property, widely available to all who wish to subscribe, rather than a profound imaginative exploration, it is not on the whole likely to have the artistic significance it acquired in

---

International Literary Annual, No. 2, edited John Wain (London, 1959). And somewhat similar comments can be found in writings by Pamela Hansford Johnson, Kingsley Amis and Philip Larkin. See R. Rabinovitz, *The Reaction Against Experiment in the English Novel: 1950–1960* (New York and London, 1967).

certain quarters in the early part of the century. What is important is that the literary response to the modern situation has taken a very varied form in England, a fact that we can attribute in part to the pattern of modern development in this country. And this means, in turn, that it is right and proper to read the 'modern element' in English writing very broadly, and not simply through the eyes of those who identify the modern world with a certain style of art. To this theme I shall return. My point here is that I am concerned in this study with an art that has manifested itself very variously. And I am interested not only in works of literature in which the extreme manifestations of modernist style are evident (in *vers libre* poetry, say, or stream-of-consciousness fiction, or works devoted to alienated heroes), but in the overall currents of writing in the period. In short, it seems to me that all the modern arts, whether modernist or not, are witnesses to the forms of cultural alteration I am speaking of. The sense of an intensified modernity is very broadly spread—as much in the 'realism' of Hardy's later novels or the works of John Galsworthy or Arnold Bennett as in T. S. Eliot's 'The Waste Land' or James Joyce's *Ulysses*. The 'modern' period is a period of profound and marked changes in the social structure and in the psychic structures of men. To such things art responds; with such things it explores. What *is* clear is that 'modernism'—an increasing self-conscious-ness in art, a concern with distilling its essence, a deliberate attempt at an aesthetic redefinition, and an overall mood of literary radicalism[1]—is not only one of the most sensitive indicators of the change into the modern arts, but the point of highest awareness of change, of being on the watershed.

III

By the end of the nineteenth century in England that sensibility, that sense of living on a turn, was very much there in English writing, but it took a wide variety of forms. We can see it taking

---

[1] Which, as I have said earlier, is not the same as political radicalism.

place with fair clarity as, after 1870 or so, the literary scene seems to lose a previously gained coherence, and the desire for a new species of art becomes widespread. 'What gives [the period 1880–1914] its distinctive character is the clear emergence in English literary consciousness of a conviction that the known bearings of literary culture, whether humanist, romantic, or Victorian, have been for ever lost,' one commentator, John A. Lester, has written.[1] W. B. Yeats speaks of this period as one of the trembling of the veil, when the age seems about to bring forth a sacred book;[2] but it is not in a single book but in an overall temper that we can sense the coming of the modern—in a number of significant and general shifts of perception and emphasis. In the systematic thought of our time, we recognize certain themes and concerns which are very much those of the twentieth-century mind—the growth of modes of knowledge like sociology and psychology, the increased emergence of secular, rational and scientific tactics of thought, and the awareness of a pluralized, complex and unifiable universe. In art, too, there are such broad and common themes that run through the literary achievement of the period, and which are expressed and contained in most of the arts of the time, whether experimental or not, whether 'serious' or not. It is finally to these broader changes of context and atmosphere, of theme and language, of sensibility and style that a 'cultural' approach to modern writing will want to draw attention. For instance, most modern writing contains—in one way or another— a testimony to the growing power of the citified society over man: the city not just as a place of rapid, communal activity and impressions but as a metaphor for new kinds of juxtapositioning, new kinds of experience, and a new secularity of experience. It contains, too, a powerful assertion of the deprivation of past centres of value: the loss of the social cohesion and rhythms of an agrarian world, of the ideas and wisdoms of an old bourgeoisie and indeed of their liberal and individual view of reality, of a poetic-religious faith that finds a unified and universal purpose in nature or human

---

[1] John A. Lester, Jr., *Journey Through Despair, 1880–1914: Transformations in British Literary Culture* (Princeton, N.J., and London, 1968).
[2] W. B. Yeats, *The Trembling of the Veil* (London, 1922).

nature. It also contains the intense effort to reach for new centres of value and unity: in the hopeful new human types or newly self-aware social strata; in the new dispositions of human relationship created by new types of contact growing up between the sexes, among the classes, and between man and a more mobile and populous world of places and things; and in the 'new' areas of unconscious prompts and principles which seemed to underlie human behaviour.

If the writer's sense of 'reality' seemed to change, then so did his very language, his capacity to structure and to symbolize. The change in languages can be followed out from those basic, almost invisible usages of journalism—in for instance the columns of *Answers* and *Tit-Bits*, where in the encapsulated sentence and the brief paragraph experience was being redefined—to the rhetoric of a novelist like H. G. Wells, working with a prose consciously made unliterary by 'modern' and 'vernacular' speech rhythms. It can be followed into writers like Hardy, whose very 'literariness' is usually an effort at converting a new, post-Darwinian sense of the operations of the universe into adequate metaphor; or into the novels of D. H. Lawrence, where the sense of 'unconscious' principles running through human behaviour compels a redefinition of the traditional idea of fictional character; or into the elaborate structures and dispositions of 'point-of-view' in Henry James's novels, which are experiments not only in formal sophistication but in redefining the relationships of consciousness.[1] It is not simply in the subject-matter of literature, then, but in its very languages—its making of metaphors, shaping of sentences, ordering of events, use of 'points-of-view', and deployment of perceptual relations between one character and another, and between characters and their author, that we will find the true flavour of change. What is apparent, very variously, in the writing of this period is the presence of new forms of imaginative power, new sense of structure and form, which—created under an intense pressure from a changing view of man's place in time, society,

---

[1] There is little space in this study to explore this crucial question of the new 'rhetoric' of literature; but it is an intensely important aspect of cultural change and one on which literary criticism could well have much to say.

history and linguistic inheritance—makes its literary works quite different from anything which preceded them.[1]

To look back over the literary achievement of England in the modern period is to be struck by how intensely rich and dense it has been—above all in the remarkable period from about 1890 to 1920, when two or three consecutive generations of writers distilled a remarkable fund of cultural material and experience, not on the basis of any single aesthetic or movement, but through a multiplicity of directions and dimensions. Its ultimate strength has been its lack of 'purism,' and its capacity to maintain a pragmatic and multi-directional momentum. It has been one of the great modern literatures, and its energies have derived not only from those writers who have stood apart from their culture, but also from those who have lived with it and from it. Many of its classic works—Conrad's *Heart of Darkness*, Lawrence's *The Rainbow*, Forster's *A Passage to India*, Yeats's 'Byzantium', Eliot's 'Waste Land', Joyce's *Ulysses*, the poems of Auden and the novels of Evelyn Waugh and Graham Greene in the 1930s—have been poised, balanced mediations of the new and the old, the idiosyn-

[1] One of the most difficult areas of critical discussion today is that of adequately relating the 'content' of literature to its entire technique and sensibility. Indeed to emphasize 'content' is, in modern literary aesthetics, to evoke a false emphasis; there is a sense, which modern writers and critics have enforced, in which there is no content which is separable from form—though critics continue to speak of 'local texture', and most still find 'characters' in novels. (It is significant that this critical emphasis really derives from the period discussed in this paragraph, is one of the marks by which we distinguish 'modernist' aesthetics from the much more 'realist' aesthetics that preceded it, and has much to do with the belief that the world has no extant orders which the poet can 'romantically' intuit, but that artistic order can only emerge from the internal structure of the work itself.)

However, this is an important crux in 'culturalist' discussion, since one inevitable area of interest is the change in the 'content' of literature. It is impossible to explore this largely theoretical topic at length in this book. But I see it as a crucial challenge to interdisciplinary studies, and have made attempts at treating it in two articles—in 'Sociology and Literary Studies, II: Romance and Reality in *Maggie*', *Journal of American Studies*, III, i (July, 1969), pp. 111–21, which considers the relationship between style and structure, consciousness and culture; and 'Towards a Poetics of Fiction, I: An Approach through Structure', *Novel: A Forum on Fiction*, I, i (Fall, 1967), pp. 45–52, which explores the problem in the reading of a novel.

cratic and the communal, in their content, vision and language. Its
sense of experiment has been held against a sense of a tradition, a
continuity; its novelties have been remarkably assimilated towards
the centre. It is a literature that has been lit by lights from
modernism, rather than a modernist literature; and it has been
considerably rooted in familiar, national, provincial experience,
rather than in arcane worlds of its own making. In this sense it has
conducted a liberal dialogue with reality and with its social
audience, its writers functioning as humanist speakers in society
while drawn beyond it both to artistic transcendence and historical desperation. That taste for anarchy that has been so important
an aspect of certain stages of modernism in other countries has
been felt, but it has been mitigated, reduced from a state of outright nihilism or desperation. And in this compensatory process the
voices of other writers less extreme in vision have played a
consistently major part in maintaining the cultural mainstream, of
occupying the highbrow-middlebrow borderland which has been
a crucial territory in the social survival of modern literature.[1]

In certain respects modern England began the century as a much-
divided culture, fairly sharply segmented into different reading
levels and brows; and we might suppose that as the years have
passed, and the division has grown less acute in cultural as it has
in social matters, the cultural benefits would grow. In fact in
cultural matters this stratification may be less of an obstruction
than it seems, since it has allowed for a dialogue among the
levels of taste, among varied audiences, which has encouraged
artistic multiplicity. Today the artistic problem is for a writer to
find his appropriate audience in an ill-defined and ill-structured
situation in which the dialogue with the cultural mainstream
may be impossible to conceive, because any living cultural centre
is impossible to find. Perhaps the real achievement of the writers
of the early part of the century was, then, to function both in the
public world of culture and the private world of art, to maintain

[1] A classic instance of this kind of writer, inclined towards modernism but
also concerned to act as a representative humanist intellectual, is E. M. Forster
—whom I have discussed in this light in 'Two Passages to India: Forster as
Victorian and Modern' in *Aspects of E. M. Forster*, ed. O. Stallybrass (London,
1969).

the role of the artist as a social intelligence while insisting on the role of the artist as the specialist of his own privatized language. At any rate, the mixture of an artistic radicalism and a cultural participation was to prove the seedbed of a major phase of literary art, co-equal with, and yet with marked national differences from, the large international effort of twentieth-century literature.

CHAPTER III

'The Impress of the Moving Age': English Culture, 1870–1914

I

I have suggested that, somewhere in the last decades of the nineteenth century and the first decades of this one, there occurs a marked change in the temper and texture of English artistic culture. Similar changes take place in other western cultures at the same time, and it is in these decades that, looking back, the literary historian normally finds one of those strange dividing lines, one of those translations of sensibility, that transfer the arts from one period to another. Yet in many other cultures this is the period of the major impact of the industrial revolution, or of other revolutionary ferment which suggests a possible cause. In England it is not. England began the Industrial Revolution and by the turn of the century many of its implications had been known for a very long time. English thought and art had been saturated, for most of the century, by concern about and imaginative comprehension of those rising forces—socially, the bourgeoisie; intellectually, the rise of utilitarian and rationalist thought; culturally, the redisposed relationships of an industrializing society—and the persistent themes of English romanticism are eminently complex artistic responses to such matters. But of course it is now romanticism, in its Victorian forms, that comes into question among the newer generations of artists; and it comes into question because the prevailing view of the 'modern' issue seems to change. And part of this change is an intensified sense of modernity itself—a sharpened consciousness of the character of the modern world as it impinges on the arts, a stronger appreciation of the powers of change at work in society, an increased sense of the need for artistic innovation, a desire to develop new themes, new concerns, and new myths. Why, in English society, should this happen when it did?

For, through most of the nineteenth century, English culture had that markedly cohesive quality that, we saw, foreign commentators tended usually to stress in observing it. What always most impresses us now, as we look at Victorian literary and intellectual culture, is its real sense of functioning close to the centre of society, of having a responsibility for its total texture. The Victorian intellectual is, of course, nothing if not critical of his society. But he persistently possesses a relative centrality and influence, a conviction of being able up to a point to command the direction and purposes of the national culture, in a spirit and tone often absent from other nineteenth-century cultures in other countries. He is part of that gradualism, that sense of community in progress, which controlled the limits of doubt and dissent, that liberal conviction that society must serve the variously different interests of its members, which we call the Victorian synthesis, and which enabled England to accommodate to the primary stages of industrial change gradually and relatively peaceably. The fact that the Victorian intellectual in the United Kingdom was not alienated is a crucial one. There was always a prospect of mobility, of access to the seats of power. The debate was therefore preserved very largely within a framework of discourse; that perhaps is best illustrated in the fortunes of the Established Religion and Dissent issue as compared with the anticlerical movement in France. It meant that intellectuals in England were less likely to be dramatic and fundamentally challenging, more likely to accept the context of argument and society as assumptions. And, finally, the absence of past breaks in the social pattern —the lack of previous radical constitutional or religious change— made the prospect of such changes seem less conceivable or even desirable. In terms of literary and intellectual culture, this confidence undoubtedly has to do with a conviction that the writer can reach and sway a general audience with ideas calculated to the betterment of all, the imaginative worth of all; the arts were part

of the common individualism of society, its pattern of collaborat-
ing *and* contending voices.

As a result, Victorian culture is a peculiarly rich artistic period,
one in which dissent and criticism flow in and out of the centre.
We must not over-estimate this coherence or suppose that the
culture was not filled with profound divisions and dissents. It
was, but by no means to the point of producing those sensations
of cultural solitude or of difficulty in the very act of making a
meaning out of art that was to touch at least some of the writing
that was to follow. The period contains most of the subsequent
doubts and disturbances, and it breaks many of the traditional
forms. But it does so without breaking completely with the
cultural past—and without seeing a cultural atomization in the
present. It does not see the modern as a violence done upon
culture itself. Indeed, it becomes possible to conceive of 'culture'
as the means of redeeming that span of scepticism, doubt and
inner anguish that lies deeply in Victorian thought. So Matthew
Arnold saw the intelligentsia as a culturally reconciling force, a
body of Guardians who transcended partisanship or class interest
by being committed to culture, 'the best that was known and
thought in the world'. Culture was the onward flow of mind and
feeling which met in a centre above politics or sectarianism; it
was the society's best expression; and it took the form of a social
debate and a spiritualization of social and human need that grew
out of exposure to variation of viewpoint and interest. The
cultural and social transitions of the era thus became a part of the
onward movement of the human mind in its growth towards
perfection, and the modernizing world could unify itself in
culture instead of dividing itself by anarchy. The arts had a
central part in this hope, which was by no means confined to
Arnold alone. One strand in Romantic thought had held that
truth, meaning and spiritual force were to be found only outside
the social order, in the realm of nature, or of human feeling. But
Romanticism itself also felt itself to be a force at work in society, a
movement of human growth that would 'spiritualize' it and make
it answer to the needs of men, would in fact make it the most
profound expression of the needs of men. Society could be

redeemed by making culture prevail as a common unity or end.[1] A moralized Romanticism could be urged on society itself; that became the prime emphasis of that extended social critique of English society from the standpoint of the literary imagination, the 'culture and society' debate that Raymond Williams has explored so well.[2] Art itself could become a species of social improvement, a reaching towards the kind of society that served, in Carlyle's phrase, 'the human being in his wholeness'. This gave the man of letters a social purpose and a social place, and it is only when this conviction starts to diminish that the idea of the 'revolutionary arts' begins to take on meaning.

But of course this does not mean that the literary intellectuals of the nineteenth century were not aware of the pressures of the modern, and the sense of strain is there in all their work. Carlyle called the Victorian period an 'age of revolutions'; Tennyson said that 'all ages are ages of transition, but this is an awful moment of transition.' 'The age then is one of *destruction*!' said Bulwer Lytton, and went on: 'Miserable would be our lot were it not also an age of preparation for reconstructing.' If the stress on transition runs deep in the Victorian era, so too does stress on the obligation towards modernity. Matthew Arnold defined the age as 'modern' and said that 'An intellectual deliverance is the peculiar demand of those ages which are called modern'; while Dickens in *Bleak House* satirizes those characters who do not receive 'any impress from the moving age'. Equally there is a stress on the anguish caused by the forces of change. 'We live in an age of visible transition—an age of disquietude and doubt . . .' said Bulwer Lytton. 'To me such epochs appear . . .

---

[1] Significantly, the belief that the culture could be transformed through the witness of the writer and intellectual never attained really powerful force in the United States, where the writer had very much less access and less influence —and where the 'nay-saying' tradition and the modernist stresses were therefore stronger. (The one obvious exception here is the culture of Boston between 1830 and 1860.) Even so, there is still an obvious imaginative difference between the literature of the first three-quarters of the nineteenth century in America, and that of the latter part of the century and the first three decades of the present one; America had its 'modernist' revaluation too.

[2] Raymond Williams, *Culture and Society* (London, 1958).

the times of greatest unhappiness to our species.'[1] Walter Pater, in his essay on Coleridge, speaks of 'that inexhaustible discontent, languor and homesickness, that endless regret, the chords of which ring all through our modern literature.' In matters of thought and literature, a modern strain is indeed apparent, though it is not what we would now call modernism. A classic statement of the Victorian view of the modern in literature is the famous lecture of 1856 by Matthew Arnold, a devout mid-century disciple of the modern, called 'On the Modern Element in Literature'. Arnold's view of culture and art depended on the sense that society was in motion and that thought, too, must be so. He recognized that 'depression and *ennui*' are characteristics stamped on many of the works of modern times. But for Arnold the 'modern element' in literature becomes the gift of intellectual maturity, the critical spirit, which leads men towards right reason. But, as Lionel Trilling has pointed out in an important essay,[2] he uses the word 'modern' in an wholly honorific sense; and if behind his ecumenical effort to reconcile the splits and schisms of culture lies a deep sense of social division, he does suggest that the literary mind can meaningfully act *in* modern society, and that to do otherwise is a loss for society and for the

[1] Walter Houghton stresses this aspect of the Victorian age in his *The Victorian Frame of Mind: 1830–1870* (New Haven, 1957); and the Victorian awareness of modernity is also very usefully discussed in Philip Collins, *The Impress of a Moving Age* (Leicester, 1965). Most of my quotations are cited in these two sources. Houghton's view that the Victorian faith that 'transition' *can* be mitigated by reason and human advance grows bleaker by the 1870s is well supported by John A. Lester, *Journey Through Despair: Transformations in British Literary Culture, 1880–1914*, cited above. Also see J. H. Buckley, *The Victorian Temper: A Study in Literary Culture* (New York, 1951), and Barbara Charlesworth, *Dark Passages: The Decadent Consciousness in Victorian Literature* (Madison, Wis., 1965).

[2] Trilling (op. cit.) stresses that in Arnold's definition of the 'modern element' there is a sense of deliverance through civilization. This is the opposite of that deep distrust of civilization that runs through modernism, as we find it in Dostoievsky, Conrad, D. H. Lawrence or Thomas Mann. Arnold in fact uses the term 'modern' as a term of praise ('So much so, indeed,' says Trilling, 'that he seems to dismiss all temporal idea from the word and make it signify certain timeless intellectual and civil virtues') where in subsequent writing it evokes the idea of a disquiet.

arts. In this, as Trilling points out, he is at odds with what we would normally think of as modernism today.

Behind the romantic desire to reform the culture—by stating the claims of the heart as opposed to the head, the rounded values of life to the mechanical views of utilitarianism, culture to the untamed and unmitigated social process—there is an element of deep independence which could easily turn in the direction of outright disaffiliation. This imaginative disaffiliation has been sketched, particularly by the romantics—by Blake and Shelley for instance—, and was always potentially there. And it is that tradition that beings to re-emerge in the arts after about 1870, as part of a general discomfort about the capacity to unify the culture and think of history as a beneficent and progressive force. The world before 1870 was not, as we have seen, a compact one, sure of its ethics, capable of holding all experience in its hand; but after 1870 it was less so than it had been, its confidence and unity shaken not simply by Darwin and the growing bulk of social and political problems attendant on expansion and industrialism, but by the capacity of growth potentially to outrun control in thought and art as well as in culture and society. W. B. Yeats found the world a bundle of fragments in his youth, and his testimony to the loss of cultural monopoly was echoed by many. A new self-awareness, which was the awareness of uncertainty, becomes apparent; and in the new systems of thought, the new notions of culture, the new species of art that began to emerge it seemed, apparently, crucial to build into them the means of their own dismantling. A new 'balkanization' shows in thought generally, in the form of an increasing specialization of mental life; a simple example would be the multiplication of triposes at the Universities of Oxford and Cambridge in the last thirty years of the century. In the same way the cultural dialogue begins to pluralize and lose its centre, producing a marked specialization and professionalization in writers and artists, and a withdrawal from the larger social life. The cultural hierarchy increasingly begins to divide into fairly sharp levels which are 'stabilized' by the multiplication of the media which arose in increasing numbers and types both to define them and to serve them.

But the most striking feature of all is a marked break in cultural continuity which occurs at this time, and leaves a void to be filled; the great Victorian literary generation gives way to a new one engaged in an endless hunt in many quarters for new styles and mannerisms. The rush to France, for realism and symbolism, for the mode of the aesthete and the impressionist; the cults of *japonaiserie* and of African or primitive art; the enhancing of aesthetic sensation and the devaluing of morality, even the quest for 'strange great sins'; the turning culture into a mystery, an individual contemplation of the beautiful, the structured and the composed; the growing ideal of the perfect exhaustion and corruption of sensibilities—all these things were not so much an attempt to define a new style and a new culture as an assertion of the thrills of the quest. Even when, in William Morris, for example, it takes the form of a radical effort to redeem the social culture, it depends upon a dream of aesthetic restoration, of dandyism for all. If traditional themes and methods will no longer cohere this shifting world, forcing the artist back either on a neo-scientific positivism or on the radiant morality of his own right sensation, then the accelerated quest for new centres of art, ideas and culture becomes not only a necessary act but a dramatization of cultural predicament. And this is what much of the new effort in the arts was to be, much of its interest today lying less in the work produced than in the producers themselves, publicly displaying the condition of artist as an epicurean manifestation. This phase in art took various forms, but its most marked feature is conscious redefinition of the idea of artistic creativity; and it was part of a broad re-alignment of the artist and intelligentsia in England towards roles more detached, socially outrageous, radical or *avant garde*.[1]

But behind them and along with them were emerging new ideas of a movement out of an old order and into a new one,

[1] For a more extensive discussion of the significance of aestheticism as a new view of the artist and the culture, see Frank Kermode, *Romantic Image* (London, 1957); and also Graham Hough, *The Last Romantics* (London, 1949) and William Gaunt, *The Aesthetic Adventure* (1945). On the broader topic of change in cultural role, see John Gross, *The Rise and Fall of the Man of Letters* (London, 1969).

intuitions that fresh forms of consciousness were breaking forth. If not revolutionary, such notions were at least evolutionary, focused in intellectual heroes like the superman, with new passions and a new psychology, or the radical, with new beliefs and hopes, or the artist, with new forms and 'instinct with the modern'. Thought and art increasingly started not only to speak on behalf of that emergence, but to try to enact it. So the modern became an intensified categorical imperative, taking on significance as an aspect of style, whether manifested personally or in the race or culture at large. So in this new cultural climate there is a growing obsession with flux—flux of sensation, moments of termination and transcendence, the cracking of an old form and the bursting forth of a new one, the possibility of possibility. There is a new reaching out for new political syntheses, or new theories of the operative principles of society, or new versions of history; there is also a new awareness of those forces which have so far been left unconscious and unexpressed, yet which must, the hope runs, really lie behind individual and social development. These theories tend, of course, to deplete individualism; they tend, particularly in neo-Darwinian and neo-Marxian form, to lead towards a more scientific view of experience and a more collective view of man. At the same time, the manifest element of despair and constraint is as important as— perhaps more important than—the element of hope. Chiliastic dreams come increasingly to merge with images of disaster, disorder and loss of control. The end of history seems in some ways more evident than the hint of a new history. Moreover, the difficulties of constructing a theory or a universe become very much more apparent, so that a profound problem exists in the realm of thought and art themselves. The marked sense of intensified crisis that sets off modern from Victorian thought comes not only from an increasing sense of the age's complexities; it also comes from the knowledge that change is disturbing and upsetting the conditions of thought and art themselves.

F

II

If part of the reason for this new awareness of change lies in diminished intellectual confidence that the culture is subject to the control of the imagination, and hence in a new relativity and subjectivism, then what are the forces in late Victorian and Edwardian society that would bring about such sentiments? The sudden sense of the Nietzschean imperative that all men must prepare themselves to reject accepted and traditional values, and face the intellectual and psychological tension of new ones, is not entirely easy to explain; this is not on the face of it a socially revolutionary period. The answer is surely that the last decades of the nineteenth century are one of those periods in history—the 1920s is another; and we seem to be moving into a like period now—when quantitative changes come suddenly to be seen as qualitative changes. It becomes clear that what has been developing and proliferating for a long time has made life so different that things must now be seen in a new way. Such intellectual ferment is not, then, necessarily entirely the product of immediate forces, but of the desire to realign old interpretations which have suddenly come to seem exposed and complete. This experience (in the United States much of it coheres neatly into the decade of the 1890s,[1] but in England it has a longer span) forces new overviews, new interpretations, new knowledge. The Victorian period in England had been one of vast acquisition, cultural, material, intellectual; but what had been acquired seemed to be outrunning knowledge and understanding. What seems to be at the centre of late Victorian intellectual ferment is the conviction that the patterns of nineteenth-century change have produced a new environment needing a different order of analysis. The change becomes seen as so sufficiently advanced as to impinge upon men in a new way. It was affecting more fortunes, producing more cultural turmoil, and transforming the visible fabric of human life. It was also making people look for

[1] Cf. Larzer Ziff, *The American 1890s: The Life and Times of a Lost Generation* (London, 1967).

the first time at what had long been there, but had not been clearly seen.

By the late decades of the century, the patterns of industrial democratic capitalism were firmly set in England—so firmly that it became harder to believe that meaningful alternatives to it existed, or that a 'change of heart' would remedy what had long been read, by intellectuals, as its defects: its mechanism and utilitarianism, or else its wealth-distribution and associated social problems. Moreover, the primary processes of industrial-capitalist society were now globally far enough developed for their nature and direction to be much more clearly visible, and analysable. It was now possible for men to envision it as a process —a tendency in historical development with its own impetus, limitations and advantages—and an all-encompassing environment, and to relate to it their hopes and fears. Fairly accurate predictions about the types and directions of social development could be made, and men like H. G. Wells won great public esteem by making them. But to see it in this way meant seeing it 'objectively', or independently of many of the beliefs of the past. Thought was freed of its old dependencies; but then, like men themselves, it was committed to new ones. And what could be explained in scientific, sociological, economic terms could not always be validated in more personal ones; indeed in many ways the rhetoric of personal and traditional values was threatened, and the metaphors of organic growth seemed inappropriate to the process of mechanical proliferation. The present was now allied to the future, and increasingly it was set off against the past, which was a static point receding into the distance. Society was agglomerating and centralizing, with industry as the centre of national endeavour and social democracy as the new human order. Men now lived not in local communities but in the context of the nation-state. With the application of technology to communications, the nation as a whole was shrinking, while the individual environment was becoming wider: the railways, from 1860 the tramways, the postal and telegraphic services, the spread of gas and electric light, the wide-circulation and national newspaper broke into separated communities, enfranchising them but producing greater social and political complexity. The need for abstract, impersonal social arrangements increased, and local and national government alike had to commit themselves to civic arrangements, services, sanitation, health matters. The hiring of labour became increasingly a matter of contract, through trades unions. Education emancipated men from old convictions and old roles; with the spread of services and the need for technical skills, new ones emerged. At the same time, there was an increasing desire for the scientific study of society itself, and both the main political parties were moving away from an individualistic or *laissez-faire* view of society, extending suffrage, education and national services and attempting to mitigate the untamed Darwinian struggle in society.

The fact that the new society, with its impersonal relationships, its new species of sensibility and possibility, its rational onward momentum, was a half-controlled growth rather than a community or a culture perhaps explains the deep vein of rural nostalgia that runs through art and sensibility in the period, expressing itself in forms as various as General William Booth's rural colonies, the search for a yeoman ideal of greatness, and such self-dependent intellectuals as Edward Carpenter, making his sandals near Sheffield. The persistence of the rural or organic image in literature runs deep, providing almost *the* essential alternative myth for the era, the only outright model of community as opposed to crowd. For England was now a post-village society, well past the stabilities of the yeoman version of England that writers like E. M. Forster or D. H. Lawrence could look back to in the course of their radical critiques of the new order. What Forster in *Howards End* (1910)—a novel which, among other things, concerns itself with this completed historical shift from yeoman England to the England of enlightened, efficient business, social stratification, and nomadic intelligence —called 'the civilization of luggage' was here to stay: a more mechanical, rational and efficient society. From the 1870s on, the industrializing, centralizing and democratizing forces took on increased momentum, as necessary aspects of national survival. Now it was possible for men to see themselves as the first waves of the coming human type, living out lives of change, pre-figuring a future in which urban living, expanding national growth, accelerating scientific advance and some sort of collectivist social pattern were part of the logical sequence of events—utopia or dystopia.[1] It was within this world of choices that human profit and loss was to be assessed, that the progress of progress was to be understood. From about 1870 to the outbreak of the First World War, the shape of this new order was, as we can now see, being increasingly exposed. Custom and inherited belief were more radically in dissolution than before; old ways of living were broken into by new ones on a large scale; the movement of change acquired the quality of a rush. The intelligentsia itself, more and more clustering towards urban centres, were losing many of their old sources of value and social place. Neither thought nor art could remain as unified as they had been; and those who carried the burden of reconciling the variety of world-views that emerged, in a culture that was questioning the place and function of the arts themselves, found themselves deeply involved in the bliss or dejection of transformation. It is not surprising that there grew up a new self-consciousness about methods, styles and structures, and, often, an emphasis on style or manner itself as a mode of self-presentation and reconcilement. The multiple origins from which thought sprang, the solvency of old ideals in new circumstances, often brought about a sense of the relativity of values, and hence encouraged new notes of cultural despair, new kinds of irony, new feelings that civilization in the traditional sense was in question.

On obvious feature of the processes at work was the growing importance of the city. In a sense it is, of course, only a spatial location of the new processes, a consequence of technological

---

[1] This was, of course, a period remarkably rich in utopian thinking and utopian writing, as well as in the reverse versions (the modern word is dystopia). See, for example, Samuel Butler's *Erewhon* (1872), William Morris's *News from Nowhere* (1891), Edward Bellamy's *Looking Backward* (1888) and Ignatius Donnelly's *Caesar's Column* (1891). Wells of course produced positive and negative versions and linked it all with science fiction (*A Modern Utopia, Anticipations, The War of the Worlds*). For a discussion of utopias real and imagined, see W. H. Armytage, *Heavens Below* (London, 1961).

development. But since culture for the arts is a matter of community, it acquired particular imaginative importance: as the place where the cultural process converged, where the writer and artist was most imposed, where the most novel impressions were to be had, where a new role might be won. Like the machine, it provided a decisive contrast to set against the more organic metaphors on which art had long depended. Always an important cultural focus in English life,[1] it now acquired new meanings. For urbanization meant not only the movement of men into cities—though with a vastly increased rate of movement to cities a new kind of hegemony was being created[2]—but their power to create particular and distinctive values which promoted the disintegration of more local values. Those who moved there were changed; those who stayed were also in a transforming environment that was breaking up traditional attitudes, so that England was in many ways becoming a nation of migrant people or migrant values. There are three important features of the urbanizing process that, becoming marked in the nineteenth century and much intensified by its end, give the city a new significance in English culture. First, the growth of the *industrial* city, the city of workers, with its white-collar suburban fringes, produced new and hardened social stratifications. Second, the national capital, London, became *the* city, diminishing the civic centrality of the provincial cities.[3] Third, London becomes not

[1] One could hardly say of England, as Richard Hofstadter (*The Age of Reform* (New York, 1955)) does of the States, that the nation was born in the country and moved to the city.

[2] So the agricultural depression of 1879 took 4 million acres out of cultivation; half a million workers left the country for the town. C. F. Masterman, in his *Condition of England* (London, 1909), reported that nine out of ten families had moved from country to town in three generations. The resulting shift in social focus is suggested by demographic figures (from Asa Briggs, *Victorian Cities* (London, 1964)). In 1841 just over one in six of the population lived in cities of 10,000 or more; in 1891 the proportion was more like one in three. The cities vastly enlarged; over the same period London grew from just over $1\frac{3}{4}$ million to just under $4\frac{1}{4}$ million.

[3] Asa Briggs (op. cit., Chap. 8) shows how London usurped many of the roles of cities like Manchester and Birmingham and began to dominate national life, eliminating local newspapers, becoming a centre of communications and focus of influence, forming something like a single cultural centre. The way in which

only the metropolis but also cosmopolis—a 'world city' which, connecting with empire and the globe, starts to represent the supreme city to men everywhere, drawing in strangers, becoming an ethnic mix and a melting pot, generating new values, new thought and new art. It becomes the city as melting pot for men and mores, forming new patterns of value-creation and trans-mission, serving in its art as a metaphor for social and intellectual flux, confusion and heterodoxy, for accelerated consciousness. It becomes a cultural frontier which the artist and thinker has to face. And at the same time, because the 'shock cities' of Victorian times were unlike previous metropolitan forms, because they were not the civilized polis but the place of manufacture and consumption, getting and spending, social problems, classes and masses, human anonymity, they crystallized many of the problems of the industrial society which created them. The new crowds, the modern masses, dominated (so Cardinal Newman feared in 1871 that the crowds might 'rise up from the depths of modern cities, and will be the new scourges of God'); and London, like Chicago, became the example of the new megalo-polis, with its endless unorganized growth, novel living patterns, marked social stratifications, and overwhelming social problems —which only reason (and sociology) might solve.[1] The city was

---

the city can become the example of cultural relativity and amorphous growth, and of a new and self-generating system of human relationships, is expounded in Georg Simmel, 'The Metropolis and Mental Life' (in *The Sociology of Georg Simmel* (ed. Kurt H. Wolff) (Glencoe, Ill., 1950), pp. 409–24). Simmel observes that the city has its own objective existence, its own cultural growth indepen-dent of the culture of its citizens: it hence can well become an image of the modern multiverse. Robert E. Park (in *Human Communities: The City and Urban Ecology* (Glencoe, Ill., 1952), pp. 138–89, and in Park, Ernest Burgess and R. D. McKenzie, *The City* (Chicago, 1925)), has also stressed that the tendency of the modern city was to produce the division and specialization of tasks, substituting secondary relationships (through jobs, schools, etc.) for primary relationships (family, church, etc.).

[1] It increasingly came to seem that the new instrumentalities which had in some respects created the problem could solve them; they could be handled by a scientific view of society itself. This was the deduction drawn from Charles Booth's sociological studies of the London poor of 1889; the same positivist deduction was being drawn in the United States.

the storm-centre of civilization;[1] it was the jungle awaiting the ministrations of the missionary;[2] it was the place of cultural confusion and cultural hope.

For beside the sense of vast indifference, distorted relationships, atomized lives, went a conviction of new possibilities—of independence, intellectual excitement, a new culture and civilization.[3] It undoubtedly accelerated the characteristic drift of the arts towards cosmopolitanism, to sophistication as opposed to local registration. Because the city seemed a context or a process rather than a human event, because it was a form of material development rather than a culture, it posed a profound problem for the arts. It could scarcely be seen as more than a condition of mind—a superfluity of experience, a permanent transience, presenting variegated, fleeting moments, a state of exposure to the unknown. It certainly invoked a new basis for cultural activity, a new notion of artistic role and experience. As George Ponderevo reflects in H. G. Wells's *Tono Bungay* (1909): 'The whole illimitable place [London] teemed with suggestions of indefinite and sometimes outrageous possibility, of hidden but magnificent meanings.' Contingent, audacious and depraved, the modern city, the frontier of cultural interaction and the ultimate expression of formlessness, was in fact not only the ideal locus for the writer to sense the nature of his society in, but the ideal metaphor for expressing it. Appropriately, in conceiving his most ironic, impressionistic and 'modern' novel, *The Secret Agent* (1907), a novel about the anarchy and the existential exposure that lies behind the face of civilization, which contains no hero, no plot in the sense of an effective resolution of the action, and no real centre of positive value, Joseph Conrad began with an image of London:

[1] So the American Joseph Strong was calling the city not only the nerve-centre but the storm-centre of civilization, because it expressed a one-sided development of material as opposed to moral and spiritual development.

[2] E.g. in General William Booth's *In Darkest England and the Way Out* (London, 1890).

[3] This of course had strong political expression. Engels saw the city as the breeding ground of a new politics; it was the purgatory of the peasant and would breed its own solutions, making the proletariat socially conscious and self-aware as a class.

the vision of an enormous town presented itself, of a monstrous town more populous than some continents, and in its man-made might as if indifferent to heaven's frowns and smiles; a cruel devourer of the world's light. There was room enough to place any story, depth enough there for any passion, variety enough there for any setting, darkness enough to bury five millions of lives.

This is a classic reversal of the ideal of the city as the locus of civilization; and it is in a line with the 'fourmillante cité' of Baudelaire, the heart with 'no pulsation of humanity' in Forster, the 'unreal city' that dominates Eliot's 'The Waste Land'. The city was a mechanical environment, a contingent disposition of multiple forces, a melting pot of human experiences, types and moral and emotional ferments. While in some sense it revealed the failure of nineteenth-century civilization—as it does for Wells in *Tono Bungay* or Conrad in *The Secret Agent*—it also, by its very tension, produced a new sense of vitality; for country living seemed to have lost its meaning and vigour, and the city, while the place of confusion and stress, offered a persistent energy and temptation, was the source of the stimulating, the intellectual, the exotic. It brought to most writers feelings of discontinuity and disconnectedness, of materialism, secularism and relativity that seemed to them logical constituents of the urban universe; yet, in their work, a comprehension of and an adaptation to the city was an essential part of an understanding. In both Lawrence and Forster, for example, we can see the industrial city, the city of Lawrence's 'town-birds', as a force for cultural discontinuity, polarized against the agrarian universe. But their response is neither simply provincial nor simply nostalgic. Both were intellectuals, mentally discrete from the values they turned to as centres of continuity, and both imaginatively entered into the city and understood it, while feeling compelled to speak of it with irony and disquiet, as a metaphor for an England destroyed or misused. But for other writers, like Wells, a different position was possible; the city may be formless, outrageous, cancerous, but its formlessness is fundamental and valuable and has its analogue in the structure of literature itself: *Tono Bungay*, Wells tells us, 'is not a constructed tale', it reaches towards 'unimaginable realities'.[1] Indeed the basic theme of that book is the groping feeling towards 'lost orientations' of those who do not lie in the shadow of the feudal, rural Bladesover system of a disappearing England.

The point was that the city incubated artistic and human novelty, encouraged, in effect, a new order of art, composed to a different and an urban historiography and structure.[2] The increasing urbanization of literature—which at once brought the writer more and more into the place and perspective of metropolitan detachment, and gave his work a panoramic multiplicity—encouraged a wide variety of modes, from realism to experimentalism. The characteristic locus of the realist-naturalist novel or play that burgeoned around the turn of the century is the large, busy, impersonal metropolis (Gissing's *New Grub Street*, Jack London's *The People of the Abyss*, G. B. Shaw's *Widower's Houses*), with deep social contrasts and juxtapositions (East End, West End), and a ferocious, Darwinian struggle for survival and supremacy at work. Here the spread of the city provides an absolute metaphor of system and process, of abstract relationship and remote responsibility, of destruction of individuality and the aimless energy of force. The other classic juxtaposition is that between country and city, producing a new pastoral in which the countryside stands for a lost organicism and the city for a new exposure (*Howards End*, *The Rainbow*). Or the myth can be more promising, as a confining past collapses and a new hope or opportunity is born as a young man strides out into a new life (*Sons and Lovers*, *Tono Bungay*). In more experimental writing, the contrasts are often not so much matters of

[1] 'Factory chimneys smoke right over against Westminster with an air of carelessly not having permission and the whole effect of industrial London and of all London east of Temple Bar and of the huge immensity of London Port is to me of something disproportionately large, something morbidly expanded without plan or intention, dark and sinister. . . .

'To this day I will ask myself will those masses ever become structural, will they indeed shape into anything new whatever or is that cancerous image their true and ultimate diagnosis. . . .' H. G. Wells, *Tono Bungay* (1909).

[2] For a more extended analysis of this, see Raymond Williams, *The English Novel from Dickens to Lawrence* (London, 1970); and the more intensive discussion still he has proposed for his forthcoming book *The Country and the City*.

objective observation—as in realism—but matters of profound irony, the city standing as a metaphor for a ghostly community of the dead (*The Secret Agent*, *Dubliners*). Or else the novel or poem of subjective consciousness catches new and flickering relationships from contingency and miscellany (*Ulysses*, 'The Waste Land'), often with an apocalyptic or diabolic association ('The City of Dreadful Night'). At any rate, it is the place of new relationships, new consciousness, and new deprivations; and the art that comes forth is frequently an art and aesthetic of new response to new situations.[1] It becomes an essential element in most literary polarizations and mythologies, and the rationale behind most expressionisms and impressionisms. Creating and diminishing possibilities, it went along with new excitements and distorted relationships, deep displacements of human resource and response. It was the centre of intellectual ferment, where ideas met and spawned, and the disorientating wilderness where culture collapsed. Such cultural ambivalence about the city is a profound part of modern sensibility; and behind it lies, clearly, an ambivalence about the modern world itself.[2]

For, of course, the city enabled the writer's own emanicpation, his expatriation from the province, his movement towards his own intellectuality and art. With the growth of London, for instance (it doubled its population in the last half of the nineteenth century, between 1841 to 1891, to become the biggest city in the world), writers were increasingly drawn towards it as a cultural focus. It had long been a centre for literature, back indeed to the Elizabethans, and certain aspects of this dialogue between city and country were not new in the least. On the other hand, the provincial centres of literary culture were being diminished as places where a successful writer might conduct his career. London provided work and the possibility of living by writing; it also became an artistic melting-pot in which cultural innovation was likely and probable. It drew artists together and

[1] Compare, for instance, Matthew Arnold's 'Lines Written in Kensington Gardens', with its dominantly pastoral imagery, and the 'new' imagery of Ezra Pound's 'The Garden'.

[2] On this general topic, see Morton and Lucia White, *The Intellectual Versus the City: From Thomas Jefferson to Frank Lloyd Wright* (Cambridge, Mass., 1962).

tended to produce artistic communities, often of a new kind. For the artist too sought his liberation; and London was the place of bohemia, those specialized artistic enclaves, cosmopolitan villages with communications out into the world but with a localized, artistic hierarchy of values, in which new movements could form and new styles evolve. The model of the artist tended to become that of the urbanized intellectual, in contact with his fellow-writers, the thought-movements not only of the city but the world, declassé, emancipated, intellectually innovative and advanced. It was an environment, too, that had to be assimilated. 'I am bound to be in London,' wrote Gissing in 1899, 'because I must work hard at gathering some new material.' Like Gissing, Henry James needed London and abhorred it: '. . . for one who takes it as I take it,' he wrote, 'London is on the whole the most possible form of life. I take it as an artist and as a bachelor; as one who has the passion of observation and whose business is the study of human life. It is the biggest aggregation of human life—the most complete compendium of the world.' Conrad saw it as an ironic masterpiece of modern civilization, the focus of an empire and a place of darkness too. Forster, in *Howards End*, represents it as the necessary intellectual centre for his heroines, the Schlegel sisters, and as a 'red rust' creeping across England for its destruction. In Gissing, Forster, James and Wells, and in the expatriate writers who came from America or the 'provincials' who came from Ireland, we can sense the profound pull of the capital, as a place of intellectual stimulus, modern thought, political activity new life-style.[1]

Writers were not the only emergent classes who were lured to the city; a whole new class of the newly educated were coming to notice and making their way, like Hardy's Clym Yeobright (*The Return of the Native*), or some of Lawrence's heroes and heroines, from 'a bucolic to an intellectual life'.

---

[1] Wells conveniently distils this experience, fictionally in *Ann Veronica* (1909), factually in *Experiment in Autobiography* (2 vols., London, 1934). See also Lovat Dickson, *H. G. Wells: His Turbulent Life and Times* (New York and London, 1969), and Bernard Bergonzi, *The Early H. G. Wells* (Manchester, 1961).

These populist figures entering various kinds of humble intellectual, service and managerial activity, under the educational
impetus of the second-stage Industrial Revolution, were men and
women seeking new horizons for themselves in schoolteaching,
journalism or writing itself: Arnold Bennett, H. G. Wells, and
Lawrence and Hardy themselves were much of this type. For
many the new way was to be, as for H. G. Wells, the way of
science and technology; Wells called these the 'new men', and
Veblen, in America, saw them as the class that would redeem
capitalist society. In England this 'rise of the technocrats' was
rather more belated than in the United States or Germany, due
to serious educational and social doubts about such developments
and the low esteem of technical training.[1] But with the rising
respectability of scientific positivism and its missionary possibilities, and with the very change in national thought towards a
much more rationalistic creed, a growing belief in the progressive value of the social and the natural and chemical sciences, th
numbers in scientific education increased.[2] While they never
acquired the conscious identity and common interest of technical
intelligentsias in some other countries, they had prestige and
influence not only in promoting national and business growth but
in promoting social reform. In intellectual bias, in their new
social origins, in their fervent scientism, the new men added new
thought to the intellectual activity of the period, offering an
important progressive context in English life. Above all they

[1] This is usually given as one reason why British national growth declined
over this period, when Germany and the United States outpaced Britain. On
this topic, see W. H. G. Armytage, *The Rise of the Technocrats: A Social History*
(London, 1965).

[2] By the 1870s, literary and philosophical societies were being replaced
locally by scientific societies, which in turn gave momentum to the foundation
of colleges (like Owen's College in Manchester or Mason's College in Birmingham) usually with a scientific emphasis. Between 1871 and 1902 eleven
new colleges (now universities) were founded. The polytechnic pattern was
also growing: the famous example was Finsbury Technical College, which has
world-wide reputation. The Webbs pressed for and achieved another sort of
scientific institute in the 1890s, the London School of Political Science. And
they along with Haldane were responsible for the Imperial College of Science
and Technology, developed in 1907 from the Royal College of Science and the
Royal School of Mines. For fuller details, see Armytage, op. cit.

seemed to cope with the dominance of the machine, which, with the city, was the other dominant point of growth in contemporary society, and which likewise meant an end to many routine concepts of the past. New concepts, new knowledge, even a new culture and society, had to emerge if it could. A new relation between self and society had to emerge, or man was a sacrifice to the machines he was making; the new men seemed to offer a way, like the commanding Holroyd in H. G. Wells's story 'The Lord of the Dynamos': 'Look at that . . . where's your 'eathen idol to match 'im? . . . that's something like a Gord.'[1]

Science and the machine were, after all, transforming not only the social but the intellectual life of late Victorian England. As Henry Adams said in America:

> One could divine pretty nearly where the force lay, since the last ten years had given to the great mechanical energies—coal, iron, steam—a distinct superiority in power over the old, independent elements—agriculture, handiwork and learning; but the results of this revolution on a survivor from the fifties resembled the action of an earth-worm; he twisted about in vain to recover his starting-point, he could no longer see his own tail, he had become an estray; a flotsam or jetsam of wreckage . . . His world was dead.[2]

The machine had dominated nineteenth-century thought: in *Signs of the Times* (1829) Carlyle had stressed, as many others were to, its significance in transforming not only the environment of but the very image of man, introducing a mechanized universe: he extended the familiar Romantic complaint to point out that men now lived in a 'Mechanical Age' not just outwardly but inwardly. The machine had been internalized and made the point of progress. Old modes of exertion were thrown aside; men were grown mechanical in head and heart as well as in hand;

[1] Donald Fleming's point that if we want to understand the intellectual ferments of the early twentieth century in America we must look to the widening of intellectual and educational possibilities in the 1890s also applies to England too. (Donald Fleming, 'Social Darwinism' in *Paths of American Thought* (ed. A. M. Schlesinger, Jr., and M. White) (Boston, Mass., 1963; London, 1964).)

[2] Henry Adams, *The Education of Henry Adams* (privately publ., 1906: Boston, 1918).

the machine was the antithesis of the 'Dynamical' and, as Ruskin said, of art itself. But at the beginning of the century the machine was the steam-pump, new methods of coal extraction, mechanization of textile industry: it was an instrument for doing more efficiently what had long been done. By the end of the century it was enabling men to move at 60 m.p.h. and fly; as writers like Henry Adams, H. G. Wells and later Lewis Mumford were to point out, the era of palaeo-technology (steam and labour) had given way to the era of neo-technology (electrical energy and streamlining). The impetus of machinery was to produce supplementary machinery. So technological innovation was bringing machines and what they made into homes, streets and cities on a new scale, transforming the visible and everyday environment. Electric light, bicycles, trains, the car or independent energy package, the motor in the home (enabling Forster's Wilcox family in *Howards End* to cross the countryside without looking at it) were spreading. More visible, dominant and personal, the machine was not only producing large changes in the environment and operation of human life; it also seemed to make man the misfit. Carlyle had contrasted the 'Mechanical' with the inward energies of self, which he called 'Dynamical'. But now the machine was itself a dynamo, was itself energetic. Machines proliferated machines; innovation produced innovation; the total fund of energy available was vastly extended, notably through thermodynamics, which allowed for the turbine, the internal combustion engine and the refrigerator, making their own independent energy. Machines were now minded by machines, producing precise and often automatic control of industrial operations. The machine was becoming an impersonal kingdom of force, proliferating indifference and mechanism, the subjection of men to things; but it was also a revolutionary instrument and an extension of man, bringing new knowledge and hope, through the new mastery over the world it gave, the new orders of society it could produce, the new men of science it could encourage.[1]

[1] There is a remarkable imaginative treatment of the ironical power of the machine in Samuel Butler's two chapters called 'The Book of the Machines' in *Erewhon* (1872).

By the end of the century, then, the machine was developing in man's consciousness as an element of tremendous power that could dictate the entire form of society and forms of environment under which the machine itself could work most successfully. It produced new models of efficiency and administration in government and business; a classic example is the Taylorist movement in the United States, whereby the model of machine operation was applied to human labour in an early form of work-study. The rhythm of the machine became a model of the human rhythm: a point that was applied precisely in some of the new art that was emerging—for instance in the mechanical dehumanization and reification of the Vorticist and Futurist painters, where the human figure becomes a mechanism.[1] Where men in the nineteenth century had tended to humanize and naturalize the mechanical object, and even to spiritualize it (hence, one presumes, St Pancras Railway station), encrusting metal with leaf-forms, the new stylists sought to mechanize the human and the natural (Wilde complained that nature had exhausted the patience of its observers). The machine, in short, offered a new mode of relation between the self and society, and between man and history. Henry Adams took the point furthest by offering an historiography based on energy-explosions; the dynamo, at the beginning of the twentieth century, representing the highest point of energy production and hence requiring a 'new social mind' which could comprehend the proliferating modern multiverse. Appropriately, he went, at the Chicago Exposition of 1893 and then again at the Paris Exhibition of 1900, to pray to the exemplary energetic machine, the dynamo: 'I go down to the Champs de Mars and sit by the hour over the great dynamos, watching them run as noiselessly and smoothly as the planets, and asking them—with infinite courtesy—where in Hell they are going.' He saw in this his own demise ('he found himself' he wrote, 'lying in the Gallery of Machines . . . , his historical neck broken by the sudden irruption of forces totally new'), the

---

[1] A classic literary instance is Wyndham Lewis's novel *Tarr* (1918), written before the First World War, which applies to its characters the Bergsonian theory that comedy is derived from their mechanization or dehumanization.

end of the past, and of a world conceived of as personal, controllable, or orderly.[1] Indeed it seemed that the machine could replace man by restricting him to those needs it could satisfy; the problem was mastery or slavery, in society and in art too. 'It is not a question of dealing with machinery in the spirit and with the methods of existing art,' said T. E. Hulme, the exponent of a new, hard classicism of art, 'but of the creation of a new art having an organization, and governed by principles, which are at present exemplified unintentionally, as it were, in machinery.'[2]

If the city became a spatial metaphor for modern man, an image of his social relations, so the machine became a temporal metaphor for him, an image of his relations with history.[3] And they afford such crucial—and ambivalent—metaphors of the dynamics of late Victorian and early-twentieth-century life because they were both spectacular instances of the forces of expansion, proliferation and standardization at work in the England of the time, and also because they were deeply bound up with the idea of liberation and innovation. They were a bounden part of the intellectual ferment of the age. They carried some of the essential fables and experiences of modernization, of changing social and environmental structure and changing consciousness; they also offered to those who understood them a new species of knowledge and discovery. They were essential parts of the transposition of national culture towards a more dynamic state, and towards secularization and scientism. They were the focal points of the second-stage Industrial Revolution

[1] Henry Adams, op. cit.

[2] T. E. Hulme, 'Modern Art and Its Philosophy', in *Speculations*, ed. Herbert Read (London, 1924). Hulme argues that geometric obstruction related to the machine is the characteristic mode of the new art. See also Siegfried Giedion, *Mechanization Takes Command* (New York, 1948). Henry L. Sussman, *Victorians and the Machine* (Cambridge, Mass., and London, 1968), gives a valuable historical perspective by following out the impact of machines and mechanical techniques on the thought of Carlyle, Dickens, Ruskin, Morris, Butler, Wells and Kipling.

[3] One could examine other things, of course, besides those I have chosen. The development of science or sociology would be obvious examples, especially with regard to the growth of unbelief. Of this there are various good discussions—I would especially cite J. Hillis Miller, *The Disappearance of God: Five Nineteenth-Century Writers* (Cambridge, Mass., 1963).

G

through which England was turning, and which led towards a particular kind of future, with new freedoms and enslavements. They were, to the men of the time, visible evidence that society had committed itself in a certain direction—that it was working by means of scientific and rational knowledge to the ends of extension and economic growth. It meant expanded intellectual opportunities, growing social reforms; but the consequences ran deep in the texture and nature of all human experience. They were that life would alter, habits change and beliefs be transformed, the complexes of power and influence in society change, the culture acquire a different temper. This would require new ethical systems, new modes of thought, new attempts at an overview. So the time seemed a time of shift, a period of take-off; moving in the direction of urbanization, technologization, secularization and the social melting-pot, it implied radical changes in morals, taste and indeed in literary and artistic structure. It is this that gives us the note of unease in the period, the sense of having reached a crisis in values. The subsequent years from 1870 throw up a new generation of men who clearly manifest the unease, and are clearly attempting a cultural reappraisal, a reaching out towards new ideas and modes. This is a period both of aestheticism and realism, the consequences in art of a growingly determinist world-view; and of a populist revaluation, when the prevailing note of many is a sense of powerlessness before and lack of access to the process, the society. 'The study of evolution,' wrote Hamlin Garland in the United States, 'has made the present the most critical and self-analytical of all ages known to us. . . . It has liberated the thought of the individual as never before, and the power of tradition grows fainter year by year.' But what was one to make of one's 'evolutionary' liberation? The time seemed one of those phases in history when the past no longer might hand on its vision to the present; where the new generation were initiated into mysteries and experiences that their predecessors could not understand. The sense of historical 'jump' produced a reaching of the imagination out beyond the existing frames of thought and the existing forms of society. The mental set of the past was no longer acceptable; but what, in a secular and increasingly rational universe, were the new myths, the new meanings? They might take the form of utopianism and revolution; they might take the form of a hunt through new forces that seemed to be apparent, the forces within the self and the consciousness. The activities of the age were often those of deconsecrating the old myths; they also involve a hunt for new mythologies and types, the intrinsic orders of a new and more sceptical realism.

This produced a strong tendency toward crisis thinking—a mood of secular millenarianism or of apocalypticism. That in its turn drew on that transitional thinking often characteristic of the turn of a century, when one cycle numerically ends and another one begins. The familiar questions come up: is the cycle turning towards a higher phase? or a lower one? or into repetition, continuation with minor differences? All these views were expressed, in fact; and cyclical and evolutionary theories took on new conviction as the end of the century loomed nearer, then turned, then began to make its own marks, with a new king, a new politics, and finally a new kind of war. These theories were also given a kind of scientific objectivity by the general intensification of cyclical and process thought which had been growing in the nineteenth-century mind—in Darwinism and Marxism, in sociological, historical and psychological thought. Evolutionary theories could lead to a joyous sense that progress was taking place; but equally despair could come when it seemed that the graph of industrialization was an independent graph. So *fin-de-siècle* decadence and *aube-de-siècle* joy begin to abound. But above all there is the central metaphor or figure: of flux and change, of plurality and discontinuity, of the loss of a single shared culture and the emergence of many new ones. So there is an intensification of style, of mannerism, of the forms that indicate novelty. So there is a yearning for the millennium or a sense of the impending apocalypse. The magazines that start up stress their novelty; and the mood suggests that the cycle of civilization is turning, the historical pendulum is swinging. We have seen such moods again since, and what goes with them: stylistic intensification, a kind of radical politics of behaviour and self-presentation, a multiplying of offered human roles. And so there is a new view of the new, a modern view of the modern, which is founded in the act of severing time, of bringing history to a point, of trying to locate the heart of 'now', of making the jump from one era into another one.

III

Changes in the character of a society are also, I have been trying to show, changes in its culture, its consciousness, its stylistic expression; and so from the arts they demand the embodiment of new meanings and metaphors, new symbols and myths. The last decades of the nineteenth century were very much decades of artistic quest, and I have attempted here to show some of the reasons why this was so. For they were years in which a relatively coherent culture, a moral and human assent, was fragmented and in many respects destroyed altogether, so that many of the values that had informed the art of nineteenth-century England were no longer alive for the artist to use. The harmonious relation between inner and outer reality, between the moral world and the world of things, between man and nature, seemed to be in disintegration: the artist could concentrate, objectively, on the outer reality, or he could turn to the world of inner consciousness, but the problems of bringing the two into relation were profound. Even the new intensity seemed persistently gained at the cost of tragedy; as in the famous 'Conclusion' Walter Pater added in 1868 to his *The Renaissance*. 'Every one of those impressions is the impression of the individual in his isolation, each mind keeping as a solitary prisoner its own dream of a world.' The end of the century was one of those times when it seemed necessary for the artist to renew the images and remake the myths, to make artistic forms and practices more consonant with his perceived experience. In the late nineteenth century, as the number of literary 'styles' and cultural levels increases, as the movements and campaigns in literature accelerate, we can see the effort being undertaken. But it is undertaken in a context of relative loss. The arts in the past had been related to the more or less invisible roots of culture, to those delicate and half-intimated forms in a society or communal experience which carry myth and meaning at their deepest levels, and to structures of human and social relationship whose significance can be suggested only by nuance and hint. But culture in that sense was precisely what the new forces of plurality and rationalism were destroying. In the arts of the period we can see a double process at work: a 'demythologizing' of the old culture, which is not consistent with experience, and an attempt at remythologizing, which becomes a crucially lonely task, since the newly dominant culture seems naturally hospitable neither to art nor humanism. The last years of the century were the years of a new realism, but it was not the realism of the great novelists of the mid-nineteenth century, like George Eliot or Balzac; it was the desperate realism of a new scepticism, making authentic in order to expose, hunting out the fact in order to reveal the inferior conditions of the universe, mapping out the forces that made men limited and individual destinies constrained. The alternative was for the poet or novelist to write out of his own personal culture, through the separate creative self that Yeats both celebrates and bemoans in poems like 'Major Robert Gregory'. The artist was forced to create, not to interpret; to act as the critic and the maker of his own tradition; to reinvent the world and substantiate aesthetic values within it, through energies appropriate to art rather than to ethics. Hence culture becomes a discontinuous sequence; even when the new art appeals to tradition, it tends to appeal to a discontinuous tradition—T. S. Eliot's tradition which must be 'sought by great labour'. Modernity in literature tends to involve, in fact, a complete change of cultural orientation, towards a culture yet unformed rather than to one that already lives.

The exposure of the modern artist was partly a universal feeling, common to many, but also it was, of course, partly one special to the arts. His immediate world was changing: not only did he get drawn more and more into the getting-and-spending city, which was not so much a cultural environment as an open, free scenario, and away from the culture of his predecessors, fading under the pressure of demographic change, science, and the growth of new and inharmonious voices, but he was tied to his audience by weaker chains of interest, looser ties of language. Cultural forms were devolving downward, towards the status of ephemeral publication; the audience for poetry in particular was declining radically, so that, as Eliot said, it had to be addressed to one hypothetical Intelligent Man 'who does not exist, and who is the audience of the artist'. The idea of culture and civilization as a communal bond was therefore weakening, and became hard to sustain. Art, which had been central to the progress of civilization, as an accessible tradition of human exploration and goodwill, as a storehouse of values, hence started to talk of its own failure. In short, if there was a radical redisposition of values in the turning decades of the century, art was deeply implicated not only because it reported, explored and extended it, but also because it was shaken by it. In the presence of science and reason its purposes and its properties became less clearcut. In the presence of a mechanical and collective age, its moral and humane resources, its commitment to individuals and inner life, also seemed threatened, to survive as precarious values or to disappear behind a total irony. The liberal and humane meaning of art, which had been its nineteenth-century meaning, therefore reached, over these years, a crisis of uncertainty. Hence the recurrent feeling that we live in the period of the disintegration of all the traditional artistic forms, that the arts have moved into a special and terrible time, when the world had let loose its own disorder: things fall apart, said Yeats, the centre cannot hold. And so the vision of chaos, a sense of anarchy, an encounter with the absurd, and a corresponding element of 'decreation' in the literature, has been an insistent theme running through the writing of the modern period—to such an extent that for many readers the word 'modern', when applied to literature, has precisely this association.[1]

[1] See, for instance, Louis Kampf, *On Modernism: The Prospects for Literature and Freedom* (Boston, Mass., 1967), which argues that art has been forced out of its frame to 'erupt into reality'.

The new arts, then, acquired a complex politics of culture, which was to a large extent a fight with history, the current of the times, the pressure of the mob. It is a striking fact that many of the great writers of the new twentieth-century arts took a conservative line on the issue of culture; make it new, said Pound, but 'it' was art and perceptual clarity, and society was to be brought into harmony with art and support it. Most of the modernist poets and novelists took the view that modernism was an attempt to transcend historicism and a positivistic view of human progress by decreating secular and historical time. And in this effort they turned to the transcendence of art, the personally achieved image, the epiphany, the ideal of metamorphosis, what Pound in a letter calls the 'bust thru from the quotidien into "divine or permanent world"'. The new arts, fed with European ideas, often out of their context, were an attempt to provide an image for a new world, but also to hold that image in suspension: these fragments shorn against my ruins. In seeking the hard, objective wholeness and energy of the independent work of art, as opposed to the softness or moralism of later romanticism, they sought to objectify the private world of culture. At the same time their fictions enact the situation of difficulty and strain in which they do so, carrying with them the modern funds of the primitive, the irrational, the uncivilized. As H. Stuart Hughes has shown, a deep challenge to rationalism runs through the thought of the late nineteenth century, in men like Bergson, Sorel, Durkheim and Pareto; in the Russian novelists and the new Futurists.[1] The dark, the primeval and the unconscious become essential forces behind the surface of civilization: the heart of darkness, and the destructive element, lie behind the cities of light. Yet these ominous presences seemed, paradoxically, a potential cure against the mechanical dehumanization of life; as the maintenance of private culture is a struggle, so the bleak promises of dark unculture seem both the old enemy and the new friend. The new art takes both culture and anti-culture as its province, giving it both a yearning for civilization and a deep distrust of civilization as it has been inherited. The

[1] H. Stuart Hughes, *Consciousness and Society*, op. cit.

liberal tradition of the past was weakened and lost, and the age of individualism seemed over; it was inevitable enough that many of the great works of art of our time were confrontations with anarchy, with springs of experience outside or beyond civilization, with the apocalypse of human enterprise. The crisis feeling runs through a good deal of the new writing; but it was not, in the end, a joyless crisis. Its writers felt the obligation, as intellectuals, to reinterpret and re-invigorate. The intellectual energy and ferment of the time abounds in it too, producing a singular literature—shaken to its roots and origins, yet energetic with ideas and possibilities. On analysis, the possibilities are frequently bleak ones, and the lesson that is manifest is of a turn in the culture profoundly disturbing and critical. But a generation emerged, and a climate evolved, around the turn of the century in which that situation could be explored deeply and seriously, and in which the effort could be made to sustain art independently of the forces that seemed so threatening to it. This is the phase of modern literature that, in the pages that follow, I want particularly to attend to—because it contains the crucial awarenesses and artistic responses that have most to tell us, and most illuminate and influence our view of the position of art from those early years of the modern arts through to the present time.

PART TWO

Modernity in Modern English Literature

CHAPTER IV

The Coming of the Modern in English Writing

I

What in fact happened in English writing in the thirty or forty years before the outbreak of the First World War was a vast stylistic upheaval—an upheaval so large as to amount to a transformation from one phase of art to another one. On a smaller scale, such upheavals take place in art all the time; as T. S. Eliot put it in a famous phrase, 'Sensibility alters from generation to generation in everybody, whether we will or no . . .' And so we can usually identify, in a rough and ready way, the work of one decade, or one literary generation, from another by its particular interests and emphases, its mood, temper and obsessions; and it is a convention of stylistic history to presume an oscillation of modes from generation to generation. What is more, certain decades, which are often times of change in other spheres, seem to have a particularly marked and distinctive temper, a particular mode of their own in the arts : the 1890s and the 1920s have some such sort of discernible unity. Both artists and their critics tend to be markedly conscious of the epochs in which they feel themselves to be working, and assume that transitions of expression are taking place in relation to them. But there are still more radical changes, changes going beyond shifts of sensibility or the dominance of particular artistic generations, that we distinguish. These are the large stylistic periods, like neo-classicism or romanticism, which establish a very varied yet still linked sequence of aesthetics, formal conventions, realms of sensibility, orders of myth and meaning, which serve for extended periods of time. And it is a change on this scale that we feel ourselves to be confronted by in the period from about 1880 to 1914. There is, as we have seen, no one clear word that suggests the nature of this movement, which seems to take shape and develop from about this time. 'Modernism' suggests it, but it is not entirely comprehensive. But it is, clearly, a change away from romanticism, and a change quite as momentous *as* romanticism— indeed, according to some critics, much *more* momentous, since it involves a total shift from the traditional idea of art, in many quarters at least.

It thus becomes possible for critics to argue that the change is one of unprecedented dimensions. So, for instance, Wylie Sypher has argued that the new movement differs from romanticism and realism in that these were, in stylistic terms, only revolts against outworn conventions, revolts which, as T. E. Hulme said, brought only artistic disorder. Hulme demanded a new convention, and Sypher believes that a major new style did emerge: he calls it *cubism*.[1] Herbert Read makes the same kind of point, arguing that modern art represents a disruption and abandonment of the tradition that had been in development over five centuries.[2] And Ortega y Gasset, like Sypher, also sees the age as one which acquired a new communal style—a style rooted in its refusal to make objective statements about reality and its willingness to make the metaphor the essential *res poetica*.[3] In fact—particularly if one emphasizes literature as opposed to painting or music—it seems rather doubtful whether such stylistic tendencies as cubism, expressionism or what Ortega calls the 'dehumanization' of art can be said to be the style of the entire age. They have, of course, had strong support from influential movements, and little art is now produced that is not aware of their significance. But even anti-representationalism does not amount to one style, and it is hardly universal. It is better to say that the age has been marked by a *will* towards style and a very high degree of artistic mannerism. But it is also marked by very

[1] Wylie Sypher, *Rococo to Cubism in Art and Literature* (New York, 1960).
[2] Herbert Read, *Art Now* (rev. ed., London, 1960).
[3] Ortega y Gasset, *The Dehumanization of Art, and Other Writings on Art and Culture* (Garden City, N.Y., 1956).

great, indeed unprecedented, artistic *variety*. This is *not* the same thing as a style for the age; and if anything modern art has been the exploration of the consequent paradox. So the truth is probably more with critics like André Malraux, who have emphasized the stylistic multiplicity of the time and the confusion that this has brought to artists.[1]

To offer a definition or a comprehensive account of the arts that emerge with our century is a problem. We cannot fail to see that a large stylistic change—possibly one of unprecedented proportions—*did* occur. (And it occurred, of course, not only or even mainly in England.) But, even given all that has been said about the changing social context in England and the west generally, which affords some explanation why a different ideological view of modern experience should tend to emerge, there is no outright reason why all this should change the arts. After all, one of the theories of art that has long been influential in the west is the idea of art's quality of universality and its permanence—its concern with the general human fate rather than with the particularities of men's fortunes, its transcendence of history, its intrinsic power to resist immediate pressure. This view of art is of course neo-classical; and its particular and obvious manifestation is in the genres of literature—tragedy and comedy, lyric and epic—which have seemed to live with archetypal permanence and to transcend historical environments in a way singular to the funds and resources that lie in great art. The view itself has had long endurance; yet it is *not* the one that has seemed to lie behind modern art and aesthetics. They, rather, have tended to see experience and consciousness as constantly changing and novel, and the artist as in some sense an accomplice of history, oriented towards the present or even the future. Indeed, it was in many ways the intensification of this conviction that lay behind the stylistic upheaval of the period. Hence there was a strengthening of the notion of a distinctively 'modern' tradition in letters; and hence the fact that one of the distinctive features of modern literature, in the west generally, is its powerful appropriation of the word 'modern' to designate itself,

[1] André Malraux, *The Voices of Silence*, trans. Stuart Gilbert (London, 1954).

as if no other literature ever was. But if one can sense a growing and fair agreement about the need for the modern in literature, one can also sense a divergence. For what the modern *was*, as a matter for the arts, is a good deal less clear.

For instance, as we have seen, the word 'modern' when applied to literature and art by many artists, critics and readers can have a special meaning: it can denote not merely a contemporary literature, not even one concerned with contemporary problems, but one with certain marks on it distinguishing it from other writing—not only in the past but in the present day itself. So, in his book *The Struggle of the Modern*, Stephen Spender can draw his clear line between 'contemporary' writers, who are engaged in a fairly prosaic way with immediate social subject-matter and whose literary structures are not notably self-conscious, and 'modern' writers who engage with inner crises of sensibility and large problems of form and language. He also tends to identify the latter with the writing of certain important figures in the early part of the century, like Joyce, Eliot, Pound, Proust and Mann, who so radically changed modern literary sensibility and transformed expression that a decisive extension of their effort was hardly possible for their successors. He also points out that an important feature of the 'moderns' is their sense of reaching very near to the edge of literature itself, their sense of literary desperation; the 'modern' artist is acutely conscious of the past and of the contemporary divorce from it, of a wholeness cut off. And in some respects he therefore suggests that the 'contemporaries' are *more* modern, since withdrawal was inevitable from the 'modernist' position into a more contemporary one, albeit one of much more consciousness than would have been possible if the moderns had not written. Both groups, he therefore recognizes, are engaged in the making of a new style, drawing on new tones of voice taken from the contemporary, new rhythms, structures and speeds.[1] Hence, whatever the differences, both groups are marked by modern manners. It has often been pointed out that the writers whom Spender calls 'contemporaries' have tended to predominate in English literature—so Graham Hough

[1] Stephen Spender, *The Struggle of the Modern* (London, 1963).

can suggest that modernism was in some sense a temporary disturbance of the literary development of English writing in the twentieth century[1]—and in fact in most literatures it is possible to discern a 'native' tradition of development coinciding with the more international characteristics of the 'moderns', many of whom in the English context were expatriate writers (James, Pound and Eliot were American; Conrad, Polish; Yeats and Joyce, Irish). And even if the two tendencies often interconnect, there are real differences between them, amounting, as Spender stresses, often to totally different views of history and the world. Hence, then, the semantic difficulty of using the word 'modernism' to describe the twentieth-century aesthetic revolution; one could easily end up with a definition of modern literature which in the English tradition was more or less exhausted by 1930. It is therefore more important to suggest the general climate of change, which is perhaps best recognized by identifying an oscillation between modernism and a changing native tradition that is rather less experimental in character and more realist in disposition. The oscillation is in fact present throughout the period in most western countries, and the disposition towards extreme experiment has in few traditions been total or absolutely continuous. But, as I have said, in England the oscillation is in fact more *marked* than in some other countries— in France, Germany and America the experimental view of the arts has held rather more sway, and for longer—and therefore the narrower definition of modernism seems particularly incomplete.

Perhaps we should employ modernism to mean this oscillation, though that is not generally how we use the word. In fact it is very vaguely defined, though what we *usually* mean to suggest by it is a whole cluster of international movements and tendencies (impressionism, post-impressionism, realism, symbolism, imagism, dadaism, surrealism and so on) which are actually often at great variance one with another. Certain discernible threads do run through them, however, one being a basically symbolist aesthetic, and another a basically experimental and *avant-garde* posture. The tendency has many different phases, waves and

[1] Graham Hough, *Image and Experience* (London, 1960).

variations, and the term includes attitudes as various as T. S. Eliot's classicism and the nihilism of Dada. But the tendency clearly stems from an international revolutionary fervour in all the arts that was associated with the new century, the new modern environment of man, the new pressures on form or literary language; and it is the most visible mark of literature and art's passing beyond the environment of Romanticism and Victorianism. Modernism reached a peak at different times in different countries—fairly early in France, Scandinavia and Russia, rather later in England, and later still in the United States —and in some of these countries, notably France and America, it found more hospitable environments than in others. Even where it existed alongside a native tradition more clearly evolved from the past, it inescapably transformed the arts of the west, and in different ways has penetrated into modern comprehension of and use of the arts. And, as the very proliferation of movements may suggest, one of its attributes has surely been in part the attempt to recreate not only the social function of art but the very degree of self-awareness involved in its creation. There is not only a change in aesthetic self-consciousness, but an actual intensification of it—an increased desire to explore art in auto-nomous terms, and at the same time an increased awareness of its methodological predicaments (so that modernism is frequently concerned with exploring the paradox of art's very existence or even with destroying many of its features). Thus seen, modernism is that movement of artistic revolutionary self-consciousness that we associate with the work of painters like Matisse and Picasso, novelists like Joyce, Proust, Mann and Gide, poets like Valéry, Apollinaire, Pound and Wallace Stevens, dramatists like Maeterlinck, Jarry and Pirandello. It is an international tendency and it derives from an international *avant garde*; it tends to emerge from cosmopolitan artistic enclaves such as grew up in culture-capitals like Berlin, Paris, London for a time, and perhaps more latterly New York.[1] It is heavily conditioned by an artistic

[1] Today, perhaps, the arts are freed from *any* such ecology—even a cosmo-politan one—by the revolution in the means of communication; the ghetto is available in the living-room.

climate that is supranational and more or less autonomous—
conditioned by that rather than the imprint of social classes,
social relationships in the sense of regional, national and class
circumstances. It seems therefore to exist rather apart from the
specific movements and tendencies of national cultures and has a
strong expatriate quality.

Modernism in England, then, can in one of its aspects be
fruitfully represented as the realization of an international movement in the arts of an already well-established character, one
which had long been exploring a variety of forms of romantic
artistic withdrawal and which is broadly distinguished by making
a cult of the artist—indeed, almost a distinct 'class' of artists.
It constitutes a point of artistic self-realization where the cult
becomes strong enough to assert itself positively as an epistemology of art. That is to say, it is very much an internal development within the history of the romantic arts themselves. But
external factors mattered too; it drew upon the cohesion of a
changing intelligentsia now fairly well divorced from its bourgeois origins, and on a life-style of urban or cosmopolitan bohemias that grew up as points of artistic confluence. Its tendency
is indeed to synthesize the arts together as common enterprise,
to draw together poetry and painting, music and fiction, sculp-
ture and drama; and to find its audience among fellow-artists
and would-be artists who are the fellow-citizens of the independent gypsy land of Bohemia. To see *how* it emerged, we have to
consider the different development of romanticism in different
countries—for it is very much from romanticism that, in the first
instance, it derives. Romanticism was, as we have seen, an international movement of revolutionary sensibility; and it certainly
marks the beginning of the aesthetic transition into the modern
age. It set out the basis of an essentially modern view of art (of
art not as the static activity of a stable society, but as an independent activity that had an oblique or futurist relationship to the
world of history and time) and a basically modern view of the
artist (that he was a free agent independent of the classes and
appealing beyond or across them). The artist now proclaimed his
role less as a conserver of culture, more as an innovator of it;

H

and his powers were associated with an open-ended, onward historical flow in the world. His role thus became heroic; and the act of creation became a high mystery performed in an aura of trance and revelation. At the same time, the widening of the audience both set him free and made it harder to see for whom he was writing. The artistic viewpoint thus became distinctive and acquired a kind of absolute morality of its own, an autonomy associated, perhaps, with the diminution of the religious view of life; for it became a secular religion. As we have seen, the independence of the artist could permit him to delve deep into his art and leave society behind as unreal; or it could provide an independent imperative from which society and life could be judged. And, as we have also seen, the English tradition in the nineteenth century tended towards the second of these two alternatives—while the assertion of an exiled independence seems more the mark of other literatures: those that moved, in fact, more rapidly toward modernism.

The Byronic or Baudelairean vein—the painful expression of irony, exposure or outright dissent as part of the artistic role—is particularly marked in nineteenth-century literatures where the artist is markedly uncertain of his social position: in the French, the Russian, the American. American nineteenth-century writing is deeply marked by a tone of uncertainty and dissent amounting to a questioning of the very possibility of artistic existence; in a phrase of Henry James's, the American writer seemed to belong to the 'disinherited of art',[1] to belong to a literature bereft by the absence of a received social tradition. It is a common assumption of critics of American literature that it is touched by a 'terrible estrangement . . . , a nameless yearning for a world no one ever really possessed';[2] and certainly

---

[1] Henry James, *The Madonna of the Future* (1873) (in *The Madonna of the Future and Other Tales*, 1879). The passage runs on to question the assumption, however. 'You seem fairly at home in exile,' is the reply received, 'and Florence seems to me a very easy Siberia. But do you want to know my own thought? Nothing is so easy as to talk about our want of nursing air, of a kindly soil, of opportunity, of inspiration, of things that help. The only thing that helps is to to do something fine. . . .'
[2] Alfred Kazin, *On Native Grounds* (New York, 1962).

we can feel in its nineteenth-century works a marked tendency
for the artist to seek transcendental truths outside and beyond
the social structure, turning to the realm of nature, the historical
future, or the self-sustaining evolution of the artistic consciousness for his subject-matter. In France, there is a similar spectacle
of artistic strain. There, as in America, we have that form of
artistic specialization which assumes that the sources of art lie
in the exploitation of the technical resources of the medium
which the artist practises, but also a strong belief in the need to
master a life-style appropriately advanced and independent
enough to allow the creative momentum to flourish. In France,
unlike America, the arts were prestigious; but they were unde-
fined in social place. By the 1830s and 1840s Paris was a city
which, though it had lost its patrons and much of its audience,
was still a centre of learning and artistic activity. So developed
a tradition of intellectual and artistic bohemianism: 'Today, as
in the past,' said Henri Murger, the great advertiser of bohemia,
'any man who enters the path of Art, with art as his sole means
of support, is bound to pass by way of Bohemia.' An over-
production of intellectual and artistic aspirants was amassed in
the city and brought about the emergence of a new type of artistic
community—that of an intellectual proletariat, living on minimal
incomes from private sources, using their freedom of situation
to create an independent style of life based on a romanticized
riotous poverty. As Gautier said, it was an environment in which
one could freely develop any intellectual fancy; and it proliferated
movements, created a peer-group of other artists, and put a high
premium on originality and artistic self-consciousness. Modernism in the arts is obviously a derivation from all these things,
though for a full flowering of the tendency, for its development
beyond romantic assumptions, we have to wait until later in the
century.

II

It is not until the late Victorian period that this broad pattern of
sensibility becomes really important in the English arts. And

when it does so, it happens partly as a derivation from what was happening within the English tradition, and partly by influence from and imitation of foreign sources. In other words, the cultural change in England is marked by a new phase of internationalism. English writers start more and more to look to Paris; at the same time London becomes more and more an hospitable centre for expatriate writers from other countries, notably from America. Indeed these late romantic and modernist developments in England must be regarded both as a development within the English tradition *and* as a borrowing from outside; hence they were not a secure artistic inheritance. Obviously they occur when the artist in England was beginning to feel growing uncertainty and disaffiliation, and when the arts were undergoing severe changes as the audience altered, the cultural symbols of the society began to shift, and the 'Victorian synthesis' was a less confident possession. What was happening in England was that the old literary-cultural critique of the romantic artists was giving way to one of two tendencies—either towards a positivist or directly political critique, usually socialist, or towards a heightened aestheticism. (William Morris is persistently interesting here, because he shows a fascinating alternation between both claims; on the one hand he speaks of the powers of the poet ('the dreamer of dreams') to redeem the culture, and on the other he speaks of the priority of politics over art ('No, rather than art should live this poor thin life among a few exceptional men, despising those beneath them for an ignorance for which they themselves are responsible . . . I would rather that the world should sweep away all art for a while.')[1]) The problem of finding a meaning for the artist and his culture in the society clearly grows as the artist becomes doubtful about his traditional social

[1] See, for instance, H. G. Wells's claims that the novel has a function in social development, and his attacks in *Boon* (1915) on 'works of art whose only claim is their art'. James's famous resistance ('it is art that *makes* life') is to be found, along with the attack, in Leon Edel and Gordon Ray (eds.), *Henry James and H. G. Wells: A Record of Their Friendship* (London, 1958). Similar debates developed between Virginia Woolf and Arnold Bennett (see Stephen Spender, *The Struggle of the Modern*). And a modern variant is of course the contemporary 'Two Cultures' controversy between C. P. Snow and F. R. Leavis.

location; and the result is a marked oscillation between the styles of realism and aestheticism—both of which could appeal to French developments. The two contrary directions—one claiming art as a species of knowledge analogous to sociology or science, and therefore capable of social analysis; the other claiming art as a form of private knowledge to be preserved and pursued for its own sake—produce an artistic debate that spilled well over into the twentieth century and makes for the artistic ferment of the 1870s, 1880s and 1890s. Hence the decades of aestheticism, decadence, art for art's sake are also the decades of a strong assertion of realism and positivism in art. So, in fact, the language of science and the language of the private artistic symbol seem to replace the broad language of shared culture; and to a considerable degree it is the loss of that culturally central language, of a shared and common reality with and through which the writer can speak, that explains the stylistic contortion that was developing and this basic oscillation within it.[1] What is apparent is that there is not only an aesthetic but an epistemological transformation—a questioning, that is, of what mode of knowledge might, in its more difficult circumstances, be held to be. To a point, at least, the shared values of a community culture, in which meaning derived from communal symbols and belief, was breaking up.

As in France, this first expressed itself in pre-modernist forms. On the one hand, there is the surge of realism, drawing on a deep-seated sense of man's being placed ironically amid a web of operative processes, whether social or biological, whose forces he could hardly influence. In many ways this becomes a populist statement, coming from writers of often lower-middle class and provincial origin who feel they are in an environment and a culture they may only partly possess. In Hardy, in Gissing, in Wells and in Lawrence a note of dispossession is sounded, sometimes despairingly, sometimes with the hope that a new kind of man or superman is emerging who can redeem this

---

[1] For the argument that realism and aestheticism are not necessarily to be seen as antithetical movements, see John A. Lester, *Journey Through Despair*, cited above.

destiny. And on the other hand there is a surge of aestheticism or artistic separatism—that emphasis on the separate and contemplative sensations that we particularly associate with Pater and the Pre-Raphaelites, that synthesis of the stoic and the epicurean that gives the perfect aesthetic form as a felt thing.[1] If realism seeks to objectify the sense of exposure, then aestheticism seeks to subjectify it, to place the weight on the rightness of individual sensations and personal relationships. Here the style points towards the artist as the mock-aristocrat or the dandy, often expressed in the form of a consciously overblown decadence or a gratuitous sensationalism.[2] So it is primarily through the achievement of a life-style that the artist becomes his own hero, making his own ethics, chasing the radiant morality of the right sensation, and redeeming the moment of aesthetic awareness, the nodal image, from the scatter of flux and time. This at least is the basis, if not the full realization, of the growing view that it is art that *creates* the world. And it depended on a close association between style and fashion, on an instinct for novelty and outrage. It involved those 'sensations of newness' that Baudelaire saw as necessary to art, and that 'quickened, multiplied consciousness' that Pater bequeathed to many later devotees of the significant form, including above all Virginia Woolf. This could lead to the idea of art as the only 'orderly product'[3] that man could possess—in short, to symbolism, the theory that the world is made by the crucial word or image.

Both tendencies looked, of course, to France; and one essential feature of the period is its new internationalism. George Moore, Wilde and Arthur Symons all brought back and adapted the modes of symbolism to England for the support and extension of what they had begun to do;[4] even as the realist writers had

[1] David Daiches has some interesting comments on this complex of sensibility in *Some Late Victorian Attitudes* (London, 1969).

[2] For a fuller discussion of the point, see Ellen Moers, *The Dandy* (New York and London, 1960).

[3] The phrase is E. M. Forster's; but the conviction of the self-inclusive unity of the work of art as a thing out of time (also present in Romanticism) is given great importance in aesthetics over this period.

[4] The classic discussion of this is Edmund Wilson, *Axel's Castle* (London, 1961).

themselves been looking to French authors, and notably to Zola, as a source for their own ways of writing. And hence a number of other developments of the French scene—the emphasis on self-conscious art and the associated patterns of bohemianism, cosmopolitanism and consciously urbanized literature—began, in a selective way, to be important in the English tradition too. The decadent symbolist phase was fairly short-lived, and its end-of-time, end-of-a-movement feeling did not last. But other aspects of the general tendency did last; and finally, perhaps, it was the idea of overcoming the idea of the literary arts as a species of rhetoric contingent with all other rhetorics that was finally to win out. Certainly as the sense of the obligation towards stylistic change grew stronger, the weight began to shift from the poet as the manifester of style to the manifester of technique. 'I believe in technique as the test of a man's sincerity,' said Ezra Pound; and this more formalist response led in its turn to a rejection of the stress on personality and emotion that had been one part of symbolism. Gradually, in this way, the 'romantic' element began to wither. Again the new ideas came partly from French and European sources, but they also involved a strong injection from another external source, the United States. As critics have been increasingly pointing out, many of the developments, though they referred to France, really involve the evolution of an Anglo-American synthesis in the arts, which of itself gave the modernism of London a destiny different from that of the modernism of Paris.[1] Indeed, a good number of American writers were acquiring many of the characteristics of modernism without benefit of Paris—for instance, by directly imitating Japanese verse-forms.[2]

In addition to the internationalism, there was also a strong attempt to unite the ferment of the various arts together, so that

[1] See, for instance, Frank Kermode, *Romantic Image* (London, 1957), Graham Hough, *Image and Experience* (London, 1960) and John Dixon Hunt's fascinating *The Pre-Raphaelite Imagination* (London, 1969). And for a detailed discussion of the new aesthetics and their development, see C. K. Stead, *The New Poetic: Yeats to Eliot* (London, 1964).

[2] See, for a fuller account, Earl Miner, *The Japanese Tradition in British and American Literature* (Princeton and London, 1958).

poetry could learn from painting and fiction from music, so that a common centre to all the artists—a 'rhythm', a 'vortex of energy', an 'Image'—could be reduced. Like the borrowing from foreign sources, this too intensified artistic self-consciousness and involved an attack on the discursive or *prose* elements of the literary work. Once again, this tended to reinforce cosmopolitanism and bohemianism, the common community of the arts. And so, by gradual acceleration from about the 1870s onward, we can see at work a growing number of literary and artistic movements, attempting to draw from the chaos of new forms and images a theoretic or aesthetic centre. So there was the Pre-Raphaelite Brotherhood; the Rhymers' Club of 1890–1894; the 'Forgotten School of 1909' around T. E. Hulme; the Georgians; the Imagists; the Vorticists. Many of these movements were of fairly brief duration, but often they handed on something to the next phase. Along with the movements came a new phenomenon, the 'little magazines' which attempted to publicize particular tendencies or groups of them to small and specialized audiences. So there was the early Pre-Raphaelite *Germ* (Jan.-May, 1850), the decadence magazines like *The Yellow Book* (1894–1897) and *The Savoy* (1896), and on through to the immediately pre-war flowering—*Rhythm* (later *The Blue Review*) (1911–1913), representing the John Middleton Murry–Katherine Mansfield–D. H. Lawrence axis; *Poetry and Drama* (1913–1914), which carried some of Imagism, some of Futurism; *The Egoist* (1914–1919), which carried Imagism in England and promoted Eliot; and the Vorticist *Blast* (1914). Most of the magazines emphasized the community of the arts and artists by carrying articles on painting and music and they stressed their separation from the growing mass of popular literature and journalism. Most emphasized the need for literary innovation and change, and the conviction that, to quote Richard Aldington, 'The arts are now divided between popular charlatans and men of talent, who, of necessity, write, think and paint only for each other, since there is no one else to understand them' ('Some Reflections on Ernest Dowson,' *Egoist*, March 1, 1915). And writers, artists and musicians were meeting one another in cafés and restaurants (the Café Royal, the Tour

D'Argent, the Kensington teashop where, according to Richard Aldington, Pound invented Imagism), displaying themselves with a new flamboyance—Pound with his single earring, Wyndham Lewis with his black coat buttoned to his chin, Lawrence with his flaming red beard—and organizing mass attacks on the public with a public-relations efficiency remarkable among groups who claimed the public as an enemy.

It had indeed all the characteristics of a bohemian environment, the artistic scene over these forty years. 'The Eighteen Nineties were the decade of a thousand "movements",' declared Holbrook Jackson;[1] so were the two decades following. The movements and display were all part of a context of innovation, though in many ways the context preceded the innovation; it is not really until after 1910 that we have any works that really fully justify it. 'If long locks and general dissoluteness were not an aid and a way to pure thought, why have they been so long [the artist's] characteristics?' asked George Mooie. But bohemianism becomes an attractive life-style in its own right, and it attracts many 'writers' who don't write but just like the life. Of course there is no causal connection between the locks and dissoluteness and the production of good art. Indeed it was not until writers of the quality and integrity of Joyce, Eliot and Pound appeared that the tendency seemed anything more than an enjoyable carnival of iconoclasm. The long locks and dissoluteness were simply the badges of subscription to a particular community or enclave —part of the desire to make the artist distinct from other performers in the field. Gradually, however, the qualitative change that takes us from late romanticism to modernism did come about. The broad tendencies of the late nineteenth-century decades—towards arts much more self-conscious, specialized, even private; towards the notion of art as a distinctive epistemology that does not mirror the world but actively recreates it; towards a manifest discontent with the settled order that took the form of a search for new ideas, new places of the mind and consciousness; towards an atmosphere of transformed knowledge—provide

[1] Holbrook Jackson, *The Eighteen Nineties* (London, 1913).

the roots of the change. In a few great artists of the late nineteenth century—in Henry James and Joseph Conrad, for
example—one can see the modernist ferment is clearly fully grown
even before the century is out. But on the whole it is not until
after the century's turn that—after a sequence of late romantic
attempts to make one or another of the various movements
'stick' as a consistent aesthetic context—one really begins to do
so. In broad terms, there emerges an intensified sense of the
writer's facing experiences and problems totally new in the
history of literature, and doing this in a context where most of
the artistic possibilities have been exhausted. Most literary
revolutions involve in some respect an appeal against the prevailing convention in the interests of realism; that was the pattern
of the Romantic revolution and the Realist revolution which was
an offshoot of it later in the century. But writers now began to
be apocalyptically urgent about the situation. T. E. Hulme, for
instance, expressed the conviction that the arts faced a totally
novel situation in which history and convention were of little
help to the contemporary artist, a view often stated (among others,
by Virginia Woolf). He said:

Each field of artistic activity is exhausted by the first great artist who
gathers a full harvest from it. This point of exhaustion seems to me to
have been reached in romanticism. We shall not get any new period of
efflorescence of verse until we get a new technique, a new convention,
to turn ourselves loose in.[1]

It was in answer to this sense of need that attention now turned,
more and more, to a revolution of technique—as opposed to a
revolution of sensibility or life-style. It is really with the specific
reaction against romanticism, which came in the shape of a
tighter and anti-discursive view of form, a stress on the impersonality of the artistic object, the growth of a sequence of means
for destroying traditional structures in art, and an increased
demand on the consumer to comply with the artist's concern
with technicality, that modernism in England begins to emerge.

[1] T. E. Hulme, 'Romanticism and Classicism', in *Speculations*, ed. Herbert
Read, op. cit.

CHAPTER V

The Making of the Modern Tradition

I

The positive assertion of the idea of a distinctively modern tradition in the arts, of a redefinition of the total artistic context, belongs in fact to a fairly narrow period of time—the last years of the nineteenth century and the first years of this. It is then that the arts begin to appropriate the word 'modern' to designate their particular claim to fresh distinctiveness. And one of the themes that begins to run through or behind the arts at this time is the theme of a new age. '[I]n or about December, 1910, human character changed,' said Virginia Woolf in a famous essay called 'Mr Bennett and Mrs Brown', 'The first signs of it are recorded in the books of Samuel Butler, in *The Way of All Flesh* in particular; the plays of Bernard Shaw continue to record it. . . . All human relations have shifted—those between masters and servants, husbands and wives, parents and children. And when human relations change there is at the same time a change in religion, conduct, politics and literature. Let us agree to place one of these changes about the year 1910.'[1] Such arbitrary dates for transformation are no more than intellectual conveniences, but they do usually have imaginative point—and 1910 was the year of a new king, George V, and so of 'Georgianism', and it was the year of the famous Post-Impressionist Exhibition at the Grafton Galleries which exposed England to *avant-garde* movements in French art.[2] But, for those who wanted to find a turn

[1] Virginia Woolf, 'Mrs Bennett and Mrs Brown' (1924), in *Collected Essays: Vol. I* (London, 1966).

[2] For an admirable discussion of this occasion and other similar events which opened the arts to continental influences see Samuel Hynes, *The Edwardian Turn*

in the gyre, as many did, there was perhaps even more point to 1900, which, as well as being imaginatively satisfying and properly millennial, was also the year of Freud's *Interpretation of Dreams*, Planck's quantum theory, and the death of Nietzsche, who himself had promised a new age in which the old forms would crack open. Henry Adams, in the United States, saw millennial meaning in 1900, as his *Education of Henry Adams* records; it was the year of 'an infinite chaos of motion' which required that mind must recognize the new conditions of discontinuity—'must merge in its supersensual universe, or succumb to it.' Gertrude Stein also opted for much the same date. 'So the twentieth century had come it began in 1901,' she said with her usual difficult simplicity, adding however that it had started in the United States long before that. But for Henry James, as for a great many other people, and perhaps for the imagination and social order generally, the real point of change was a truly apocalyptic moment for western civilization—the First World War, a very recognizable point of transition in ideology, mores and social change, and possibly the mark of the collapse of an entire civilized order. 'The plunge of civilization into this abyss of blood and darkness by the wanton feat of those two infamous autocrats,' he wrote in a letter of August, 1914, to Howard Sturgis, 'is a thing that so gives away the whole long age during which we have supposed the world to be, with whatever abatement, gradually bettering, that to have to take it all now for what the treacherous years were all the while really making for and *meaning* is too tragic for any words.'[1] The war made the progressive hope cynical and its version of history uneasy; it made the modern an abyss; the points of change a disaster or crisis. It redirected all the futurist hope in the arts and made it doubtful, soured its direction. D. H. Lawrence picked a similar date for his apocalypse. 'It was in 1915 the old world ended,' he said in

---

of Mind (Princeton and London, 1968): especially the chapter 'Human Character Changes' and the appendix listing the contents of the First and Second Post-Impressionist Shows.

[1] Henry James in *The Letters of Henry James*, selected and edited by Percy Lubbock (2 vols., New York, 1920), Vol. II, p. 384.

Kangaroo. And though he saw, with various degrees of hope, the possibility of a phoenix rebirth, he, like others, created a familiar imaginative pattern for the century[1]—that of an historical process caught between two moments of turn with both purgative and disastrous meanings.

There is, of course, no one date that will really give us the turning point into a modern awareness or a modern style. One can only think of the whole tendency as a development that occurs in England from somewhere around 1870 and which has various points of acceleration and deceleration. In the 1870s, there are certain obvious signals of the new taste for the new: a stress on the way art might serve the taste of an audience itself demanding stylistic outrage, novelty of form, or Pater's recognition in *Studies in the History of the Renaissance* (1873) of the relativism of modern thought, and its consequences for human sensibility, as for the criticism of art. As one nears the turn of the century, which as we have seen tended to become sharply associated with a notion of the turn of the historical wheel, there is a further marked emphasis on the emergence of new styles, typologies, and thrusts of the evolutionary principle, often taking the form of a decadent sensationalism. More and more there is persistent appeal to the principle of the 'new' and the 'modern', and, as Holbrook Jackson points out in his book *The Eighteen Nineties* (1913), the word 'new' starts to acquire a special resonance, perhaps acquired from the French *art nouveau.* 'The range of the adjective gradually spread until it embraced the ideas of the whole period, and we find innumerable references to the "New Spirit", the "New Humour", the "New Realism", the "New Hedonism", the "New Drama", the "New Unionism", the "New Party", and the "New Woman",' he points out, and quotes H. D. Traill beginning an essay on the 'New Fiction', saying 'Not to be *new* is, in these days, to be nothing.' Modern—perhaps borrowed from Germany and Scandinavia—also had some of the

---

[1] This aspect of Lawrence is discussed in Frank Kermode, 'Lawrence and the Apocalyptic Types', *Critical Quarterly*, X, 1 & 2 (Spring and Summer, 1968), pp. 14–38. And there is a brilliant account of the way the mood of crisis and apocalypse affected the modern arts in Kermode's *The Sense of an Ending.*

same cachet; in 1894 John Lane said his *Yellow Book* would have 'the courage of its modernness'. What was meant by newness and modernness clearly varied; *fin-de-siècle* pessimism, dandyish decadence, the bright hope of the Georgian poets. But the growing need for novelty of style is all a recognizable part of the radical spirit that touches thought and art over the decade and passes through into the ones that follow. From about 1908 onward, another new phase of conviction about the urgency of the modern begins to suffuse the arts and the world of ideas in England, this time with a rather less 'decadent' and rather more optimistic bias. The theme comes back again in the twenties with yet another change of temper, one that now emphasizes a species of disillusionment and despair.

These different versions of the 'modern' were, of course, often very different; so different as to be incompatible one with another. In some quarters the emphasis fell on naturalistic realism, in others on the evanescence of consciousness; some writers stress a hard, spare classicism appropriate to the post-sentimental age of the machine, others a new romanticism and subjectivism. What they shared in common was the belief that a new art must emerge to fit a new age; and their strong conviction about the turn of an historical wheel is obviously a species of crisis thought. For a specific apocalypse in history, the modernist mind had to wait until 1914— the outbreak of a war which functioned not only as a holocaust and an image of apocalypse, but as the end of a phase in western civilization, so making a sharp break between the past and the present. But imaginatively that transition had been prepared for over the previous thirty or forty years[1]—in the repeated figures of consciousness struggling forward towards a new stage of existence, or facing a new reality, or producing a new historical type (like the Shavian superman, the Hardy 'new woman' or the Wellsian 'new scientist'). And of course one of

---

[1] For one important aspect of this 'prefiguring', the way in which images of a vast new war abound in earlier literature, see I. F. Clarke, *Voices Prophesying War* (London, 1966; New York, 1967). (Bernard Bergonzi also explores the point in his *Heroes' Twilight: A Study of the Literature of the Great War* (London, 1965).) There is a similar prefiguration in the fact that Wyndham Lewis called his new magazine, appearing in mid-1914, *Blast*.

the most persistent and central of the images was of the new artist himself, feeling his way through the morass of forms and styles to a yearning new mode of expression. Wyndham Lewis seeks to portray him in *Tarr* (1918), Ezra Pound in *Hugh Selwyn Mauberley* (1920) and of course he seeks to portray himself in the various phases of extravagant artistic display that were associated with what Wyndham Lewis called the 'rebel arts'. Many of these developments were 'borrowed' ones, and they depended upon the growing or renewed 'internationalism' of the arts; in many respects they gain their momentum from a sudden new exposure to some outside influence or movement. But, again, the propensity to borrow, to accept the force of a new French movement or to provide an atmosphere sufficiently attractive to draw in writers and artists from other countries (like James and Conrad, Pound and Eliot) does mark a new expansiveness in the climate and a desire for change in the arts.

The notion of an emergence from one phase of culture to another pervades the arts in this period—viewed joyously or sadly, as growth or dissolution. Nor do we find it only in the work of those writers who insist on a technical novelty, those who at their most extreme we should now call 'modernists'. Modernism itself is part of the process, but that comes in various waves interspersed with others that do not quite belong to that tendency, yet which are of undoubted importance in the development. We should probably not now call George Bernard Shaw or Thomas Hardy 'modernist', but their art was radical and their realism the subject of profound controversy; equally H. G. Wells and Arnold Bennett were clearly in the line of what Zola in 1880 had called 'le roman experimental', meaning a novel exhibiting a circumstantial realism and a sense of the hereditary and physiological determinants affecting human character. The feeling for the modern was often a feeling for transition into a new environment in society, a conviction of an explosion of social forces which had produced the need for artistic change. Inevitably, as we shall see, some of this feeling must have derived from the specific conditions—in changing audiences, changing publishing practices, changing literary economics—affecting art itself; and certainly some of it takes the form of an extreme artistic self-consciousness. But in stressing that the change was historical as well as stylistic, Virginia Woolf ('. . . human character changed . . . all human relations have shifted . . .') was indicating not only the basis of the novelty of her own art, but the presence of a whole new environment which involved all other writers too. What happens, in fact, over this span of years is not so much the emergence of a new movement as a vast stylistic upheaval, the consequences of which permeate all the literature written since and are still part of the context of writing today. It was an upheaval that gave literature a much more oblique and complex place in society, one of the most oblique and complex forms of its existence that has ever been.

As these chapters have been suggesting, this large stylistic change, this remaking of the literary environment, comes out of the rapid social alteration and modernization that occurred in England from about 1870, and brought about a new flowing of consciousness, a new massing of forces that required expression and development. The specific consequences for writers of those changes in the culture of late-nineteenth-century England that made life and thought so temperamentally different will be explored in fully detail in later parts of this book; but some feautres of the broad texture of this change should be stressed. For over this period the qualities of a new spirit in the arts do begin clearly to emerge, as much that had made the arts of the earlier part of the century began to pass away. The intelligentsia itself was now growing increasingly urbanized and had so lost many of its own sources of value and its old social place. It had to create new relationships to its culture and to the growing heterodoxy of the audience within it, an audience both socially more plural and in many ways much more 'mass'. It had to come to terms with the extending patterns of communication in the society, as with the newly articulate sectors in the community. Much previous thought and art had emerged out of a provincial or pastoral culture, but that was really no longer the case. The post-village character of the modern England had eliminated much of that sense of cultural stability and organic and felt community, that agrarian centre that, for many writers, provided a contrasting pastoral image against which to contrast the processes of urban change. And the pattern of growing religious doubt, increasing secularization and newer species of intellectual rationalism also had the same effect of creating a sense of transition and uncertainty. Though among intellectuals and artists agnosticism or atheism were prevalent, this was less important than the general weakening of a religious interpretation of the human situation which questioned the status of myth and fiction itself. And the spirit of individualistic romanticism which had so deeply marked the art and thought of the nineteenth century began therefore to give way to a new rationalism and realism, to much more 'conditioned' views of man. Then, too, the very working conditions of artists and writers were altering. The texture of the reading public was being transformed: by education and literacy and the expanded need for printed communication. Intellectual and literary culture tended to become both more proletarian and more metropolitan; and new roles for writers and journalists abounded in this phase of literary expansion. And the new technology not only changed printing methods but came to the writer's fingertips: in 1874 Mark Twain wrote a letter on a new typewriter and said 'I believe it will print faster than I can write. One may lean back in his chair and work it. It piles an awful stack of words on one page.'

Perhaps the largest consequence of the mood of change was the growing pluralism of the culture. More than ever, you could divide it up between the various brows—high, middle and low—and in doing so conceive of many different modes of existence for the arts and the artist. And it became less and less possible to think in terms of a single and shared culture, national and international, on which the arts might draw. Thought and art could therefore no longer remain as unified as they had been, and those who carried the burden of reconciling the variety of world-views that arose—that is to say, the intellectuals and 'serious' artists—found themselves having to come to terms with an environment that questioned in many respects the very origins of art and thought themselves. In some quarters, this produced a new self-consciousness about language, methods, styles, and

I

often a committed emphasis on style or manner itself. It also involved a growing relativity of values which encouraged new notes of despair or new species of irony, new feelings that civilization in the traditional sense was under question. But if anything marks the new mood in the arts it is the very pluralism of art itself—the very heterodoxy of the forms of the new, the very breadth of expression involved in the conviction that the modern was here. Hence the difficulty of identifying the 'modern' in literature with any one particular style, any one mode of the new. If the changed mood is marked by anything, it is not by a single new style or manner or movement, but by the way the developing situation seemed to throw any single tendency into question.

II

Just as there is in fact no precise date for modernism so there is no ready causal explanation for its emergence. It is simply the crystallization in the arts of the tendencies developing through nineteenth-century literature, the changing viewpoint turned in a certain direction and then explored and re-explored in more convincing ways by men of genius. Nonetheless there *is* one literary generation that seems to carry the experience of modernism most: the generation that came to maturity and notice in a few brief years immediately before the 1914–1918 War. This is the period that Ford Madox Ford fixes on for the emergence of 'Les Jeunes' ('It was—truly—like an opening world,' he said);[1] that Pound dates as the period of his Risorgimento; that Wyndham Lewis has spoken of as the lost chance of a great new art (' *We are the first men of a Future that has not materialized,*' he wrote).[2] It is certainly the most active period of stylistic change in the modern arts in England—a period in which, in the course of four or five years, many of the traditional norms of literature

[1] Ford Madox Ford (later Hueffer), *Thus to Revisit* (London, 1921).
[2] Wyndham Lewis, *Blasting and Bombardiering* (London, 1937).

were seriously subverted, the atmosphere of Victorianism faded, and the romantic inheritance seems in many respects to have gone into flight. These are the years of the early work of Ezra Pound and T. S. Eliot, and of Yeats's emergence from his late Victorian and Celtic twilight phase. In fiction they see the later work of Henry James, some of Conrad's finest fiction, and the coming to notice of E. M. Forster, D. H. Lawrence, Katherine Mansfield and Wyndham Lewis, as well as the appearance of James Joyce's *Dubliners* and the writing of his *A Portrait of the Artist as a Young Man* (1916). In both poetry and fiction it is a period of marked technical experiment, coupled with the emergence of a whole new body of influential ideas that were to affect literature; the theories of Bergson about interior time, the stress on the intrinsic orders of consciousness that owe a great deal to William James[1] and come to owe even more to Freud and Jung, the turning away from a liberal progressive view of history, the growing distrust of the realism of art. In 1910, the year Virginia Woolf picked out, two important events did happen—the Edwardian period gave way to the Georgian with the death of King Edward ('If it is felt, as it is clearly felt, that the era of Victoria is indeed at last over, who is so bold as to dare forecast the nature of the epoch that is to come?' asked A. R. Orage in his magazine *The New Age* that year), and Roger Fry put on his exhibition of the Post-Impressionist painters, containing work from Van Gogh to Picasso, at the Grafton Galleries, which caused general ferment. '. . . I have permitted myself to suspect,' wrote Arnold Bennett, also in *The New Age*, 'that supposing some writer were to come along and do in words what these men have done in paint, I might conceivably be disgusted with nearly the whole of modern fiction, and I might have to begin again. . . . Supposing a young writer turned up and forced me, and some of my contemporaries —us who fancy ourselves a bit—to admit that we had been concerning ourselves unduly with essentials, that we had been

[1] It was William James who provided the famous idea of a 'stream' of consciousness: 'A "river" or a "stream" are the metaphors by which it [consciousness] is most naturally described. In talking of it hereafter, let us agree to call it the stream of thought, of consciousness, or of subjective life.' (*Principles of Psychology*, 1890).

worrying ourselves to achieve infantile realisms? Well, that day would be a great and disturbing day—for us.'[1] These are, indeed, the years of a large-scale change of mood in the English arts.

The Tradition of the New in England does indeed reach a kind of peak at this time, though many of its elements go back to much earlier activity; in the novel, for instance, which tended to be the first form in England to become self-consciously experimental in the modernist way, it reaches back a bit further, certainly to the middle work of Henry James. But out of the past a new model of the artistic situation had emerged—one in which art was the product of a kind of creative ferment analogous to rebellion in other spheres; in which it was problematically placed, and must struggle to ensure the language, the structure and even the historical survival of the formal object, the work of art; in which the artist was socially isolated, in communion not with the contingencies of immediate history but with some primary, distant artistic utopia. By the outbreak of war the intellectual obsessions of this tendency had been laid down, and the new influences—intellectual, artistic and literary—assimilated. By the same time there existed a body of inescapable artistic performances—the novels of James, George Moore, Conrad, early Lawrence, Joyce; the poetry of T. E. Hulme, early Pound, and the minor Imagists—which pointed a direction. There were a number of explicit statements—by James, Pound, F. S. Flint and others—suggesting what the aesthetic was. There were certain basic figures who had been established as influences —the unmaskers of process, like Darwin, Marx and above all Freud; the cyclical historiographers, such as Spengler (though the tradition goes back at least to Vico); the new 'intuitionalists', like Bergson and Remy de Gourmont; the Russian novelists of consciousness, notably Dostoevsky; some of the later French symbolist poets, like Mallarmé and Laforgue; and the Post-Impressionist painters, whose techniques were considered to be adaptable by analogy to literature. The emphasis on technique, or on the perceptual resources of the artist himself as a subjective

---

[1] For a fuller discussion of the ferment and the part played in it by Orage's magazine, see Wallace Martin, *The New Age Under Orage: Chapters in English Cultural History* (Manchester and New York, 1967).

consciousness; the emphasis on rendering, or the heightened resonance that might be attached to certain observed objects; the emphasis on the medium of art itself as the artist's essential subject-matter; the stress on a literature that was, in Ortega y Gasset's phrase, an art of figures rather than an art of adventures —all these pieties of the artistic apocalypse of modernism were established in many advanced quarters by this time. The registering of modern consciousness had now become not a representational matter but an aesthetic matter, a problem in the making of literary structures, in the employment of language and finally in the social role of the artist himself. Hence the search for a style and a typology becomes the most emphatic element in the work of literature as such.

If the overall tendency was one of a number of competing tendencies in the period, there can be little doubt that it does reach a kind of optimum point at around this time. Indeed one could argue, as some critics have,[1] that by about 1925 the whole movement was more or less exhausted; though of course if it was it had been deeply assimilated into literary practice generally. In England, certainly, it was in many respects declining from the end of the war onward. Between 1908 and 1915 London had been an international capital of the tendency, drawing in writers from several countries; but after the war Paris reverted to being the focus. Ezra Pound left England for Paris in 1919, complaining that England was finished as an artistic centre. James Joyce and Ford Madox Ford went too. D. H. Lawrence, also sure that England had 'died', travelled elsewhere. Henry James had died in 1916. Of course some of the major works of modernism in the English line were yet to appear: T. S. Eliot's 'The Waste Land', W. B. Yeats's middle work, James Joyce's *Ulysses*, Ford Madox Ford's *Parade's End* tetralogy, and the major novels of Virginia Woolf. But the cosmopolitan atmosphere in England, though not yet in Paris, had started to fade: the new mood was rather set by the emergence of 'Bloomsbury', a polite,

---

[1] See, for instance, Harry Levin, 'What Was Modernism?' in *Refractions: Essays in Comparative Literature* (New York and London, 1966); Bernard Bergonzi, 'Introduction' to *Innovations: Essays in Art and Ideas* (London, 1968), edited by himself.

upper-middle-class and national bohemia, with strong connections, however, with European writing. In some respects at least
modernism now seemed like a tendency which had visited and
gone. The truth is perhaps the one that T. S. Eliot stressed: that
what had to follow was a critical consolidation of the creative
passions that had gone before. So, if the main magazines of 1908–
1915 were essentially devoted to creative ferment, the main ones
of the twenties were reviews like Eliot's own *Criterion*, heavily
devoted to critical articles and debate. As for the newer writers
who emerged in the twenties, they tended to assimilate many
aspects of modernism without in most cases being modernist.
What *they* confronted was a world rapidly modernized in a new
way, by war: a period of accelerating change in mores and social
arrangements, a period of a new kind of 'Bright Young Thing'
who regarded himself or herself as emancipated and advanced, a
period in which the revolution of consciousness seemed to lie
not so much in art as in social style. So now the task of the modern
was at least in part to catch the nature of the new social temper
or tone; and in the work of novelists like Aldous Huxley or
Evelyn Waugh or of poets like the Sitwells and, later, Auden and
MacNeice, the increased fashionable acceptance of the 'advanced'
intellectual by a society fascinated by its own social turmoil is
clear. So, by the end of the 1920s, there had been a considerable
remaking of modernism, as the general ferment reached deeper
into more people's experience and was reflected in more people's
mores, and as the immediate stuff and conditions of the modern
world became part of the substance of its art.

The tone was different, too, as social change, reflected in this
period of shifting styles, provided a consumable, fashionable sense
of being modern. Improvisation, cynicism and self-destructiveness
provided acceptable psychological means of dealing with a disturbed history, as in Aldous Huxley's *Those Barren Leaves*:

> 'I don't see that it would be possible to live in a more exciting age,'
> said Calamy. 'The sense that everything's perfectly provisional and
> temporary—everything, from social institutions to what we've hitherto
> regarded as the most sacred scientific truths—the feeling that nothing,
> from the Treaty of Versailles to the rationally explicable universe, is

really safe, the intimate conviction that anything may happen, anything may be discovered—another war, the artificial creation of life, the proof of continued existence after death—why it is all infinitely exhilarating.'

'And the possibility that everything may be destroyed?' questioned Mr. Cardan.

'That's exhilarating too,' Calamy answered, smiling.

It was possible for a young writer to enact his sense of the modern through the world, to internalize the decade. So the problems of 'structuring' history in literature began to be solved in rather a different way—for instance, by allowing the concern with crisis and change to become part of the matter of literature, rather than as a feature of its experimental form. This may suggest a decline in modernism; this is to miss the persistence of modernism's sense of an ironic era of art and the way it has turned to new forms. In most of the writers of the decade, the detachment of the author, the devaluation of his heroes, the loss of a sense of logic in history or society, are manifest. The world created is one growing less rational, less ordered, more impermanent, more disposed to boredom, loneliness, uncertainty and despair; and it is a world of new mores, new consciousness, new social conflicts. The age is an age of new barbarism, and the writer can include the barbarity and immerse himself in it, or stand back to condemn it in the 'classicist' way. But this is the time in which many of the modern themes—of desperation, civilized misery, the sacrifice of self and society to irrational forces, the contingency of history become confirmed among a generation of writers who had grown up in the 'modern'.[1]

By the 1930s, after the World Slump, the theme and the bias was given a much more political and often a more documentary slant. Sociology and psychology were brought together in a prevalent style that mixed a realistic and surrealistic vision of a disturbed and disordered world. The revolutionary state of

[1] For a much more extensive discussion of my argument here, see my essay 'The Novel in the 1920s' in *The Sphere History of Literature in the English Language: Vol. VII, The Twentieth Century*, ed. Bernard Bergonzi (London and New York, 1970) (on which I have slightly drawn for the above discussion). Also see Sean O'Faolain, *The Vanishing Hero: Studies in the Novel of the Twenties* (London, 1951).

transition was now the accepted state of affairs, and the literary images of machinery and waste were images of a world that had lost purpose or meaning. 'Bloomsbury' remains, still, the central meeting place of writers, but it was now hunting for an uneasy marriage of aestheticism and social realism, or what it liked to think of as 'responsibility'.[1] The novelty of literature was derived from the novelty of the world; history had taken over as the great experimentalist. By the Second World War, Cyril Connolly was arguing in his magazine *Horizon* that 'such a thing as *avant garde* in literature has ceased to exist'. Experiment had become associated with withdrawal; writing had passed on beyond the modernist generation; and social realism and writers from new social backgrounds were the points of progression. Though the literary critics and academics had now entirely accepted the modernist writers, and indeed had deeply assimilated the neo-symbolist norms of modernism into their own theory,[2] the younger English writers clearly tended to regard the movement as one belonging essentially to a previous generation. Indeed, it has become usual to characterize the English postwar literary scene as one of a reaction against experiment.[3] Certainly in the provincial, lower-middle-class novels of the 1950s and in, for instance, Philip Larkin's presentation of the poet as the ordinary man embarrassed by the large 'myth-kitty' on which the poets of the twentieth-century past have drawn, one can see a

[1] As an instance here, see the contents of John Lehmann's magazines *New Writing* and *Penguin New Writing*, with their strong proletarian fascination linked with a Bloomsbury inheritance; and his book *New Writing in Europe* (London, 1940).

[2] The degree to which modernism has been accredited—both by literary critics and then in due course by the general public—constitutes a fascinating issue in itself. To the question of popular acceptance I shall return; of critical acceptance one might briefly say that much of New Critical theory in the United States and England, both in its treatment of literature of the present and the past, has derived from certain aspects of the modernist aesthetic. The height of its acceptance came in the 1940s and 1950s—just at the time when writers themselves seemed to be turning *away* from modernism.

[3] See, for instance, Frederick J. Karl, *A Reader's Guide to the Contemporary English Novel* (New York, 1959; London, 1963); and R. Rabinovitz, *The Reaction Against Experiment in the English Novel: 1950–1960* (New York and London, 1967).

reaction against experimentalism and bohemianism *and* a kind of resigned acceptance of the fact that the artist is—like all the rest of us—the victim of history, unable to transcend, by a great effort of art, the determinations of historical and social process. That transcendance, in part, modernism did achieve; it was profoundly anti-historical and anti-determinist, and that is one of the reasons why it is hard to define its complicated social place. Nonetheless, modernism played an enormous part in the transformation of the cultural environment and in the forms and assumptions of modern artistic activity. Even critics who, like Frederick J. Karl, have noted that the tendency of post-1930 English writing has been 'to bring back traditional character and plot rather than to speak the inexpressible', have also observed that they have done this while retaining 'many of the technical developments of the major moderns'.[1] If it is true that the reaction against some aspects of modernism has been stronger in the English than in some other literatures, and that English writing has lost some of the *avant-gardist* disposition evident in other traditions to the point of disappointing some present-day critics,[2] the fact remains that modernism has been only one of the twentieth-century styles. Its intense sense of crisis, its feeling that it was at the end of the line of culture, its persistent attempts to make the final artistic statement before the deluge came, gave it a completeness and finality. Where forms of modernism have occurred since, they have really appeared as one of a variety of technical species and social postures open to the modern writer.

This is perhaps particularly apparent today, when there has been a marked atmosphere of stylistic ferment, especially among

[1] Karl, op. cit.

[2] So Richard Kostelanetz can suggest, in his introductory essay to his anthology *On Contemporary Literature* (New York, 1964), that much contemporary English writing has lacked 'the scope and urgent contemporaneousness that are the prime characteristics of truly significant contemporary writing'. The same disappointment is expressed, in more ambivalent terms, in Bernard Bergonzi, *The Situation of the Novel* (London, 1970)—though he recognizes that the character of recent English writing is conditioned by a valuable, if apparently technically unambitious, liberalism. But both writers seem to imply that only an urgently apocalyptic art can meet the contemporary state of affairs—a somewhat limiting version of the modernist argument.

young people, and a kind of generalized bohemianism has become the fashion. But this has been much more a broad cultural manifestation rather than a specialized artistic manifestation. Art has been involved, but as a kind of secondary feature of the situation. For bohemianism has been much more important as a new, free life-style borrowed from writers; there are now bohemians on every street corner. Most are 'writers' who don't write; a few of them, by further extension, become, so to speak, 'writers who don't write' who write. They become, that is, artists in a culture that is not primarily conceived in artistic terms; and the art they produce tends often—as in the happening, in op art and pop art, in the psychedelic merging of poetry and music, in the art of immediacy—to be momentary stylizations of the broader environment. As Bernard Bergonzi has said, there is in this contemporary activity an *avant-garde* element, but also a 'widespread shift from the traditional concept of the work of art (whether "minority" or "popular" art is immaterial) as an *artefact* to that of art as *performance*'.[1] In this sense, and in the relatively disposable nature of much of this activity, it is much more a manifestation of mass rather than high culture. In this situation, certain of the techniques, styles and postures of earlier modernism do become available again. But, as Al Alvarez has argued, this seems to be, as earlier modernism was not, the expression of a totally open stylistic field, an Age of No Style, in which all past styles are laid open for inspection and re-use simultaneously.[2] The new stylists are again cosmopolitan, but they are usually cosmopolitans of the internationality of mass-media and modern youth; and there is a case for saying that the best example of the tendency in England is the Beatles. In certain of this writing, though not notably in the English variants (which have in any case been few), some of the modernist themes have been sounded again and a certain continuity can be established.[3]

[1] Bernard Bergonzi, 'Introduction' to *Innovations: Essays in Art and Ideas* (London, 1968), edited by himself.

[2] Al Alvarez, various essays in *Beyond All This Fiddle: Essays 1955–1967* (London, 1968).

[3] Frank Kermode has brilliant discussions of these matters in *The Sense of an Ending* and in his essay 'Modernisms', reprinted in Bergonzi's anthology

Here, too, the fascination with an historical apocalypse, the search for new order or mutation of consciousness, the conviction of a crisis of the word, is to be found among some of the more prestigious exponents (like William Burroughs, for instance). That strong sense of transition that lay behind the early phases of modernism does undoubtedly run today through the western cultures, and it is producing striking upheaval in the arts. But one difference from earlier modernism is that the battle for the *avant garde* is won: novelty is an achieved convention. And, since the activity exists in a climate of more or less instant acceptance, in a period of institutionalized bohemia, certain other themes that mark the great modernist works are a good deal less apparent—those essential themes of the preservation of the artist and high culture in a specialized and private world; the withdrawal from politics and history; the belief in art as a totally distinct and separate order of knowledge. In many respects, it seems right to say, as Harry Levin says, that the new bohemianism marks the cultural lag rather than the advance-guard.[1] In any case, precisely because of the obvious elements of play and impermanence, the lack of concern for standards or perpetuation, in such of their work as has taken literary form, it would be difficult to say that it dominated the current scene. It has indeed become one part of the general multiplicity of artistic activity that has welled up in a time when a proliferation of media and presentational techniques (themselves machineries that demand styles) have coincided with changes in social mores and structures, when individuals have more identities available and a choice of new life-styles. Perhaps more than anything what these contemporary phenomena do is to remind us that we have still some evidence that there is a certain irreducible minimum surviving in art as there is in language. We still, despite Pinter, talk *to* one another and are understood; we still, despite modernism at the point (as in Beckett) where it is most convinced that art

---

Innovations and in Kermode's collection of his own essays, *Continuities* (London and New York, 1968).

[1] Harry Levin, 'What Was Modernism?' in *Refractions: Essays in Comparative Literature* (New York and London, 1966).

has almost reached the silence of the word, find narrative fascinating, and its power to treat recognizable life in a recognizable way to recreate the particular feel of this or that experience, to act contiguously with shared and familiar knowledge, to apprehend reality rather than transform it a recurrent pleasure. And, through the phases of beginning-of-the-century modernism and the latter revival of semi-modernist features—what Frank Kermode calls 'palaeo-modernism' and 'neo-modernism'[1]—that minimum has persisted: persisted in a form no more traditional, in my view, than traditional modernism. The art of extremes may now be undergoing a revival; but there is nothing in the record of the modern century to say it is the only true art. And the art which still asserts the reality of language or the recognizableness of human character is not therefore a provenly outmoded form. To persist, of course, literature of this temper has necessarily found much change in the world it treats and, in finding that, it has changed the forms and structures by which the writer communicates with our own changing structures of perception; but it has done so with a degree of linguistic and structural community foreign to much art in the modernist modes. Hence the importance of that 'oscillation' of which I have several times spoken.

III

To sum up briefly. The style of modern literature needs to be tracked by looking at its extreme manifestations *and* at its more ordinary and familiar ones—those that belong to what is sometimes thought of as realism and sometimes as literary traditionalism and sometimes as 'liberal' or 'formless' art. This means that two kinds of change have taken place in twentieth-century literature. One is towards representing or structuring contemporary reality, experience or feeling without any notably spectacular display of the artistic difficulties of doing so; here art is relatively contiguous with the general culture and finds its resources in its languages and tones of voice, its ways of value-creation and value-

[1] Kermode, 'Modernisms', cited above.

transmission. The other is towards mutating consciousness or decreating extant artistic orders to make each work a totally new perceptual field which we may or may not feel ourselves able to decode. Both involve responses to the modern cultural situation which are comprehensible, though the latter is of course vastly more oblique and requires comprehension not only of the state of culture but of one of the most difficult contours art has ever performed. The emergence of the latter as a conspicuous tendency is, in the English tradition, roughly datable somewhere just before the First World War; but it depends on an accelerating development in literature from which, in many respects, the other tendency is *also* derived. There is some community to the broad stylistic age, as there are to all ages, but it must be sought very generally and include both species of artistic development. When a critic like Northrop Frye defines ours as an age of the 'low mimetic'—an age, that is, in which the structures of literature deal in heroes very like ourselves, or inferior to ourselves; when he and Sean O'Faolain note the disappearance of the hero from literature; when critics like Alan Friedman observe how much twentieth-century fictional writing depends upon the internalization of consciousness within characters[1]—then they touch on factors which most modern literature manifests, and which can be generally recognized as part of the total temper. In the long-term history of styles ours is a distinctive age; but within the age there is unprecedented variation. And though historicism is itself part of the temper of this age, and though a strong sense to exposure to historical necessity is a marked feature of its art, it is in fact, and for these reasons, harder to 'explain' contextually than most artistic eras. Its very proliferation of forms is in fact a testimony to the complexity of the modern world, and the many sources of value in it. And in many respects it is an age of a new internationalism in art, so that national cultural interpretations of art no longer can be entirely satisfactory, so that its remarkable interfusion is drawn from all compass-points.

[1] Northrop Frye, *Anatomy of Criticism* (Princeton and London, 1957); Sean O'Faolain, *The Vanishing Hero*, cited above; Alan Friedman, *The Turn of the Novel* (New York and London, 1960).

Equally briefly, we may point to the presence in the twentieth-century arts of two contrasted functions. One is art in its liberal function; the artist is essentially the humanist, and his art is a species of disinterested knowledge. The traditional obligations of the artist towards civilization and learning make him a moral agent in the society. His concern is neither simply to represent life nor newly to create it, but to criticize it from the standpoint of that disinterested right reason, to which the writer by virtue of his calling is bound. Art and education are intimately linked here, in a common aspiration for and enlargement of the full human spirit. In this tradition, which reaches back at least a hundred and fifty years and indeed has its roots in the Renaissance, art is a permanent and universally valid epistemology for the society. It is not a matter of individual works created and evaluated at random, but a sustained tradition which involves a system of meanings and comprehensions of man, society and life. It is, in I. A. Richards's phrase, 'a storehouse of recorded values', an instrument in the advancement of human understanding. The artist is a man of intelligence engaged *as* an intelligence, with serious responsibility for values and judgments; the body of artists are a kind of secular clergy, a group of 'guardians', practising and disseminating a special wisdom founded in the arts. The other tendency is art in its formalist function; it believes in the distinctiveness of its own way of knowing and may be seriously concerned for the fortunes of civilization, but it postulates an anarchistic environment in society in which certain aspects of the traditional activity are no longer possible. Instead of acting within history and culture, the artist must, if he is to survive, escape from it. The specific problems of being an artist become paramount and art is seen not as a general activity of the intelligence but a highly specialized and arcane form of knowledge; it should not mean but *be*. Its works are in some sense purified of life, and they cease, as Ortega y Gasset has put it, to be of 'a generally human kind'.[1] They become aesthetic objects for contemplation, or they enact the leap out of time to the enduring artistic moment: the Joycean epiphany, the Imagist

[1] Ortega y Gasset, 'The Dehumanization of Art', cited above.

image, moments of statis or aesthetic equipoise caught from the 'brutal chaos' of reality. There is little doubt that the liberal function of art in our century has been reduced, under the pressures of a democratizing culture and the overweaning distrust of 'bourgeois' civilization that has marked much intellectual activity in our time. But it has also been pined for and at times recovered in English writing, and it has certainly modified the extremes of modernism in the English tradition.

PART THREE

The Writer Today

CHAPTER VI

The Place of the Artist in Liberal Society

I

It will be apparent, from all that has been said so far, that I am assuming the existence of literature to be a social fact of an extremely complex kind. As a social fact, it involves at the minimum an author, a work, a means for its distribution, and a reader, webbed together in a complex circuit of communication. More broadly, it also involves a culture in which literature has more or less prestige; a cumulative tradition of literary roles and practices; a body of ways of knowing experience and reality which is the mark of a cultural community and in which literature has an epistemological function which can be centrally important or highly marginal. It is clear enough, when we look backwards through history, or comparatively across different countries and cultures, that different kinds of social organization produce different kinds of writer, support different kinds of writing, and involve wide variations of regard for the literary act. In some cultures the book has small place or none at all; in others it has a high place and the producers of books have high prestige. There are in fact enormous ranges of assumption about what art is for and what needs the artist serves. His role can be priestly or menial; he may exist as a distinct personality or his work may be a folk-product unmarked by any personal signature. So De Tocqueville, in his *Democracy in America*, tellingly observed that the status of the artist and the arts there would be very different from that in Europe: excellence and tradition would be less cultivated, and the artist would be regarded as an ordinary man.[1] Karl Mannheim also once remarked that the status of the arts in a

[1] This contrast is of course no longer so marked: Tocqueville wrote in the 1830s.

particular society is closely associated with the status of those who produce and consume it; in societies where it is produced by slaves it is thought to be an activity of the inferior. And even today, when the international arts are marked by a high degree of similarity and inter-influence, we can still see, as we look from society to society, very marked variations in the situations of artists and the arts. The contemporary Russian writer clearly works in a context in which a different view of the writer exists than that which prevails in our society, or even in Russian society before the Revolution. We expect our writers to be free to appeal to their own distinctive experience, to explore their own individual terms of creativity or their own passions and impulses and neuroses, to exorcise their devil; after all, creativity is virtuous of itself. In Russian society the writer is not of course free in that sense; though in not being so he is a good deal more fully integrated with certain other aspects of his culture than is a writer in England, the United States or France.

There are, then, large-scale variations of the role of the arts and the artist, even in societies that enjoy a high degree of literacy, which of course not all societies do. Then again there are more subtle variations that affect literature very considerably, existing between similar societies (the French tend to view the writer as an intellectual, the Americans as a specialist practitioner) or in the same society between one generation and the next (so at the end of the Civil War American writing moved rapidly from its centre in New England culture and became a much more provincial and populist phenomenon). The status of particular art-forms can change suddenly, so that in England in the late nineteenth century poetry declines rapidly in popularity and importance and attention tends to shift to the novel. The habit of reading may suddenly become the possession of a new class; the rise of the novel in England in the eighteenth century clearly has much to do with the emergence of a new audience (the rising, mainly urban bourgeoisie) as well as that of a new medium (the commercial, easily available printed book following on cheaper paper, moveable type and the growth of means of circulation) and a new empiricism at work generally in the culture.

The prestige of writing can be affected by the social status of those who produce it and the implications of this for indicating what abilities are necessary to acquire the appropriate skills. Creativity may appear extremely rare and mysterious, or highly common. In short, the nature of writing and its cultural place and meaning is very much affected by all sorts of delicate transformations in the conditions of production and consumption—in changes of class-origin among writers, in their sense of addressing a new audience, even when the price of books goes up or down. Indeed, part of literature's way of growth and change is by its way of drawing upon the exploration and exploitation of such delicately shifting possibilities in the literary environment.

II

I want here to concentrate on such matters as they affect the writer in our kind of society; and I want in due course to look at the nature of the literary profession in England, in terms of the kind of recruitment, rewards and status it possesses. But it is best to begin by looking at the question from the broadest possible view. What is the place of the writer in western democratic society? At first sight it is a free and at the same time a fairly eminent one. In England, at least (the situation was somewhat different in America, for the simple reason that the literary profession had no existence prior to Independence), the great beneficiary of Romanticism was the writer and the literary intelligence; indeed one of the changes wrought by Romanticism was an extension of the claims of the power of art. Until the romantics, the chief impetus of most western art had been that of adding humanistically to the traditional experience and inherited imaginings of mankind, of recreating old stories out of the shared patrimony of the culture. Art now ceased to be a ritualization of the known world and a distillation of experience universally recognizable; it became a distinctive and special form of knowing that was, nonetheless, held to be central to the onward needs of society. The imagination became a creative and reconciling principle which afforded, by wide agreement, supreme faculties for apprehending truth; the artist was, as Sir Isaiah Berlin puts it, 'the highest manifestation of the ever-active spirit' and he existed above and beyond the classes in a state of imaginative disinterestedness. The relevance of such a notion could only emerge after the disappearance of the patron and with the rise of an anonymous and multi-class audience.[1] Now the artist could act as an independent intellectual and state his obligation as primarily one to art itself, art as a large ideal of culture, a world-spirit, an expanding human awareness. As Sartre puts the point in his *What Is Literature?*, there grew up, he says, with the breakdown in the church's claim to contest for spirituality and truth, the belief that this was literature's function—a writer could, by the practice of his art, become the timeless and unlocalized mind, the universal man. The appeal he made to his readers and the part he took in their fortunes and misfortunes was dictated by generosity and free judgment; his position was therefore critical. In this sense the writer became not the expert practitioner of the formal aspects of his art, but a humanist still—a central social intelligence. In the English nineteenth century the intelligentsia generally was heavily literary in orientation, and was involved with society through a cultural point of view. That is to say, its aims were not directly political but rather educational. So Matthew Arnold's view in *Culture and Anarchy* that culture is a social concern: 'the moment . . . culture is considered not merely as the endeavour to *see* and *learn* [total and harmonious perfection], but the endeavour, also, to make it *prevail*, the moral, social and beneficent character of culture becomes manifest'. This involves the association of the writer with the liberalism of much English intellectual thought, and places the literary intelligentsia in a more or less educational role. Of course from this view (as we have already seen) there comes a marked divergence. The artist's move towards the ideal of culture could lead him to sacrifice cultural involvement for even more specialized

[1] See Raymond Williams's fuller discussion of this situation in *Culture and Society*, Chapter 2.

functions of art, while at the same time other forms of knowledge, like politics or sociology or Northcliffe's *Daily Mail*, could contend for the place of being the humanist scripture.

The western writer, then, has been a man allowed many privileges—privileges conferred on him because he represents a highly regarded kind of intelligence or the mysterious and valued practices of art. He has the traditional freedom to criticize and attack the society, and he has the right to be dissident, deviant and bizarre. Not all writers take advantage of these privileges at their extreme, of course; even so, we sometimes assume, almost as a matter of cliché, that the more eccentric or deviant a writer is, the better the art he will produce. Now all this represents the furthest edge of our liberal presumption that personal creativity has a high value in its own right, and obviously one of the attractions of the extremist writer is that he encourages us in the thought that our kind of society does freely release the resources of the creative imagination and the critical vision. Jean-Paul Sartre once said, very finely, that all literary work is an appeal offering itself on behalf of the reader's own freedom; it offers us the promise of expression, of our own 'opening out' as individuals.[1] That obviously is one reason why we do read literature, and why we think it worthy of study and analysis. This is why we grant special dispensation to genius, and why at times (as in the case of the gradual repeal of legislation about obscenity in literature, or the ending of the surveillance of the Lord Chamberlain over the English theatre) we are prepared to make social adaptations to tolerate it better. The conventional humanist reason behind our greater tolerance of sexual frankness or deviant ethics in literature is that literature educates and enlarges our knowledge of life, our sensitive awareness, our consciousness. (No doubt it would be logical to assume that if literature can influence us for the good it can also affect us to the bad; that, curiously, is a less widespread assumption among the coteries supporting art.)[2] Now one result of the situation of

[1] Jean-Paul Sartre, *What Is Literature?* (London, 1950).
[2] Though George Steiner uses aspects of this argument in *Language and Silence: Essays 1958–1966* (London, 1967).

the writer in western liberal society is that it is in fact one of the most attractive careers available—creative, tolerantly regarded and prestigious. There are few posts more worth having, though talent is normally (but not always) necessary. So, in this sort of society, there is no shortage of aspirants. In fact, just now, when there is no very great evidence that readers of imaginative literature are increasing substantially in number, there is an obvious expansion going on in the numbers of artists and would-be artists. As the art-schools produce more and more painters, so the open educational system produces more poets, novelists and dramatists. There are poetry magazines with more poets submitting to them than readers; and the coffee-bars, clubs and pubs, even the labour-exchanges, are well stocked with writers, not all of them notably productive. 'It is easy to see why there is a longstanding association between literature and riotous poverty,' Frank Kermode once remarked, 'as soon as it becomes even remotely possible to live by writing it turns out that far too many people have the basic equipment to try it.' Consequently marginal literary roles (advertising copywriting, journalism, publishing, scriptwriting, researching) are easily filled from the ranks of 'writers', while quantitatively literary production is in ceaseless increase. Not only is the life attractive and valued; it also has social space in which to exist.

In liberal western society, then, the artist's role is recognized and respected but it is not institutionalized; it functions on a *laissez-faire* basis. If he can find the means to exist, in the economics of the market or by some form of patronage, he has great independence of creative action. He need not live in the same country as his audience or serve them in any other way than by impersonal publication. He can, through that market, make considerable profit and win considerable prestige. The situation has been one favourable to the production of a major art, expansive, varied, original, qualitatively and humanly dense and rich. The classically successful environment for the liberal artist is of course that of the nineteenth century: in that environment art became a centrally independent way of knowing, acquiring many of the functions formerly associated with religion and religious wisdom, enlightening men and alleviating their sorrows, advancing their comprehension and their sensibilities. To read any major study of the mid-Victorian literary scene—for instance, Gordon Haight's recent brilliant life of George Eliot[1]—is to discover how a liberal exercise of the artistic function could produce writing consonant with the shared intellectual and emotional activity of a literate, intelligent and inquisitive middle class. That sort of expanding community between a freely placed writer and an audience themselves humanistically engaged with art obviously represents an ideal version of the liberal relationship between artist and society. But this humanist view of art—an art that contained and lived alongside man, enlarging his conduct and sympathies, testifying to his humanity, introducing him to sectors of the world of which he had no experience, serving as a secular and open-ended wisdom—now seems to us to have been thrown into doubt. A number of important modern writers have embodied it with a profound authority—E. M. Forster or George Orwell, for instance—but many have not.

Hence another aspect of our modern view of the arts. For, while we believe that art should and can be free, we also believe that we live in a time and society exceptionally difficult for the production of art—a view that has also played a big part in our expectation about writers and the work they give us. I have shown that there are sound enough reasons for this belief, just as there are for the conviction that the free writer has the profoundest significance for us. Now both of these two views—that writers are free, and that they live in profoundly unfortunate circumstances—reach back to the Romantic movement, in this country and even more in America, Russia or France. For the right to freedom was often held to involve a necessary quest into loneliness, and to involve a risky journey into the dangerous, Promethean dimensions of artistic knowledge. In Romantic fable, the risk often takes the form—as in say Hawthorne's story 'Ethan Brand'—of a loss of necessary human sympathy and community, though it also had profound virtuous associations in shattering false visions and blind delights. This lore comes through into

[1] Gordon S. Haight, *George Eliot: A Biography* (New York and London, 1968).

modern art, though often with a changed dimension; separation is the only virtuous posture.[1] This situation contained obvious risks: as literature grew more marginal and the audience for it more dispersed and specialized, a parallel dispersion and marginality emerged in the mind and work of the writer. For, of course, if the writer was entitled to take his independence and disinterestedness to the extreme, so of course was the audience. It can choose not to attend to his work. The kind of knowledge and awareness that somehow seems inherently literary can lose its prestige even while the writer's privileges remain as they were; science and sociology, journalism and sport can take over various traditional functions of literature. The writer may choose, then, to move towards mystery or obscurity in order to gain the fullest possible exploration of his art as an aspect of his own growth and curiosity; but then art's social functions become associated with individual rather than communal action. So the decline of the humane and mimetic dimensions of art, its diminished concern with a moral commitment and its growing obsession with its own form, its self-conscious aestheticism and élitism, its willingness to take art as a species of neurosis, sublimation or fantasy, could all seem to emphasize the personal over the public satisfactions of creativity—to have the a-cultural interest of a symptomatic piece of creativity like a kindergarten drawing. This was the situation that was idealized by Hegel, who argued that once art forwent its sense of social obligation and moved to the margin it would become a more perfect art. Its rewards for the writer pyschologically could doubtless increase, allowing him to explore his consciousness and medium to new depths and intensities. The danger is that proposed by Wyndham Lewis, in *The Diabolic Principle*, where he argues that the modern arts persist where the need for them is absent—they are perpetuated for their own sake.[2]

The perpetuation, of course, can have long-term value. Clearly, like any specialist in new and difficult forms of conscious-

[1] The great transitional fable is surely James Joyce's *Portrait of the Artist as a Young Man* (1916), where Stephen Dedalus makes his Promethean journey, severing the ties of family, religion and race, and moving towards impersonality in exile, in order that he can *become* a dedicated artist.

[2] Wyndham Lewis, *The Diabolic Principle* (London, 1931).

ness—or unconsciousness made conscious—the artist of this
kind is likely to be understood only by a few who can adjust
to his distinctive, self-created, self-determined activity. But
this in turn can make the functions of art he explores become
increasingly more significant and possibly in due course culturally
dominant, at which point his acclaim will come. There is no
doubt that this has always been a crucial aspect of artistic development, and what is more that society does have a way of discover-
ing that arts that once seemed arcane are really continuous with its
own experience, once their new nature has been comprehended,
assimilated and understood. The danger comes only really when
this becomes the *dominant* and prevailing definition of art. It is,
of course, a notion of art that has been explored a good deal
in this century, and there are many different forms of the aesthetic. Many of them have sought to restore a measure of objectivity
to the creative process again by claims about the 'objectivity'
of the unconscious; a classic instance is that systematic dis-
arrangement of the senses for which Rimbaud sought, when the
poet becomes an instrument: 'C'est faux de dire: Je pense. On
devrait dire: On me pense.'[1] The same search for the forms of
the formless runs through surrealism, with its theories of automatic writing, and with the entire aesthetic of the nature of art
as the enclosure of an artistic space in which the spectator or
participant happens to be included.[2] In short, it has to do with
the notion of art not as a form of the continuous cultural community but as an open-ended form of knowledge, derived partly
from the offered consciousness of the artist but as much from his
openness to anything novel that it can consume. In short, it is an
attempt at framing or formulating the 'unconscious' of literature

---

[1] Rimbaud in his letters, 1871; quoted in Stephen Spender, *The Struggle of the
Modern* (London, 1963), p. 140, who comments well on this aspect of modern
art.

[2] As in the modern happening or a Living Theatre 'event'. On this aspect of
modernist literature, see Louis Kampf, *On Modernism: The Prospects for Literature
and Freedom* (Cambridge, Mass., and London, 1967), which argues that there
is a danger of the modern artist forgoing his most important faculty—his free
will, felt at the depths of his personal creativity—in the interests of letting art
'happen'.

and art, through a species of contained subjectivism. None the less, the degree of subjectivism involved is great enough to raise problems not only of criticism and assessment but of direct appreciation; art simply becomes an undifferentiated manifestation. As Raymond Williams observes: 'There is great danger in the assumption that art serves only on the frontiers of knowledge. It serves on these frontiers, particularly in disturbed and rapidly changing societies. Yet it serves, also, at the very centre of societies. It is often through art that the society expresses its sense of being a society.'[1] There can be little doubt that this paradoxical expression of the freedom of the artist is a radical move onward from the liberal humanistic function of art, and postulates a quite different function for the arts in modern society.

The 'liberal' situation of the artist in our century, then, has hardly been that of the liberal artist of the past. It is hardly surprising, therefore, that our tolerance sometimes has a bemused air to it, as our humanistic expectations are persistently baffled. Indeed it may be that we as readers have lost some of those humanistic expectations ourselves. For the task of maintaining the significance of past literature as a species of central social knowledge and imagination has itself tended to grow specialized. It has shifted into the school and the university; the century of the modern arts has also been the century of the rise of literary study. But perhaps this need to teach and interpret literature is itself a signal of its increasing specialization. T. S. Eliot once said: 'The important moment for the appearance of criticism seems to be the time when poetry ceases to be the expression of the mind of a whole people.' So, perhaps, one reason for the great spread of literature as a subject for the academy is that common pools of value no longer exist out of which general critical standards of judgment can come; we must be *taught* what is good, and how to read it, by objective specialists. More and more, then, literature has been mediated by an expert interpreter (called a teacher) to an expert consumer (called a student). We

[1] Raymond Williams, *The Long Revolution* (London, 1961). Quotation from p. 47 of the Penguin edition.

accept that literature is difficult, even the literature of the past, which was not once thought to be so. At the same time there is a humanist paradox in this activity, too. We assume that the educational value of doing this is to convey the wise past of our culture; but, as modern literature itself becomes an essential part of what is taught, then we tend to teach a revulsion against that humanism itself. I suppose that means that the modern arts are now taken as the new humanism; it is not a view its creators have always taken.[1] Perhaps the point is rather that a democratic society, strongly oriented towards the future, feels that it needs its intellectuals and artists precisely for the dissident functions they are often apt to pursue. On the other hand, they may simply exist as a half-noticed by-product of that larger and more serviceable intelligentsia of scientists and administrators which a 'progressive' social order requires for its operational functioning. Certainly the modern writer and artist is likely to find an ambiguity built into the terms of his very existence. Moreover, he himself is likely to live off the benefits of his paradoxical situation, for his sense of plight and uncertainty may well be as necessary to him as an artist as a pen used to be.

Something of the broad change in temper I am trying to convey can be suggested by comparing the words which have had vogue for describing the sense of distance between the liberal writer and society. Matthew Arnold's word, which obviously represented a deep nineteenth-century value, was *disinterestedness*, and by it he meant to say that the writer was independent of particular class or sectarian interests in society, particular social needs and urgencies, and committed to the ideal realm of art and the wish to make it prevail in society. The modern word is more commonly *alienation*, a word so over-used, in political, psychological and religious connotations, as to be almost beyond definition.[2] We may use it to suggest the emptiness and lack of

---

[1] Lionel Trilling makes this point in several essays in *Beyond Culture* (New York and London, 1966).

[2] For an excellent discussion of the career of this fashionable modern concept, see Lewis Feuer, 'What Is Alienation? The Career of a Concept', in *Sociology on Trial*, ed. Maurice Stein and Arnold Vidich (Englewood Cliffs, N.J., 1963). Feuer points out that the concept is historically far from novel;

resources of the modern writer, the deprivation of funds that
he needs to create an adequate art; or we may mean it, much more
honorifically, to suggest that internal independence and scepticism
which enables him to *create* an adequate art. Then again we may
refer to a detachment which is separate from society in wanting
to rebuke it, reform it, and make it liberally whole again; or we
may be speaking of a revolutionary alienation which seeks a
totally different state of affairs in which liberalism has no place
at all. So we may be speaking of the artist or intellectual who seeks
to preserve a disinterested overview of society in order to maintain that kind of spirit and value that belongs to the inheritance
of liberal art; or we may be referring to an absolute and thorough-
going nihilism in artists for whom plight, degradation and despair
are a *modus vivendi*. There have been innumerable accounts—
some of them literary-historical, some psychological, some
sociological; but what is striking about most of them is that they
assume the state to be likely or inevitable. And though there is
normally an assumption of neurosis or social dislocation, there
is a tendency to associate this with the *fortunate* disability. Edmund
Wilson, in his title-essay in *The Wound and the Bow*, cites the
classical story of Philoctetes as a myth of the artist: isolated by
his wound, he is redeemed by his skill with his bow—the power
of artistic creativity.[1] In short, we can take alienation as a force
from outside, driving the writer away and into exile; or we can
regard it as something internal and structural to the artistic
condition in particular individuals or in artists generally, that
quality Plato saw in the poet which made him a dangerous
member of his ideal Republic.

  The latter view may be the most logical one, though if it is

---

that we use it in a bewildering variety of ways; that it hardly represents an
effective characterization of distinctively modern experience; and that—by
implication—the modern peculiarity is really that we suppose that there is some
alternative to this condition.

  For an interesting study of the literary application of the idea, see Solomon
Fishman, *The Disinherited of Art* (Berkeley and Los Angeles, 1953). The classic
'popular' version of the theme is of course Colin Wilson's *The Outsider* (London,
1956).

  [1] Edmund Wilson, *The Wound and the Bow* (New York and London, 1941).

true it is certainly the case that writers have felt more at odds with their society in some periods and nations than others. Artists have, though, long been wanderers and expatriates; and alienation, as a certain sort of separatism, has long been their inheritance. Moreover, as it becomes more possible to think of art as a kind of religious discipline, demanding that kind of absolute dedication manifest, say, in James Joyce's Stephen Dedalus, this aspect will increase. Art may genuinely benefit from its freedom and difficulties; it may enlarge itself by creating an absolute demand to be taken in and for itself, 'refusing' a public in order to establish its own laws. But the pursuit of the independent morality of the arts can lead to something much more flamboyant: to the stylish artist who, by virtue of his calling, affronts the social norms and customs, or to the *poète maudit*, splendid and damned. But here too there can be two directions of separation. The aim can be culturally preservative: a desire to maintain the elitism and selectivity of the arts. Or it can be culturally subversive: the desire to disintegrate traditional culture, traditional expectation, all past norms. It can lead into the assumption that art can be produced only under conditions not just of independence but extreme deviance or criminality. The artist is the down-and-out, the perpetual proletarian; so, says Henry Miller, the great geniuses always 'lived like scarecrows, amid the abundant riches of the cultural world'. Art, he suggests, manifests not the culture but the anti-culture, and it is wildly destructive energy that expresses itself itself in violent opposition.[1] It is associated with deviant and hostile emotions, with an intrinsic nihilism, or is the product of neurosis and disorder. All this is consistent with a growing 'proletarianization' of the writer; and it is undoubtedly the case that this whole pattern of artistic emotions and assumptions

---

[1] Henry Miller, *The Time of the Assassins: A Study of Rimbaud* (New York and London, 1956). Miller's own work—like that of Celine and Genet, and the early work of his English disciple Lawrence Durrell—is in the same tradition: 'This', he begins *Tropic of Cancer*, 'is a gob in the face of Art . . .'. George Orwell has an interesting view of this 'type' of alienation in his essay 'Inside the Whale' in *Collected Essays, Journalism and Letters of George Orwell*, Vol. I (London, 1968).

—about the independence of art, and its possible relationship with anarchy or neurosis—acquired an expanding currency in the late nineteenth and early twentieth century in England. As Erich Auerbach notes in his great study of western literary forms and modes, *Mimesis*, one can find uniquely in the arts of our century 'a hatred of culture and civilization, brought about by means of the subtlest stylistic devices which culture and civilization have developed, and often a radical and fanatical urge to destroy'.[1] The ideal of cultivating outrage, hostility and hardness of heart has occurred time and again; Wyndham Lewis explores it in *Tarr* (1918). So does the idea of breaking the ties and bonds, religious and familial, of western life; it is there in D. H. Lawrence and a lot of latter-day radical ideology. But behind these passions lie two different motives: the desire to be for art, and the desire to be against prevalent society. It can be the expression of the extreme logic of what society allows (and this is surely the character of a good deal of modern pornography); or it can be an assault on what it seems to forbid.

For us, as observers, it would be appropriate to note that 'alienation' is in fact as much an expression of liberal society as a protest against that society. As such, it can, of course, be taken as a symptom of that degeneration that Max Nordau saw in the decadence of the 1890s, in which the arts were—Nordau suggests in an illusory way—gesturing towards hope while manifesting a good deal of the decay.[2] That sort of view is interestingly echoed by the Marxist critic Georg Lukács, who has seen 'modernist

[1] Erich Auerbach, *Mimesis: The Representation of Reality in Western Literature* (Princeton and London, 1953).

[2] 'One epoch of history is unmistakably in its decline, and another is announcing its approach. There is a sound of rending in every tradition, and it is as though the morrow would not link itself with today. Things as they are totter and plunge, and they are suffered to reel and fall, because man is weary, and there is no faith that is worth the effort to uphold them. . . . Men look with longing for whatever new things are at hand, without presage whence they will come or what they will be. They have hope that in the chaos of thought, art may yield revelations of the order that is to follow on this tangled web. The poet, the musician, is to announce, or divine, or at least suggest in what forms civilization will further be evolved.'—Max Nordau, *Degeneration* (London, 1895), pp. 5–6.

anti-realism' as a manifestation of bourgeois culture, alienated from true consciousness, ridden with an exaggerated devotion to a static and sensational view of the world, a solitary and individualistic version of the human condition, and a flight from outward reality into psycho-pathology.[1] But intelligent (as opposed to routine ideological) Marxist criticism has been compelled to admit to a paradox. Sartre, who notes that most modern writing is nowhere near an identification with the proletariat, and a good deal closer to identification with a dis-appeared aristocracy, also notes that in many ways it contains the fullest embodiments of modern freedom.[2] Obviously a good deal of modern western writing does possess—as I have already argued—the despair and unease of the cultural individual in modernizing industrial society. A sense of disintegration and division is a familiar enough feature of a response, and modern writers may indeed, as Solomon Fishman says, be touched by 'the stigmata of modern consciousness, among which are a sense of social disintegration, of cultural decadence, and of the widen-ing chasm between the individual and his moral and material environment'.[3] But the important point is that they have, often, created this consciousness for themselves as a metaphor for independence. When the modern writer thinks of himself as an 'outsider', this is not by any means necessarily because he finds himself in hostile detestation of liberal culture. Rather he often sees himself as the continuation of it into unpropitious circum-stances. As I have said, in English literary culture the extremes of outrage have not been very marked and the writer has more commonly sought, in cultural unease, to remake the tradition, to recover the texture, of the 'botched civilization'—the phrase is Pound's—in which he finds himself. If this is a form or expres-sion of liberalism, it is obviously a very different one from that of the writer who feels unequivocally benefited by his freedom or finds himself informed and illuminated by the basic currents

[1] Georg Lukács, *The Meaning of Contemporary Realism* (London, 1963). (American ed.: *Realism in Our Time* (New York, 1964)).

[2] Jean-Paul Sartre, *What Is Literature?*, cited above.

[3] Solomon Fishman, *The Disinherited of Art*, cited above.

L

of expression of his society. But the liberal-critical function has held its place against the claims either of a more outright nihilism or outright politicism; and it is still very much alive in the novels of Angus Wilson, Kingsley Amis or John Braine, or the plays of John Osborne, Arnold Wesker or Peter Terson. And even in that art of accelerated modern consciousness, with its vision of chaos, of a civilization in Yeats's phrase 'much divided', the liberal-artistic ideal of redeeming the culture through the transcendence of art runs deep. In short, the marks of alienation on modern English writing are less those of a retreat into the 'unreality' of neurosis or the over-reality of a revolutionary politics, but more commonly an expression of the possibilities of artistic independence and a desire to use it to reach towards metaphors of a desirable wholeness.

III

According to Marxist theory (in some branches at least), as the society grows more classless, literature should be able to move towards its fullest expression and fullest significance. This hope has hardly been satisfied in practice, if modern Russian literature is to serve as an example. And it is equally noteworthy that in our own culture the highest points of modern artistic achievement came when English society, though liberal, was stratified into fairly distinct classes and cultural sectors over which the great artists sought to reach. But in the course of the last hundred years, the years of our 'modern' literature, that class-stratification has very much diminished; and literature today is created not against the liberal variety of a multi-class society but against the much more standardized order of a relatively egalitarian one. One important element in the cultural critique of many modern writers has in fact been a protest against this kind of standardiz-ation, which is to suggest that, while they have resisted many features of the modern world, they have resisted it in the spirit of an aristocratic rejection of its overall cultural processes. There are in fact clear reasons why this should be so, though in an age of routine egalitarianism they are not always easily comprehended. For if a culture is to be more than the personal attribute of those artists who speak for it, and if art is to have a public meaning beyond that of accepting anything by an accredited artist *as* art, then these things must exist within a stable sector of society in whom particular cultural values are embedded. In our society for two centuries, this has essentially been in the middle class, on which the principles, standards and myths of a liberal art had essentially drawn. But the cultural condition of an egalitarian society seems to be not that restoration of cultural community which equality has often been assumed to bring with it, but, instead, the proletarianization of the entire culture: a state of affairs that many earlier writers had foreshadowed and feared. By the postwar period, social change and inflation had diminished the cultural confidence and influence of those classes, accelerating a process that had been going on throughout the century. Many of their traditional cultural contexts faded under inflationary pressures: theatres closed, literary magazines could no longer afford rising printers' bills, and the uniformities of broad-scale cultural provision in the form of mass-culture rushed in to take their places. The difficulties of creating new cultural contexts vastly increased. Publishing expanded, new media emerged, but all on a large-scale and centralized basis, while attempts at institutional provision of culture by government were small and not notably successful. In inflationary periods it is the independent operators who suffer, particularly those on small private incomes; and this includes most writers. Nor did they have cheap-living communities to retire to, like the American writers of the 1920s who had fled to Paris. Their careers necessarily became less independent and more vocational. New service industries were coming into being in the vastly more centralized and affluent society; the writer could find jobs in television, advertising and teaching. His creativity was at least a marketable commodity; he could appeal to a general and fairly educated audience, but not one in whom clear cultural norms were embedded, nor one in which his serious role as a part of the 'high' culture could be recognized.

Though culturally tolerant and permissive, the culture also grew increasingly culturally uniform. Over this period, then, the writer undoubtedly lost some of his traditional prestige, independence, and area of cultural reference.

I have argued that the conditions for the literature of the twentieth century were those of a commitment to an idea of free creativity often coupled with an idea of 'alienation' or difficult separatism. In the egalitarian environment both of these two aspects of art seem to diminish. The writer feels less alienated from the climate of his culture, but at the same time he feels less capable of committing himself fully to the claims of art either as an essential mode of social intelligence or as a commitment to absolute formalism. As the novelist-heroine of Doris Lessing's *The Golden Notebook* (1963), Anna, observes: '. . . I am incapable of writing the only kind of novel which interests me: a book powered with an intellectual and moral passion strong enough to create order, to create a new way of looking at life'— incapable because the contemporary world is too fragmentary, too contingent, too 'real' to permit the performance of the task which many of the earlier writers of the century had undertaken, the fragmentation into a world of form. Though today's writer may be a radical, his radicalism is usually a form of politics rather than of culture; and even when, after a period of relative contentment with the state of the culture in the 1950s, there followed a marked return to bohemianism in the next decade, it was rather the bohemianism of an affluent, political younger generation seeking to accelerate social change than the bohemianism of a primarily artistic community—while the constituency for novelty was rather an elite of protestors rather than an artistic sector.[1] Indeed if anything marks the character of 'underground' art it is its in-built quality of evanescence and its social functionality as an instrument for changing consciousness and producing reform. To the two types of writer already mentioned—the liberal and the 'alienated'—we perhaps therefore should add a third, the egalitarian: who, though he may derive to some extent from both, finally belongs to a much less liberal-artistic climate.

[1] For an 'inside' view, see Jeff Nuttall, *Bomb Culture* (London, 1968).

With the changes that have taken place in the composition and character of the reading public; with the relative decline of imaginative written literature in favour either of other forms of expression or other media; with the disappearance of the social conditions that made literary elitism an effective possibility; and with the fading of a clearly defined and selective notion of 'high' culture—with all these shifts, the situation of the postwar writer seems very much to have changed. His own writing becomes much more a phenomenon among many 'cultural' artefacts; his role and self-image seems different, and he manifests the role of 'poet', 'playwright' or 'novelist' differently now, less monopolizing those roles than serving in them. Indeed there is every sign that literature in the present context is being reshaped, as the writer in egalitarian democracy becomes—as De Tocqueville predicted he would[1]—the ordinary man. As the written work loses some of its numinous power and eternity, as an appeal to transcendence or posterity yields to an environment of immediate consumption, as the book itself becomes one form of communication, relative to others and potentially replaced by them, then the writer—like the rest of us—tends to become historicist, a man consciously conditioned by his immediate environment in the particular task that he professes.

A hundred years, from 1870 to 1970, is a long time in the history of a literature, and we may expect such changes in function to occur. But of course they do not occur in neat logical sequence; and the three broad 'types' of writer I have spoken of clearly exist simultaneously in our society. In many respects the tradition of the liberal arts survives in our culture, and the great works of the early modern period still have, for the contemporary writer, significance and propinquity. In other ways they are infinitely remote, as, especially since the war, a new order in English society has grown into being. So, while many of the most marked changes that affect the English writer today occurred eighty or a hundred years ago, there are many that have happened since. This is my theme in the rest of this section. For behind such changes there lie, I think, many very specific

[1] Alexis de Tocqueville, *Democracy in America* (1835: 1840).

and detailed shifts—in the ways writers find their careers, make their income, acquire their reputations, live—both publicly and privately—their lives. Many of the changes around 1870 and since in literature reach down to changes at this level—to shifts in the actual composition of the literary profession, the degree to which it has been an attractive life-style and the way that style has taken different forms and guises, the nature of the social and financial rewards of being a writer. I take it, therefore, that an obvious part of the writer's nature lies in his way of exploring the particular possibilities of the role in which he acts in the culture in which he acts it. He has both to find and to extend the prevailing possibilities of expression, in relation to audiences and publishers and the needs he ascribes to himself as a writer. Among the most important areas of such exploration in our culture are changes in relation to an audience as a result of the expansion of literacy and shifts in social stratification; changes in the literary profession itself, which have made it both attractive but financially precarious; changes in the social value of the literary arts and in general taste. All these things have meant real changes in the opportunities for each writer's own growth and career, and for the broader literary profession and the community of artists of which he is part. So I turn, in these following pages, to consider what kinds of people our serious modern writers have been, what kinds of life they have lived, and what sorts of role for the writer they have developed, in the broad environment of a modernizing liberal society.

CHAPTER VII

Who Our Writers Are

I

It is probably because of our present cultural uncertainty that in
our time students of literature have become very much aware of
the way literature is formed by its context, by its immediate
environment and the forces, general and specific, which determine our existence as men. They have been very attentive to
the fact that works of literature, and men of letters, are not
entirely stable and unchanging phenomena, and equally that
literary development does not only derive from the internal
momentum of the literary tradition as such. Today we are
strikingly interested in the very idea of a culture as a body of
shared practices and values, and of literary culture as a peculiarly
rich and dense form of such patterns and meanings; but we are
also strikingly attentive to the change in these things, and the
mutability of even the most monumental civilization. Interests of
this sort can engage us in very broad questions about the state
of the culture and the relative claims of art and life, about the
social meaning and function of education and humane learning
and the way it interfuses with more mundane and practical
matters, or with other social-historical needs we come to formu-
late. Part of the validity and value of the artist is that he raises
our eyes to matters of worth which lie finally beyond any of the
political or historical reckonings we want to make, any of the
more immediate imperatives we want to serve. But what is
equally valuable about him is that he acts within his specific
cultural environment, serving as an explorer of its particular
possibilities and limitations, and so constantly rediscovering
experience for himself and others by finding the tones and

nuances that bind him to those novel communities which constitute his particular audience. In our own century, we have seen
the writer doing these things in a context and a culture in which
there has been a vast expansion of literacy, so extending but also
in many ways dividing the audience and the nature of literary
usage; in which there has been a strong value attached to the
literary arts for their educational and humane significance, but
also for their use as entertainment or as crude stimulus; in which
there has been vast and varied literary flowering, and yet an
enormous uncertainty about the financial and cultural viability of
the literary forms.

An interest in the particular fortunes of our literary culture
can lead us towards many large and theoretical matters about the
virtues and vices of our particular kind of society and the social
and cultural choices we have made. It can also lead us towards
very much more specific questions about the closer context in
which writers write—questions about their social origins, their
typical trainings, their financial rewards, their methods of
publication, the general relation of writer to audience, the
general role and status of the literary profession—and the way
these things have altered to the good or the bad the cultural
aspects of our society. For, as is apparent, the immediate
conditions of literary creation and consumption do affect and
shape the character of a period's writing deeply; and for the
writer as individual this is perhaps finally where the heart of the
issue lies. Yet the practical features of the literary career are
not always easy to determine; and it is striking that, although a
good deal of distinguished research has been done to explore
these matters for earlier periods,[1] not a great deal of material
has been amassed for the present day.[2] If part of the data here

[1] I am thinking particularly of such studies as Edwin H. Miller, *The Profes-
sional Writer in Elizabethan England* (Cambridge, Mass., 1959); the brilliant
pioneering work of A. S. Collins, in *Authorship in the Days of Johnson* (London,
1927) and *The Profession of Letters: 1780–1832* (London, 1928); Ian Watt, *The
Rise of the Novel* (London, 1957); Richard D. Altick, *The English Common Reader:
A Social History of the Mass Reading Public: 1800–1900* (Chicago, 1957); and
J. W. Saunders's recent valuable valuable survey, *The Profession of English Letters*
(London/Toronto, 1964).

[2] So in Saunders's book there is much more material on the earlier period

must be a history and analysis of the modern literary intelligentsia, such as has been touched on by sociologists of knowledge and others,[1] then another important part is the detailing of the actual working conditions of the writer, his sense of his own role and possibilities, and the simple facts of his income and rewards. Though the changing function of intellectuals and writers in relation to the culture and knowledge they reflect and create, interpret and administer is an important part of the picture, so are the practical details of the aspects of literary production. Part of the general restructuring of the literary climate that we discern in these changeable years between 1870 and 1914, and then again since, obviously has much to do with changes at this level—changes in the actual composition of the profession, the degree to which it has served for certain kinds of people as an attractive life-style and a means of social mobility and so on, are part of the story. Here the writer is the explorer of his culture in a very practical sense, creating his own means of survival and existence out of the possibilities or their absence. It is to these more practical aspects of the writer's situation that I now want to turn.

II

What is the literary profession in our society? We had better begin by saying that the writer's profession is not, of course, in the strict sense a profession at all. It is very much less formal than most of the professions, which have standards of access, selectivity of entry, norms of conduct. Anyone who writes can be a writer. Moreover, the skills are not normally supposed to be ones that can be directly taught, although we have seen attempts at times

---

than on our own time. And most of the important information comes from writers themselves or others concerned for their interests, like the Society of Authors.

[1] See, for instance, Jean-Paul Sartre, *What Is Literature?* (London, 1950); Colin Wilson, *The Outsider* (London, 1956); John Gross, *The Rise and Fall of the Man of Letters* (London, 1969); and T. R. Fyvel, *Intellectuals Today* (London, 1968).

to teach them—from the postal courses advertised in weekly magazines to the growth, particularly in the United States but now in England too, of the creative writing class. But writing remains still primarily an activity which depends very much upon intuitions and imaginative gifts that may be stimulated and encouraged, but which cannot normally be easily passed on. In journalism, one of the expanding trades of this and the last century, some instruction exists; and in certain forms of writing like television script writing a good deal of the practice becomes codified so that instruction can occur. But a distinction is normally made between such 'practical' forms of writing and 'imaginative' writing, with the latter regarded as a matter of personal human quality, inspiration and self-acquired skills. From time to time, patterns of apprenticeship have emerged in some form among serious writers, somewhat on the model of the visual arts; writers have gathered in coteries and acolytes have joined the numbers to be instructed in elements of their craft. In particular, this has occurred in bohemian groups; for instance, there was a notable instructional element in the literary expatriate scene in Paris in the 1920s, when writers like Gertrude Stein and Ford Madox Ford issued aphoristic advice. But there have been no writing schools, as there have been schools of art, ballet or acting. And the teachable elements in literary creation have always been thought to be the subsidiary ones—grammar, rhetoric and the like. The study of literature abounds, of course, in schools and universities (though only really in our own century has the study of the native literature been very strongly emphasized); but of course its purpose is not to produce writers but generally educated men or critics and scholars. And it is not, in fact, notably from those who study literature that writers are recruited. A good many of our writers are university graduates, and in particular the products of the ancient universities. But more often than not they have studied history or classics rather than English, and when English has been studied it has not been normally studied with a modern, or a particularly creative, emphasis.

The writer in our society is normally the product of his own motivation, and there is no clearcut path to competence or success. The literary hopeful may acquire some unsystematic support from certain types of patron—from publishers, editors, reviewers and already successful writers. But as a profession of sorts, literature has been both a very open profession and, from the outsider's point of view, a mysteriously closed one. There is no handy advice that can be given to the entrant beyond the most simple: type clearly on one side of the page, and the like. There are few places to find sophisticated discussion of literary practice. It normally exists only among coteries of the relatively successful, which have never really been particularly open groups. And if the methods of entry to writing in our culture seem somewhat perplexing, so too do the methods by which success is determined. The tests here are complicated. On the one hand there is the test of public acceptance in a commercial market, and on the other there is critical success, which involves an elaborate complex of often very varied judgment derived from other artists, reviewers at various levels and the literary critics—who may themselves be independent agents or academic professionals. One level of success may automatically cancel out another; it is well known that critical taste and standards are matters of dispute. In our own century we have seen a remarkable professionalization of the critic at the university level, and more and more he has become the custodian of long-term reputation. In fact, of course, he is himself somewhat the product of his own professional duties; the writers he prefers, and the judgments he advances, often have a great deal to do with a broad historical assessment of cultural significance, though there can be little doubt that he has a certain vested interest in devoting himself to works that are by nature complex and subject to elaborate decoding. But as, in a context of change, long-term assents about standards and values seem to have seriously declined in the culture, he carries a large burden of responsibility. And there can be little doubt that a certain part of minority literature is now written for the critic and the students whom he teaches. In fact they are now a basic sector of the book-buying public, and the £35 which local authorities grant students for book purchase is something of a factor in modern literary economics. There are, however, other constituencies the writer can appeal to—the young, for instance—and considerable success with them may give the writer a second chance with the serious critics. Normally, however, most books published in England, as in most countries, are ephemeral and more or less unnoticed. In short, most writers are forgotten.

But if literature is only dubiously a profession, it does have a number of professional or institutional features. It has behind it an inheritance of practices and assumptions to which most writers of serious disposition seek in some way both to contribute as well as to extend. It lives by an acquired body of forms and conventions of a very sophisticated kind—from such simple formal assumptions as that most novels are (in our day at least) about 75,000 words long to such complex ones as we have seen at work in the aesthetics of modernism. Moreover, we have noted the institutionalization and professionalization of the literary critic in the university; a similar institutionalization seems to have taken place among writers themselves in the same conditions of cultural uncertainty. Writers have begun increasingly to organize in order to protect their interests. In 1883 Walter Besant founded the Society of Authors, specifically to safeguard their needs and position. The rewards of writers had been declining since the beginning of the nineteenth century, partly in consequence of the expansion of the profession, and publishers appeared to be making disproportionate profits. At about the same time, in response to similar needs, another agency for protection of the writer began to become important —the official literary agent (there had long been unofficial versions of this kind of middleman). The famous agents of this period—A. P. Watt, Curtis Brown and J. B. Pinker, for instance— were, of course, not simply concerned with writers' profits but with protecting the writer in some respects from commercial pressures endangering his reputation. None the less, they did serve to systematize the conditions of writing and to make it possible for writing to be conducted primarily for economic motives. At the same time, as we shall see, the book-market was itself expanding in directions that encouraged the writer to think of his task in terms of a higher trade in which there was the opportunity delicately to balance the social and critical prestige of high seriousness and dedication with the profits of commerce. However, because of the increasing segmentation of the market the balance was becoming harder to achieve; and in the view of many writers the choice was between one end or the other. Indeed, the tendency towards professionalisation among writers often simply encouraged mercantilism. George Gissing joined the Society of Authors and found it seriously disappointing, 'a mere gathering of tradesmen'. It was hard to institutionalize the distinction; even such accolades as the Order of Merit or the Poet Laureateship began to seem compromised. So, as we have seen, there was a tendency for the serious artist to withdraw to a very narrow constituency of peers and supporters in bohemia, and to hope that posterity would do him justice.

But these conditions derived from an expanding use of literary skills in the society, coupled with a marked expansion of literary producers. This was particularly evident at two periods in recent literary history—the period of the expansion of the journalistic media between 1855 and 1870; and the expansion of television between 1950 and the present. In both periods it was generally agreed that the writers needed for such rapid expansion could not be found, and in both periods they easily were. In both cases, the basis of the expansion was an increase in the number of working writers, with dubious benefit for more serious ones. At any rate, the records suggest a very considerable expansion of the numbers of those in the society who called themselves 'writers'. The number of professional writers in English society has grown vastly since 1800. The census returns show, for instance, expansions of more than 200% between 1841 and 1851, and again between 1851 and 1861, of those calling themselves writers. Such figures must always be doubtful—as anyone who has met a self-described 'writer' at a party will know—and they were made more so by the inclusion in various censuses of 'students', 'reporters', and 'shorthand writers' as part of the same category. Nonetheless, they clearly indicate a trend, and they clearly have some significance if we can make the proper reservations. In 1841, the census records 167 authors; in 1851, 2,671 'authors, editors, writers' are counted; in 1901 the number of 'authors, editors, journalists, reporters' is 11,060; in 1931 there are 20,599 'authors, editors, journalists, publicists'; in 1951 the same category contains 23,822; in 1961, the similar category contains 37,460.[1] Richard Findlater has noted that *Whitaker's Reference Catalogue of Current Literature* in fact lists 55,000 to 60,000 writers, of whom perhaps 45,000 to 50,000 are both alive and British. But, as he says, most are not professional authors; and his own estimate, based on reckoning this and the 1951 census return against the records of the Society of Authors, is that there are probably about 6,500–7,000 writers in England producing books, film-scripts or plays with some degree of continuity and productivity.[2] That must modify the figures, but it still means a remarkable expansion.

So the profession is bigger and it is more professional. But that does not of course mean that the numbers of serious writers have vastly increased or that outright genius is easier to come by. Indeed for serious writers it may well be that this expansion is one of the things that has made their own existence less secure and the possibilities of serious dedication less high. The very size and the prevailing general competence of modern literary activity makes distinction harder to define and harder to achieve. The largest part of the growth has been in the expansion of communication tasks involving literary skills: in journalism, television writing, advertising. But as writing has more and more found its professional centre in large, institutional and often commercially-oriented activities, the preservation of a context for independent creation has become harder, and very much more difficult to finance. In many respects, the conditions of literary independence that are normally associated with the production

---

[1] Details from Richard D. Altick, 'The Sociology of Authorship: The Social Origins, Education, and Occupations of 1,100 British Authors, 1800–1935', *The Bulletin of the New York Public Library*, LXVI, vi (June 1962), pp. 389–404. Also see W. J. Reader, *Professional Men: The Rise of the Professional Classes in Nineteenth-Century England* (London, 1966).

[2] Richard Findlater, *What Are Writers Worth? A Survey of Authorship* (London, Society of Authors, 1963).

of the most considered, serious and enduring writing are those that come from leisure coupled with reasonable lack of economic exposure. But the writer in our time is more and more tempted to put his skills into the employment market, and so to regard them as saleable commodities. In short, the real expansion is the expansion of Grub Street, which is now a good address. But an expanding profession declines in status and mystique; and it tends to set as its standard efficiency and competence rather than remarkable and rare powers. At one time the constraints here could be conveniently seen as those of bourgeois civilization, and it was often in the escape from *its* view of the artist that our more sophisticated art came. Since the war it can no longer seem that it is the bourgeois society that is to blame, but rather the assault upon its economics by the much more rationalized and centralized state. The managerial revolution has occurred among writers too; they less and less administer their own production. Our main interest here is of course with the 'serious' writer; and here, I think, the significant story is of his difficulties in finding a role within this overall expansion. Nonetheless, there does remain in our literature an important body of writers whom we do regard seriously; and it is basically with the impact of the modern social situation on them that I shall here be concerned.

III

Where do our writers come from? Who were their fathers? How were they educated? One marked feature of the English twentieth-century cultural scene is that although the audience for the written word has expanded vastly in the last 150 years,[1] the culture-makers have come from a much narrower social range. Writing may not necessarily be an activity of the educated, but in our society it has tended to be so. For instance, if we take as a representative sample of the important figures in modern literature the writers listed in the *Concise Cambridge Bibliography of English Literature*

---

[1] See Richard D. Altick, *The English Common Reader*, for an extended documentation.

for the period since 1900, we will find that, of the 72 'imaginative' writers listed (i.e. those who are primarily poets, novelists
or dramatists), 44 went to public schools of some kind, 14 to
grammar schools, and 9 had private educations; the rest had little
formal secondary schooling or are inadequately documented.[1]
Forty-four went to universities, with the two ancient universities
taking most of them (Oxford 21, Cambridge 15). The figures deal
essentially with reputations made before 1945, after which the
grammar schools and the provincial—and now even the new—
universities will no doubt be better represented. A high degree of
education is in fact the most common factor among the writers
listed, but, as one would expect, this does mean that the writers
were substantially drawn from the middle and upper middle
classes of society. If we roughly distinguish the wealthy and
professional middle classes from the lower middle classes of
clerks, shopkeepers, ordinary schoolteachers, dissenting ministers
clerks and lower civil servants, we find that the fathers of 41 of
our 'sample' fall in the higher part of that group (professional
middle classes or above), while distinguishing the working class
we will find that only five fathers clearly belong there.

So it would seem to be true that, as other surveys using
different samples have suggested,[2] that the main sources of serious
literature in English society has been the 'solid' middle classes.
One would expect this to be true, but it seems even more true
in England than in, say, France or the United States. What is
more, the social range from which writers are drawn in England
in the nineteenth century would seem to be actually wider than
it was in the twentieth, at least up to 1945. By the 1930s, many

[1] These comments and the ones that follow are based on a survey, done by
Bryan R. Wilson and the present author, to form part of a forthcoming book.
The survey is of English authors between 1660 and the present and uses as its
'sample' the writers listed in George Watson, *The Concise Cambridge Bibliography
of English Literature* (2nd edition) (Cambridge, 1965). (It is hardly necessary to
note that Watson's listing of important writers does contain names that could
well be replaced by others: but it remains a significant guide.)

[2] Raymond Williams, 'The Social History of English Writers', Part II,
Chapter 5, of *The Long Revolution* (London, 1961); and Richard D. Altick, 'The
Sociology of Authorship: The Social Origins, Education and Occupations of
1,100 British Writers, 1800–1935' (cited above).

writers were obviously embarrassed by their bourgeois personalities, and even, like Orwell, took on proletarian personalities
to conceal it. (The same style still prevails.) Yet clearly literature
does tend to derive from groups in which literature has somewhat
more than usual significance, and who also have the opportunities
to sustain that significance by income and life-pattern. And,
since writing is in fact more or less an open profession, it does
mean that the responsibility for the creation of culture, in its
immediate sense of a written imaginative literature, has been in
our time very unevenly spread across the society. On the evidence
of the *Concise Cambridge Bibliography* and the similar sources used
by Williams and Altick, it would be possible to create a kind of
profile of a typical writer that would serve until after the Second
World War. His parents would come from various levels of the
professional middle classes; his father is likely to be a surgeon
or a doctor, a lawyer or a solicitor, a clergyman or a dissenting
minister, a merchant or a businessman, a schoolmaster in a
private or a state school, a civil servant or an army officer. He
stands a very good chance of having gone to a public school, and
then he very probably went to a university, most likely an
ancient university. He then himself probably entered one of the
professional occupations: teaching, journalism, the civil service
or the law. He may later have become a full-time writer, but in
many cases it was a part-time occupation and not his primary
source of income.

   This pattern persists until 1945, when there are signs that it
becomes modified. Part of the postwar reaction against Bloomsbury was a class-reaction, as, with the expansion of general and
higher education and the growth of meritocratic opportunity,
the social range of authors begins to widen. Writing in *Encounter*
in the 1950s, Stephen Spender observed that the dominance
of the middle or upper-middle-class writer was being threatened
by the 'angry' generation, who were rebelling against the literary
scene and style of the previous generation. Spender called it a
'rebellion of the lower middlebrows' and remarked that there
was 'an aroma of inferiority about its protest'. He also pointed
out that it tended to derive from the self-conscious provincialism

M

of writers not in London, and that these writers tended to have less positive commitments to writing as a cultural or formal expression. Reading through the novels and poems of the 1950s, with their celebration of local ordinariness, we can sense the nature of this fairly new type of writer. He was by no means entirely new; the novels of H. G. Wells, C. P. Snow (for instance, Snow's *The Search* (1934)) and of an older postwar writer like William Cooper[1] are also very much the products of the lower-middle-class, provincial boy moving his way into the society suspiciously, sceptically—with, perhaps, new forms of knowledge which will bring him the rewards of mobility, and an appropriate doubt about whether they are worth having. And the early letters of Dylan Thomas likewise show him as a very recognizable type of the young, lower-middle-class provincial boy from the grammar-school plotting his way towards literary success.[2] As we have already seen, this kind of populist writer has played a fair part in modern writing; but now he acquires increasing confidence. And, as Spender said, behind him lay a grammar-school and university or technical-college education which laid often a new stress on literature as a way both of understanding and criticizing society and getting on in it. Today this kind of writer is familiar and exists in large numbers; he tends to be rather more bohemianized, often in regional communities like Liverpool.[3] But the contemporary classlessness of education, the less defined stratifications of taste, and the depersonalization of publishing have all weakened some of the sentiments of class-consciousness that existed in literature in the 1950s, when entry into the profession seemed selective and there was an obvious feeling in some quarters that the culture was being monopolized

[1] On this see my introduction to the reissue of William Cooper's *Scenes from Provincial Life* (London, 1969).

[2] Dylan Thomas, *Selected Letters*, ed. Constantine Fitzgibbon (London, 1966).

[3] For an interesting comment on recent regional 'bohemias', see Jim Burns, 'La Vie de Bohème', *New Society*, 239 (April 27, 1967), p. 619. Dudley Andrew and I discussed earlier versions of the 1940s and 1950s in an article, 'The Sugar-Beet Generation', *Texas Quarterly*, III, 4 (Winter, 1960), pp. 38–47 (Special issue on 'Britain'). (Our title derives from the fact that bohemian existence was often financed by working long hours on the sugar-beet harvest!)

by particular classes and tendencies. If the 'emergence' of new sectors into cultural expression was something of a novelty twenty years ago, it has now ceased to be so. Nor are the links between writing and education quite as tight-knit as they used to be. In an era of expanded universities, many writers have attended universities. But many have not. In any case, such an education is less expected of today's writer, since the traditional benefits of an education—which once helped writers to relate themselves towards the classical past of literary practice—are less urgent needs in the present literary climate. For today culture tends to be increasingly conceived as a mode of personal expression, or the expression of a new and self-aware age-group. Even writers who have been to university are nowadays likely to get more of their literary experience out of the generational sub-cultures through which, with little class differentiation, they move.

It would be mistaken to conclude from this account that the origins of writers deeply determine the nature of the literature they produce; a great many other factors are important too. For instance, writers in the nineteenth century, largely drawn from middle-class origins, clearly often have a a sense of being part of the majority culture of their times, and draw effectively on the enlightened and expansive aspects of their background. By the beginning of this century, this tie had been considerably weakened. Most of our important writers were much more aware of belonging to a literary cultural minority. Their background may have made them feel particularly responsible for it, and they were able to support it by a relative degree of financial and social independence. To a considerable extent it was such writers who maintained the survival of poetry—which had ceased to be a profitable activity—and the minority novel. Yet they also often were in marked revolt against their own class, as for instance the writers of the Auden group in the 1930s, and regarded themselves as members of the sceptical general intelligentsia. Even more important, throughout this period there is a constant infusion of writers from what Raymond Williams calls 'minority' sources in the society. Not only is there a large 'populist' contingent, from working or lower-middle-class sources, containing some of our most important writers (Lawrence, Hardy, Wells, Gissing), and gaining considerable currency in certain periods—in the 1930s and in the climate of *New Writing*, for instance. There is also a high level of cosmopolitan interaction between cultures in the west, and at the same time a considerable proportion of writers who are foreign born or part-foreign, or from the regions and commonwealth, or from America or Ireland. This is particularly marked over the turn of the century, when there was of course the remarkable 'Celtic Twilight' contribution from Ireland (the important Irish figures include George Moore, Wilde, Yeats, Shaw, Lady Gregory, Joyce, Synge, O'Casey and Frank O'Connor) and from the Commonwealth (Katherine Mansfield), a very large contribution from American expatriates (Henry James, Henry Harland, Stephen Crane, Harold Frederic, Pound, John Gould Fletcher, Robert Frost, T. S. Eliot), a good number of part-foreign writers (Ford Madox Hueffer, Wyndham Lewis, Hilaire Belloc) and several continental writers (most notably Joseph Conrad). One can hardly doubt (as Raymond Williams suggests) one's general literary critical impression that the literature of this period draws singularly and extensively for its pattern of development on cultural funds and attitudes that come from outside the mainstream of the established national cutlure. Add to this the number of English writers who were themselves for a time expatriates elsewhere (Norman Douglas, Arnold Bennett, George Gissing, Robert Louis Stevenson, D. H. Lawrence) and a wide class-range and culture-range becomes apparent. A not dissimilar pattern has developed postwar. It would seem, in fact, that the ranks of English writers—perhaps, in fact, of writers generally—have tended to come from emergent, culturally uncertain or assertive, sectors in the social community: rather as with boxers and professional entertainers. And in periods of special fluidity and change —the turn-of-the-century period, and then again the postwar period—one notices the phenomenon particularly.

Altogether the portrait of modern literature adds up to one in which the fact that the middle classes have made themselves particularly responsible for our literature has inhibited neither its growth or its range. Indeed it seems to have created a pattern in which a belief in literature's worth and social value (which tends in our society to reside particularly in these classes) has been coupled with a desire to expand it imaginatively and socially. As we have seen, statistical details of this sort tell us only so much; they finally reveal only a little about the values and perspectives embodied in the writing that is done. They usually remind us, though, that modern writing has not simply been an activity of those who have grounds for radical dissent with the nature of our culture and society. Indeed, as I say, it would seem that good writing depends at least to a point on those who value it as a *traditional* activity. The result is that modern English literary culture has been formed out of a pattern of interplay between writers who have sought to find the roots and sources of art in new and different places, and those who have felt themselves to be maintaining the humanistic stock of the tradition: both groups have lived in common contact and dialogue. The sense of difficulty or anguish in the culture has thus alternated with a sense of its stability. If one of the essential aspects of twentieth-century writing is a revulsion from bourgeois values ('The artist's exile from middle-class society accounts in part for the character of our literature,' says William York Tindall in a fairly representative judgment)[1] then another important aspect is its deep derivation *from* bourgeois society, in which, on the whole, the values of literary culture have been particularly well sustained.

[1] William York Tindall, *Forces in Modern British Literature: 1885–1956* (New York, revised ed. 1956).

CHAPTER VIII

How Our Writers Live

I

In English society, as in most western societies, the most familiar idea of the writer is of the writer as a free agent, enabled to sustain his literary activity over a lifetime—either from the income he makes from selling his writing, or from some form of patronage. In this society, most writers in our century have tended to begin writing early, and to regard their work as a dedication or a career; their usual hope has been to continue with that work as little disturbed by other obligations as possible. And although quite a lot of our writing is in fact produced by people who write only incidentally or occasionally, we still tend to see as the ideal type the writer who is full-time, dedicated and spectacularly individual. Not in all societies is this economically possible; but England over the last two centuries has sustained a large number of writers who have been able to make writing their sole career and the basis of their life-style. Not all of these have been supported directly by the market; a good number, both in the last and the present century, have been sustained by their own independent incomes. There has in fact been no steady correlation between literary quality and financial success; writing has long been a notably insecure and risky career in which not only the under-qualified fell by the wayside; and the 'indirect' financing of inherited income has much to do with our literature. On the other hand, the pattern has also given a number of very important writers a great financial success. And with the success has usually gone great public prestige; in the last century and the early part of this, the activities and personalities of writers became matters of great public fascination. Part literary life here normally lies somewhere between personal self-extension and social action, between a mission and a career. We sometimes assume that success in the market is destructive of literary excellence, and often this is true. (Sometimes it indicates the absence of such excellence.) Many writers have feared success for that reason. But many others have grown through their success and the resulting independence. There is in fact no single version of the worthwhile literary life in our time.

But it does exist within a particular pattern of opportunities and possibilities; it is a stylized form of social communication. For instance, the literary career in England normally involves a fairly gradual process of acceptance. A writer will produce his work and then submit it to a publisher or publishers, who are the usual first court of appeal. He may already have made some reputation before this, often through periodical publication, or else among other writers who have seen his work in manuscript. If the publisher decides to accept his work, he may very well do so with no expectation that it will sell profitably; indeed he may be prepared to make a loss, in order to nurture an author he expects to be successful later, or simply as part of his 'prestige' list. (The situation here is somewhat different in the theatre, where until recently the work that was not commercially promising had few outlets.) Some writers will remain 'prestige' writers for the rest of their writing days, making little or no profit for their publisher and themselves from work which might, none the less, have critical success. Others may achieve considerable success and income—suddenly, with a best-seller, or slowly, by a gradual process of winning a name and an audience. This is the literary process as it operates through the commercial publisher; but in this century we have seen a considerable growth in the number of small presses, many of them short-lived, which have enabled writers to be published outside the normal commercial market. Normally, however, a writer who first publishes with a small press will move to the commercial market in due course. In short, our 'form of social communication' is normally a version of the commercial process, mitigated by the willingness of some publishers to print deserving authors at a loss and by a

fringe of non-commercial ventures which encourage talent outside the familiar channels.

To begin with, at least, the writer normally requires a source
of income which will support him in his early writing days; that,
perhaps, is one reason why so many writers come from social
backgrounds where independent means are a possibility. He
may have a small private income, as a fair proportion of the
modern writers listed in the *Concise Cambridge Bibliography of
English Literature* in fact had. He may extend the value of this by
going to live in another country where the living is cheap and
the rate of exchange favourable; that is one reason why many
writers are brief or long-term expatriates. On the other hand,
he may take a job which allows him time for writing, and it will
usually be some kind of professional job. At one time the church
was the familiar sponsor of literary activity; in the modern
period, that pattern has more or less completely disappeared.
Richard Altick, in his survey, notes the change in the pattern of
these associated professions; in the nineteenth century the church,
the arts and the government were the three main sources of
literary sponsorship, while in the twentieth century the two
main other professions are professional, salaried journalism or
teaching, in schools or universities. He also notes the increase in
those who did make their living from writing, though as he
observes this body includes many whose source of income is
considerably from *free-lance* journalism.[1] And, we might add for
the later periods, from film or television writing, which, at
least until very latterly, were usually regarded among writers as
forms of hack-work.[2] In certain cases, it is apparent that a serious
literary interest has developed late among those who entered
these professions and careers as their sole professions. But in
many other cases—and it is, as I have said, very notable that most
writers, in the modern period at least, began to write early and
presumably sustained the hope of finally living by it—the other

[1] Altick, 'The Sociology of Authorship', cited above.
[2] Today the careers of writers like David Mercer and Dennis Potter represent
a marked change in this pattern, and suggest that it has become possible for
writers to find that media like television and film are culturally flexible enough
to offer whole new sets of exciting possibilities for artistic exploration.

profession has been in part a form of assistance. At any rate, it has normally been assumed that in order to write one needed the guarantee of a small income—Virginia Woolf's £500 a year and a room of one's own—and the social system has normally been flexible enough to allow this. In the twentieth-century heyday of literary journalism, which comes in the 1920s, many writers were able to sustain themselves by writing literary journalism for papers like *The Athenaeum* or *The London Mercury*. In recent years, with the decline of such journalism and the increasing professionalization of all the professions, including teaching in universities, finding a sustaining and attractive atmosphere that produces an income and allows one time to write has been harder. (Often writing becomes very much the *secondary* activity.) And this has undoubtedly a good deal to do with the fact that nowadays many writers go into professional writing jobs—in television, journalism, or advertising—early on and tend to stay there. By selling the same skills they hope to use independently, they tend to become, in fact, much less independent agents. And in the long run this increasing professionalization of the writer himself may be one of the most significant developments affecting the freedom and liberalism of literature.

In many respects, the opportunities for commercial success from literature have grown greater in the last hundred years. With the expanding machinery of communications, and the extending audience for them, many more people are making profit from literary skill than ever before. Despite the fact that many of these are simply serving the market, the possibility of balancing literary merit and financial opportunity have grown— certainly earlier in the century, though there has been an increase of difficulty in recent years when there has been a recession of interest in imaginative literature. These expanding opportunities became particularly clear at the end of the last century, and a number of important writers, like Wells, Shaw, and Arnold Bennett, seized on them. Often these were writers of fairly poor social background whose interests were almost necessarily at once serious *and* commercial. They were writers with new opinions and attitudes to express, and they aspired to lead taste and reform opinion without wanting to violate entirely their relationship with a potential audience. They assumed that the new difficulties of art in a more mercantile age and the presence of the new audiences represented a challenge that could be met and explored to the long-term good of art and the influence of the artist. So, indeed, the literary life could become, as Wells said, 'one of the modern forms of adventure'. Since then, many very good writers, like Graham Greene, Evelyn Waugh and Iris Murdoch, have succeeded in maintaining a fair balance between merit and success in the market. Others have not: Virginia Woolf earned only £228 from her first three novels, and by the age of 47 was earning only £520 a year from her books (she had, of course, independent means). In a high proportion of the cases in fiction and drama, though not in poetry, the important writers listed in the *Concise Cambridge Bibliography* did succeed in making literature their full profession; they managed to live by writing from early middle age onward. For many writers of serious bent the pattern of risking early poverty or spending income as a gamble on the future has worked well. It has usually depended on the writer's being willing to undertake many different kinds of writing, often of a journalistic kind, in order to support more dedicated activity. But, at least as regards writers earlier in the century, once critical success has come and a reputation has been won, there has been a commensurate financial success, allowing the writer to produce his later work in independence or even considerable comfort. Of course such successes conceal a large class of the failed, but the failure has commonly been both critical as well as financial. The essential risks are high, and they may nowadays be higher than they were. For instance, a recent survey of 1,587 members of the Society of Authors, a relatively select group of restricted entry, showed that only a sixth of these earned more than £1,050 a year from writing; a third made less than £312 a year; and *another* third made less than £78 a year.[1] Certainly the difficulties of independent free-lancing have increased, as the market for literary journalism has declined and as, at the same time, the public has turned away somewhat

[1] Richard Findlater, *The Book Writers: Who Are They?* (London, 1966).

from imaginative literature. The high rewards of men like Arnold Bennett or Bernard Shaw, who mediated seriousness and popularity, have not totally disappeared (as we can see in the case of John Osborne or Kingsley Amis). But their life-style has. As Richard Findlater says: 'In 1938 a young aspiring writer without dependants, without influence and with only his talent for capital, could get by on £4 a week. This was enough for a furnished bed-sitter in central London, for keeping in touch with films and plays, and for a weekly meal out in Soho; and it could be earned with relative ease on the fringe of the literary world so that he had time for his own writing. By 1952, however, a young man living in that way would have needed at least £9 a week; while by 1962 the minimum was £12 a week, for a Spartan existence without much to spare for playgoing (or smoking). In tax alone, he would have to pay twice as big a share of his earnings as in 1938. . . . .'[1]

Not surprisingly, then, the literary scene in this century has always contained a large neo-bohemian contingent, normally consisting of two types of writer—those who, in the interests of protecting their art, have made a deliberate choice of semi-poverty; and those who, by not succeeding, have been forced into it. All have in their different ways explored the economics of uncertainty. The writer of this kind may do occasional casual work, or, postwar, live on National Assistance; or be supported by a husband or wife. He may, in recent years, get a creative writing fellowship in a university, often in the U.S.A., or a grant from the Arts Council. He may, as was notably possible in the early part of the century, live in cheap country cottages, perhaps even borrowing these from friends. He may, again particularly early in the century, live in bohemia itself, a cheap-rent urban area with a cosmopolitan flavour and a group of other writers around. Soho and Bloomsbury, Montmartre or Montparnasse, were the possibilities most available to the English writer. The pattern usually involved a cheap room, an approach to patrons, and the undertaking of small literary tasks from which money could be earned. It may—as is the case often with the present

[1] Richard Findlater, *What Are Writers Worth?* (London, 1963).

semi-bohemian Underground—or it may not depend on a policy of deliberately exploiting society. Many of those in bohemia were short-term members, who moved on in due course to a commercial success; others were more permanent, either through necessity or choice. Most bohemian environments tend to begin as cheap-living communities and then to acquire a general attraction and draw in many followers, who then drive up the rents. In this case, the bohemian group may re-form elsewhere, or it may become a more expensive type of *avant-garde*. The capacity of bohemia to attract many writers who are not financially ill-placed should not, indeed, be forgotten, since it also functions as a place for making reputations. It normally works through little magazines, small presses, and clique reputations, and as such it is one of the forming grounds for writers who are not necessarily financially forced to be there. Many, indeed, are those on private incomes, seeking a context of other writers, moving into the city. Bohemia has been importantly associated with the early careers and first reputations of a significant number of English writers, and in certain important periods—particularly, as we have seen, between 1908 and 1914, when many of the new reputations were made through the little magazines—it has produced a large number of the new writers. On the other hand, its real production is often much smaller than the impression it creates. It is often a stylization of the writer's life among groups containing only a small number of serious or practising writers. Its presses and periodicals are often very short-lived and financially shaky. It contains large numbers of literary aspirants who quickly withdraw from their ambitions. Indeed, much of our important literature comes from quite other environments; and most of it has come from writers producing relatively independently of one another and publishing through established channels.

The writer's life in England seems to lie typically somewhere between the semi-commercial and the semi-bohemian modes. But it has tended, until latterly, to be a fairly independent form of life, once the commitment to a literary career has been taken. We have not had, like the United States in the 1920s, large numbers of writers deliberately exiling themselves in another country, though quite a number of our writers have, for various reasons, often economic, lived abroad. But many others have not, and indeed have played an important part in our social, educational and political affairs. And, in different ways, they have manifested a serious and committed responsibility to literature, and spoken in the culture on behalf of culture. However, it may be that, in the growing atmosphere of literary professionalism, and the increase in the literary salariat produced by television, this will be less possible and likely, especially as pressure grows upon the independence not only of the writer but of the written work, the book itself.

II

How do our writers earn? We have seen that the writer's life has a tendency to be financially precarious but also to be potentially profitable. How does this, in fact, work out in terms of life-patterns for our writers? It is, of course, well known that the literary profession is financially uncertain and full of financial inequalities: so Sir Walter Scott built Abbotsford from his novels, and could earn £5,000 for one of them, while Jane Austen earned no more than £700 from hers in her lifetime. But, at the end of the nineteenth century, the writer became increasingly exposed to the market, and the financial opportunities of literature became much more arbitrary. Books, as we shall see in a later chapter, became much cheaper at this time and a part of the retail trade, a situation which tended to accentuate the discrepancy between merit and income. At the same time the market for them became much larger, and it consumed a great deal of writing. Most of what it consumed was ephemeral, work normally written specifically to satisfy its assumed immediate needs. Journalism of the book was encouraged, as well as all the other forms of journalism, which were expanding rapidly to satisfy the outlets created by the rise of the popular press, magazine and book. All this tended to produce a surplus of writers, and what George Gissing called the 'New Grub Street' became more significant than ever in literary life. Remarkable rewards were possible, but the overall market was a depressed one, especially for those who had serious ambitions and little private money to support them. Publishers and editors were able to buy the work of writers of whatever quality for remarkably little, and by the late years of the century it was undoubtedly true that, as Arnold Bennett pointed out, the prevailing publishing system worked against the writer's earning much from literature unless he had 'strong mercantile interests'. The gap between what Richard Findlater has called 'authorship by activity' and 'authorship by income' could and did grow wider. Even the author who hoped to find and please a market felt himself to be in difficulties, while for the more serious author the outlets for more good poetry and fiction were also decreasing. It is certainly the case that the change in the literary climate over these years is partly due to the growing sense of literary difficulty.

As we have seen, one of the effects of this was to encourage writers to organize to protect their interests; and the foundation of the Society of Authors and the official literary agencies date from this period. It is not hard to see why. With many seeking the prestige of publication, and with the expansion of the numbers of the literary profession and the intelligentsia, books could become cheap fare. Many books appeared at the expense of the author: Thomas Hardy published his first novel, *Desperate Remedies* (1871), at a cost to himself of £75. In his book *Methods of Publishing* (1891), Samuel Squire Sprigge pointed out that three-quarters of all novels were published on terms requiring authors' payments. In these cases, the author usually received royalties (though these were often dishonestly computed, resulting in low profits even on a successful book). Otherwise, publishers adopted the system of requiring an author to make an outright sale to them of his work (a familiar nineteenth-century pattern which was open to increasing abuse), relinquishing his copyright entirely so that no royalties could be earned from success. George Gissing, for instance, received an outright sum of £150 for his *New Grub Street* (1891)—a novel about the difficulties of writers. Earlier in the century, such practices had helped serious writers; now, with the expansion of the profession and the cheapening of the book, they simply encouraged literary poverty. Even writers who were cushioned financially found a gap between what they wanted to write and the taste of the publisher and the public. At the same time, the environment of publishing expansion was also one in which large profits were possible with success.[1] Arnold Bennett, for instance, was reporting his earnings in 1913 as over £300 per week, from a diversified output in journalism and fiction, and from a consistently high rate of production (he records in his journal at the end of 1910, for instance, that he had written 355,900 words in the year).

As a result, many of the writers of the period evince many of the attitudes of a new commercialism, even if they also protest against certain features of it. The sense of a gap between what one wanted to write and what one had to write was strong; this is the theme of Gissing's *New Grub Street*, and the book embodies all the uncertainties of direction and conviction the situation could produce. The hero, Edward Reardon, refuses to supply the 'good, coarse, marketable stuff for the world's vulgar' that the situation invites, despite the pressure of his wife, who claims that 'Art must be practised as a trade, at all events in our time. This is the age of trade.' Around him are a gallery of opportunist writers, exploiting expanding literacy and the taste for superficial reading matter, professionals responding to the demands of the market, and a general decline of cultural values. But Reardon's problem, amid the financial worries he suffers, is defining his seriousness, his sense of separateness from the crowds that surround him. One of the persistent issues of conscience and integrity in the period was, in fact, the interest in a new realism. We have already seen that one of the literary tendencies of the period was towards a new and neo-scientific realism of viewpoint— it was partly the result, perhaps, of the broader social origins of writers and their exposure to a broader social experience, partly the result of the way neo-science was penetrating intellectual thought, and partly the result of the growing secularization of writers—and writers like Gissing, Hardy and Wells were all

[1] This environment is much more fully discussed in Chapter IX of this book.

N

engaged in battling not only against financial difficulty but the pressure of demand, from publishers and lending libraries in particular, for a more edifying literature. Hardy's experiences with his last novel, *Jude the Obscure* (1894), 'completely cure[d] me of further interest in novel-writing,' he said, and he turned to poetry entirely. For writers even more positively committed to the idea of the perfection of the art, like Henry James, the difficulties were the greater. James's later income from writing was very low indeed, and his friend Edith Wharton even diverted some of her royalties into his to conceal the smallness of his audience. But it is less financial worry, or a feeling of not being permitted expression, then a deep sense of the loneliness of the serious artist that haunts his writing (as in, for instance, 'The Lesson of the Master'); he has no true audience, no effective criticism or understanding of his work to support and justify him. Hence his sense of the need to 'give up' everything in the interests of art; hence his profound sense of cultural loss.

However, it is in fact the writers who were most exposed to the market who offer the fullest exploration of it; and these are normally the writers who come from poorer backgrounds and so are not financially cushioned from its implications. Frequently their story—the story of those who try to live by writing or to support it on a small private income—is one of a long struggle with poverty, sometimes later mitigated, and sometimes not. Gissing, for instance, has left us fairly clear records of his financial transactions, on which he depended, since he was committed to a professional literary career. He spent all his life on the edge of poverty—in part, certainly, because of his unwillingness to meet the demands of the market. He invested £125 of his own money in his first novel, *Workers in the Dawn* (1880), on an agreement which gave him two-thirds of the profits, and earned him £2. Later he turned to selling his novels outright: *Demos: A Story of English Socialism* (1886), brought him £100 and, a little later, working under pressure and producing a novel a year, he earned £150 outright for each. He felt his position to be contradictory, as it was; for instance, he joined the Society of Authors (and was disappointed to find it a gathering of tradesmen) and in 1891 turned to a literary agent, A. P. Watt. This didn't raise his income, but he later turned to dealing, more profitably, with another major agent of the day, J. B. Pinker.[1] Arnold Bennett was vastly more successful, partly because—as we can see from his *The Truth About an Author*—he was able to reconcile his strong mercantile concerns ('I am a writer, just as I might be a hotel-keeper, a solicitor, a doctor, a grocer, or an earthenware manufacturer') with the equally strong desire to be a great artist. He was throughout his life a professional journalist, drawing a high income from that source, and he skilfully used the services of J. B. Pinker until by about 1926 he was earning some £20,000 a year. It was Pinker's way to support his writers in the early days of their career in the hope of recouping his loans later; this he did with Stephen Crane, Joseph Conrad and D. H. Lawrence. In Bennett's case his early assistance was clearly a success; by this process, clearly recognized on both sides as an investment, an effective modern form of patronage emerged. At least in this case; not all of Pinker's authors were to prove so profitable.[2]

The problems of adopting the motivations of art to a climate of extreme mercantilism had many subtle consequences and produced many different views of the artist. One inevitable consequence was that the writer, particularly the novelist, tended to see himself in the same verbal and perceptual world as the journalist; this, too, is one of the stimuli of realism. The very difficulties of defining the authorial role became greatly increased; and the swashbuckling, reformist journalist with his standards of truth and integrity and his curiosity about the way systems and institutions worked, about the poor and about social conditions generally, encouraged a new kind of social involvement and even a distrust of the arcaneness of art as such; hence the famous disagreement between H. G. Wells and Henry James about the relative claims of art and life. Certainly writers like

[1] See the excellent account of this in Jacob Korg, *George Gissing: A Critical Biography* (Seattle, Washington, 1963).
[2] See James Hepburn's edition of *The Letters of Arnold Bennett: I. Letters to J. B. Pinker* (London and New York, 1966). Also the letters of D. H. Lawrence and Stephen Crane, which make it apparent that Pinker was often rather more a disinterested patron than perhaps my comments suggest. In Crane's case, it seems impossible to avoid the view that Crane regarded Pinker as precisely a financial support.

Wells and Bennett found that the intermittent satisfaction of the claims of seriousness and those of trade provided an alluring form of the literary life. Wells, like Bennett, was proud to assert that he was both an artist *and* a journalist, and the attack in *Boon* on the overwrought consciousness of James was part of a general conviction about the best way of serving the prevailing literary scene. In his early reviewing, he made it clear that he considered the literary scene to be debased, and very much by people who had similar education and background to his own. 'The coming to reading age in 1886–1888 of multitudes of boys and girls . . . changed the conditions of journalism and literature in much the same way as the French Revolution changed the conditions of political thought and action,' he said, referring to the consequences of the Education Act of 1870 which established the Board schools. One consequence was the popularity of works 'whose connection with art is purely accidental. It is scarcely too much to say that every writer of our time who can be called popular owes three-quarters of his or her fame to the girls who have been taught in Board Schools.'[1] And his career is clearly one in which he accepted that situation as an opportunity while, at the same time, feeling the profoundest reservations about it. And, like Wells, Bernard Shaw equally resolved to use the prevailing situation to exercise his maximum influence consonant with the winning of a large audience. He too began writing fiction, and in his first nine years in London earned only £6 from writing; his *Collected Letters* show how strongly he protested about the prevailing financial environment of fiction. In 1881 he rejected an offer to publish *Immaturity* if he would pay £95 with: 'If I am to be a capitalist as well as artist, might I not as well publish on commission and retain my copyright entire?' 'I object to publishers,' he also wrote, 'the one service they have done me is to teach me to do without them. They combine commercial rascality with artistic touchiness and pettishness, without being either

[1] Quoted in Gordon N. Ray, 'H. G. Wells Tries to Be a Novelist', cited above. Raymond Williams (in *The Long Revolution*) resists the view that the 1870 Act 'opened the floodgates of literacy'. But the significance of the Act was perhaps symbolic; it suggested to publishers, editors and writers a large change in the market and increased their efforts to reach it.

good business men or fine judges of literature.'[1] But after a wealthy marriage in 1898, which freed him from a heavy burden of reviewing, he turned away from fiction to the theatre, where he could both appeal to and affront the middlebrow standards more easily and, it proved, with vastly greater profit. In 1914 he had enormous success with *Pygmalion*, and by 1931 he was earning £16,000 in the United States alone; he left a six-figure fortune.[2]

Writers like Bennett, Wells and Shaw, who were so successful commercially, represent the spectacular successes, and behind them lay as many spectacular failures, sad instances of poverty and insecurity. All were sufficiently radical writers to extend and develop the prevailing artistic conventions and possibilities, but they were at least fortunate in that the forms in which they wrote—the novel and the play—were still effective media of social communication, and they had no modernist desire to exhaust them. But in the course of the century their success has become less and less repeatable, as the profits of the single book go down and down in an expanding but commercially competitive market. And, of course, many of the most interesting literary forms have tended, partly because of the complexity of artists, partly because of the decline of serious audiences, to become minority forms. This has been particularly true of poetry, which in this century has become less and less popular. By the turn of the century the days when a Tennyson could sell 60,000 copies of the first edition of *Enoch Arden*, earn £500 for a single poem and £20,000 for an American lecture-tour, were obviously over. This was partly because poetry was ceasing, as Professor V. de S. Pinto has put it, to 'represent the equilibrium of a society that had achieved some degree of integration' and was becoming increasingly a matter of private artistic sensibility;[3] it was partly because some of its functions were being yielded up to the novel in a more realistic and secularistic age; it was

---

[1] George Bernard Shaw, *Collected Letters: 1874–1897*, ed. Dan H. Laurence (London, 1965), pp. 543–4.

[2] Saunders, *Profession of English Letters*, cited above, pp. 205–10.

[3] V. de Sola Pinto, *Crisis in English Poetry: 1880–1940* (London, 1951).

partly because poetry—in some ways the most 'literary' of all literary procedures, marked by methods of distillation and compression of linguistic effect, having behind it a powerful tradition of self-consciousness and a view of the poet as the exploratory artistic hero—particularly tends to be the focus of a sense of artistic difficulty. The eighteen-nineties markedly dramatized poetic poverty ('Nine-tenths of my time,' wrote John Davidson, 'and that which is more precious, have been wasted in the endeavour to earn a livelihood. In a world of my own making I should have been writing only what should have been written') and assumed the minor audience. And though the situation in poetry had not reached its present state, where a volume of new poetry is almost necessarily a non-commercial proposition, and where scarcely any poet makes anything like an income from poetry alone, it became markedly insecure.[1] Poets like Kipling, Masefield and Hardy all profited considerably from verse, and collections of poetry were still potentially a source of some profit for publishers, and there was an audience which could be captured even for poetry of a markedly novel kind.[2] But as Ezra Pound, in this as in so many things a remarkable cultural explorer of the era, stressed, the poet had to find new ways of support. He himself worked hard to hunt out new ways of financing the poets around him in London, getting them jobs on magazines, accosting potential patrons, and starting a fund to get T. S. Eliot out of the bank where he worked to let him live by writing (in fact Eliot became a publisher for his support). Patronage came back again, either indirectly, through the founding of magazines which paid poets, or directly, through outright payments. It was part of the economics of bohemia, part of financing the novel writer until his broader-based reputation had time to emerge.

We can see the neo-bohemian pattern at work in the case of many of the poets and the self-conscious novelists of the period.

[1] This situation may, however, be reversing somewhat; poetry sales in some areas have been increasing over the last three years or so; and a recent Penguin Modern Poets volume devoted to the Liverpool poets has sold 70,000 copies in two years. Indeed paperbacks seem to have extended the poetry reading audience significantly.

[2] On this see C. K. Stead, *The New Poetic*, cited above, and Joy Grant, *Harold Monro and the Poetry Bookshop* (London, 1967).

James Joyce, who came of a background of reduced circumstances and like his hero, Stephen Dedalus, left Dublin to fulfil literary ambitions in Paris, lived there on less than a pound a week. After that he earned £80 a year teaching at the Berlitz Institute in Zürich. Having made nothing from his first volume, *Chamber Music* (1907), but an *avant-garde* reputation, reinforced by the publication of *Dubliners* (1914), he began, largely through the efforts of Ezra Pound, to acquire patrons and supporters. During the war he was assisted by, among others, Harriet Shaw Weaver, who also helped Eliot and Pound and supported the magazine *The Egoist*. But the patronage also extended to assistance in the publication of his books—in *The Egoist* and the American *Little Review*. Another patron, Sylvia Beach, who ran the expatriate bookshop called Shakespeare and Company in Paris, published *Ulysses* for him. Despite obscenity difficulties both in England and the States, it began to produce a considerable income. But Joyce, like D. H. Lawrence, did not live long enough to acquire the real rewards his writing was to bring; Lawrence at his death in 1930 had £4,000, but the sale of the Penguin paperback *Lady Chatterley's Lover* alone (and it was one of a number of different hardback and paperback editions) has totalled over three and a half million.[1] Here, we might say then, are two writers who were not bound by the market; the rewards of their work came, but the pattern failed to provide the income that sponsors the writer when he is most in need of it. By the fortunes of patronage, and in Joyce's case through doing other work, both of these two writers were able to live as writers. With the decline of the cultivated rich in England, this form of personal patronage has tended to disappear; and various writers more latterly have sought to find institutional equivalents for it. Some writers have sought to be put on a salary basis by their publishers. Others have drawn on Arts Council bursaries. Latterly, too, patronage from universities, particularly American ones, has been important. Indeed, the postwar equivalent to the expatriation of Joyce and Lawrence, which had among other things the advantages of cheaper living costs, has tended to be the voyage to the United States, or even

[1] Figures here from J. W. Saunders, *The Profession of English Letters* (London, 1964).

the sale of manuscripts and work-sheets to American libraries.[1] A notable instance here is Dylan Thomas, a good deal of whose income derived in different ways from American sources, and who in his middle age found himself heavily dependent on American lecture-tours.[2] Otherwise, literary economics in England have grown in the last twenty years even tighter than before. The independent novelist or poet is a much rarer figure. And the two most important and flamboyant life-styles of writers in the earlier part of the century—that of the commercially successful man-of-letters; and that of the literary bohemian— have tended to give way to a phase in which literature is produced by what is, in effect, a literary salariat.

Large rewards from writing are possible today. Richard Findlater has pointed out in a recent article that rich authors are getting richer, and poor authors getting poorer. For the writer in tune with the market, its possibilities are greater than ever. There are various remarkably successful multi-media figures, like Jacqueline Susann, whose work is patterned to the conditions of modern success in a market effectively geared to large-scale production. As a result it is serialized, paperbacked, sold on a global overseas market, made into films and even television serials. Such writers may even become incorporated companies (Agatha Christie Ltd., Ian Fleming Ltd.). But at the level of medium success, where most of the better literature fits, conditions are a good deal more marginal, as the print-order needed for a success-ful book rises and the number of purchasers falls. In some ways, says Findlater, the prospects for the serious independent writer of high reputation but low income, a staple type in the market, have improved lately: 'With the advent of the Arts Council grants and such sizable new prizes as those awarded by Bookers and W. H. Smith, writers like V. S. Naipaul have a better hope of augmenting their relatively meagre return from their books

[1] For a more extended discussion of the importance of American economics in modern English writing, see the article by Bryan Wilson and the present author, 'Why Young Writers Emigrate: The Away Game', *Twentieth Century*, Vol. 169 (Jan. 1961), pp. 69–80. There is a fictional treatment in my novel *Stepping Westward* (1965); and in Thomas Hinde's *High* (1968).

[2] See, for a fuller account, John Malcolm Brinnin, *Dylan Thomas in America* (London, 1956).

with bonuses which will not only buy them writing time but, for a period, may boost their advances and even their sales.'[1] They also have the chance of gaining writerships-in-residence in universities, selling their manuscripts,[2] or appearing on television. In other ways, because of a shift away from imaginative literature, and the general reduction of outlets for it—a declining number of serious literary reviews, a reduction in the book-pages of newspapers and weekend reviews, a threatened decline of serious broadcasting in the BBC—the prospects grow worse. The practical consequences for a competent, busy and serious writer were laid out in some detail a few years ago by David Holbrook, who reported that after completing nine books (in eleven volumes) he was beginning to feel secure as an author. His career, divided between teaching and writing, but with about 25 hours a week spent on writing, showed almost no writing profits for the first nine years for which he charts it, and did not rise above about £600 a year for another three. 'Only now, 14 years after I started, can I contemplate becoming a full-time professional writer,' he notes, adding 'my choice . . . is between living on royalties at about £1,500 a year plus part-time journalistic earnings, or to take an educational post, earning, say, £2,225—and paying tax at the full rate on my £1,500 royalties, the product of so many years when my earnings were below a factory worker's wages.'[3] This brings David Holbrook into what Richard Findlater has called the 'lucky sixth' of professional writers today.

However, the writing of books, particularly imaginative books, is less likely than ever to attract those who enter the profession to live by writing. Not all are interested in it in this light; writing

[1] Richard Findlater, 'The Writer Considered as Wage-Earner', *Times Literary Supplement*, 3517 (July 24, 1969) (Money in Writing issue No. 1). He concludes: 'If anything is clear, it is that there is going to be an increasingly painful process of adjustment between British authors on the one hand, and, on the other, the further extensions of the education system, of state investments in the arts, of printing technology, and of the concentration of ownership in the publishing industry. It is the author who will have to do most of the adjusting: meanwhile, the wage rate—unlike the casualty rate—remains low.' To some of these matters I return in Chapter X.

[2] On this see Jenny Stratford, 'The Market in Authors' Manuscripts', in the same issue of *The Times Literary Supplement*.

[3] David Holbrook, 'An Author's Apprenticeship', *Guardian*, March 28, 1963.

still has something of the character of a cottage industry, and its roots strike down into many local writers' circles, many part-time writers who write as a spare-time activity, and, of course, many married women writing at home. Many writers have also tried to break out of the professional pattern by pursuing new forms of publishing structure, from the cyclostyled circulation of books to the development of writers' cooperatives, often in conscious rejection of the idea of the word as a commodity. Some live on National Assistance, and it is true that there are in the modern industrial state various economic lacunae in which activities like writing can be exercised. However, writing is even more than ever linked to a large expansion of the media, written, aural and visual, most of it produced on a large and costly scale. One consequence of the situation is that writers have shifted increasingly towards media other than books.[1]

The real benefits of writing today, as J. W. Saunders points out, tend to go to those writing for film and television; he notes, for instance, that the Television and Screenwriters' Guild (another feature of the highly professional organization of writing today) has more than 500 full-time writers among its members, 11% of whom earn over £80 a week, and more than 40% of whom earn more than £20 a week, from their writing.[2] A writer can often earn more from writing an hour-long television play (perhaps £500) than he can from writing a novel; and he can write the television play very much more quickly. The writing of books is likely, in fact, to attract only those who feel some urgency about writing individualistically and seriously. In these days, when not only patronage is hard to come by but private income is rarer and savings themselves in an inflationary situation hardly support any career, the independent writer is something of a threatened figure; and the career is to some extent a declining career—despite the evidence of a high rate of publication in

[1] Richard Findlater ('The Writer Considered as Wage-Earner', cited above) quotes the literary agent Michael Sissons: 'The authors of most of the first novels for which we have been responsible in 1967 are now involved either in a film treatment, or a television play, in which they are working out themes which would previously have been presented as short stories.'

[2] Saunders, *The Profession of English Letters*, p. 238.

fiction and poetry. Even the appeal to literary values is itself harder to make, in a democratizing and, increasingly, a highly politicized age. As Findlater points out, the prewar writer still tended to think of himself in terms of four literary categories: the novel, poetry, drama and journalism. Now there are many more, making demands on writers, but offering them a different kind of role.[1] The technocrat writer, visibly emerging in the 1920s and 1930s—reported in fiction by Evelyn Waugh in England, and Scott Fitzgerald and others in the U.S.A.[2]—is now a familiar type. The situation of the writer in film, radio or television is one that demands a high level of skill in the manipulation of technical equipment. This means, to a fair degree, that experiment within the media is determined (more so than in most modes of writing) by developments taking place outside the actual writing situation—by technological advances made by engineers, and applied by a team of persons of whom the writer is only one. In the characteristic hierarchy of such media (which are complex institutions in their own right) the writer is, of course, usually in a team-situation, and in effect an employee. As such, he is not necessarily highly regarded and is subservient to direction. He may assert commitments to 'literature' but these will not be taken at all seriously; he is there for his skills, not because of his integrity.

In this sort of situation, the contemporary writer can be thought of as both more and less professional than his predecessors. *More* so, because he has considerable technical mastery, is often highly trained, and is increasingly 'unionized' and supported by a well-developed system of agents and contracts for his protection. In all these ways he grows closer to the model of the other professions and his circumstances become bureaucratic ones. But in the traditional sense he is obviously *less* professional—less committed to literature as culture, as a mode of individualism, as the expression of his own art and his own literary aims (which in today's situation become very hard to define). Most of our full-time writers now must relate in some way or other to this large world

---

[1] Findlater, *What Are Writers Worth?*

[2] See, for instance, F. Scott Fitzgerald, *The Pat Hobby Stories* (London, 1967).

of the media or the services. Though many writers start on the bohemian model, it remains rare as a long-term prospect.[1] Today it is not difficult for writers to make the transition from the *avant-garde* world to that of the technological writer; they can even appear to have much in common. The changing patterns of reward make writing for the technical media the most attractive and secure of contemporary careers in writing,[2] but there are other attractions. The media offer direct confrontation with an audience; and they are novel and changing enough to permit experimental relationships with it to exist, to permit the exercise of daring ideas and new techniques. Because of this high degree of immediate contact and the relative neutrality of the content, which ranges freely from traditional to advanced, even writers not seeking success find television or film tempting. Technology itself becomes, moreover, an obsessive instrumentality. The inevitable effect of all this is to make writers concerned much more with the 'radical' means and techniques of distribution than with the 'purity' of their work. These media are by their nature very much less 'perpetual' than the book. The time of the period of exposure is very much more limited; the technical media tend to create for the moment, and to work on a principle of very high artistic wastage. But of course this situation tends to reduce a writer's feeling of commitment to the long-term impact of his work, his sense of writing for posterity. It even reduces, generally across the literary scene, the distinctiveness and individuality of writers; and in a time when many are writing it becomes very hard for a writer to acquire a distinct individual reputation, to stand out from the general group. So everything encourages the writer to move away from an 'aesthetic' approach to his work,

[1] 'Novelist Brian S. Johnson last week signed an £800-a-year contract with Secker and Warburg to write two novels in three years, putting him in the exceptional class of being a salaried novelist. . . . He thinks it is appropriate that an experimental writer should have an experimental contract.' *Observer*, June 6, 1965. Johnson, more experimentally, proposed a consortium of writers publishing their own books in 'A Living for Writers', *New Society*, 9 January 1969.

[2] For instance, a writer can earn as much or more from a television play, which may take him three months to write, as from a novel which may take two years. Fees of £750 for a one-hour television script are not now uncommon.

and towards a much more directly professional one. A further significant factor is the disappearance of the significance of the printed book as an object, and of the private reading situation as the basic point of contact between writer and reader. So the writer has tended to turn from the more permanent written word to the more ephemeral spoken word, from the considered to the impromptu, from the work written for long-term use to work written for the occasion. The changes that have taken place lately in the composition of the reading public, away from the old stratifications of 'high', 'middle' and 'low' towards an undifferentiated centre; the relative decline of 'imaginative' writing in relation to other forms of writing; the disappearance of the financial conditions encouraging to literary bohemianism; the fading of a clearly defined notion of 'high' culture; and perhaps, above all, the removal of literature from the context of literacy to a context with a different technology and different relations between creators, transmitters and receivers—all are crucial factors in a situation in which the writer's role and self-image are again visibly changing.

One might put the point in a rather different way. We live in a culture which is strongly oriented towards achievement, and our view of literature is one that emphasizes its nature as a public thing, requires an objective assessment of it. In more placid societies the emphasis can be on the creation rather the consumption of art; there are new sects in Japan, with millions of followers, which see art as part of man's religious sense, not something made for consumption by others. So the followers will go out and look at (and occasionally draw) a tree, studying it for hours together. We tend to regard art in a much more instrumental way, and this can well be turned readily into an economic formulation; it is the act of creating for others, finally for a market which can be emphasized, even among bohemian writers. It becomes part of Marx's fetishism of commodities. So, even for the bohemian writer, art becomes a livelihood, an instrument as well as a dedication, subject to the assessment of the critical if not the mercantile market. And, as more and more our place and worth in society comes to depend upon instrumental skills, on what one does rather than what one is, then so has writing tended to become more instrumental, less concerned with communicating perceptions of truth than with finding more functional and immediate ways of existence. And this situation is intensified rather than reduced in our kind of 'mass' society, when the private intuitions, impulses and motives involved in creativity are less and less prized for their own sake, and the writer's relationship with his audience tends to become much more formalized, more remote, more competitive with other writers, more business-like.

PART FOUR

Communications

CHAPTER IX

The Climate of Literary Culture
and the Literary Periodical

I

At best writing is a solitary and self-directed activity, most satisfyingly done, as Virginia Woolf said, on a private income in a room of one's own. Though a good deal of literary work is produced under commission or under pressure, the ideal of most writers is to win their representativeness through their own independence—setting their own work-rhythms, being responsive to their own pace, inclinations and observations, creating out of a self-made, personal and uninterrupted climate in the circumstances that suit them best. For the creative process is a strange one; it is psychologically mysterious and in many respects unbidden. Even in its conscious aspects it is much more than socially or culturally determined, having to do with what Henry James once called 'the beautiful difficulties of art'. Writers may seek the ideal environment, the perfect sources for their stimulus; but even then art is in no sense guaranteed. But unless the creative process is conducted with an absolute integrity it easily becomes impure; and we respect that purity because it is essential to the human spirit, because it involves an interplay between objective reality and the process of subjective selection, exploration and interpretation which has to do not only with the central philosophical conundrum but the most extensive pace for free expression and manoeuvre in man. In all these ways, then, writing, at its best, is a very individualized and individualistic activity indeed: an outright example of our humanism and freedom. But if that humanism and freedom has been one of the main themes

o

of art for the last 150 years, this is precisely because it is precarious. And it is precarious both psychologically, as an aspect of
the creative self, and socially. Hence over the same period many
writers have felt that the essential context of such art—a liberal
freedom and a degree of preserved autonomy—is threatened. This
has been particularly true in this century, when many activities
of an autonomous and privately sanctioned kind seemed to have
come under threat, not simply from totalitarianism but from more
subtle incursions into the idea of individual identity.[1]

It would seem to me that the ideal of the freely creative individual has an absolute value, and that it is closely bound up with
the nature of great art. Yet there is another sense in which the
writer is neither solitary nor autonomous: the cultural and sociological sense. Any satisfactory artistic realization is, as Matthew
Arnold said, a coming together of the power of the man and the
power of the moment. Although art has the capacity to transcend
the environment it inhabits, it is never independent of it. The
writer exists within a culture, in all the various senses—literary,
linguistic, historical, sociological—in which we use that word.
That culture, of course, he also helps to create; indeed in the
idealization of his own freedom he accepts the responsibility
for doing that. But he lives and works through a body of traditions, practices and insights; through a system of naming,
meaning and sharing, called a language; and through a set of
styles and gestures of contact which form the basis for the two

---

[1] An interesting expression of the case for and need for literary autonomy—
though there are many—occurs in *The Selected Letters of Stephen Vincent Benet*, ed.
Charles A. Fenton (New Haven, Conn., 1960), where Benet writes:

'The artist . . . is a tough kind of plant in general and will grow on unfavour-
able soil. . . . But when the world reverts to a certain kind of barbarism—and
that does not necessarily mean the Cro-Magnons—they cannot function. They
cannot function because they cannot exist. As Mr Justice Holmes once remarked
(I am quoting incorrectly and from memory), "the machinery of government
must be allowed a certain amount of play in its joints". When there is no play
in its joints, the artist is one of the first people to be crushed between the cogs.
He needs very little room, at least, but that much he must have.

'What gives him that little room? A certain, admitted respect on the part
of rulers and states for civilized things, for the work of the mind. A certain
hard-bought tolerance—even a certain neglect.'

sets of relationships in which he is necessarily involved—those within the work of art (between sentence and sentence, character and character), and those that reach out from it, relationships with the reader or audience. The language and its concepts; the sense of reality and of fiction; the orders and structures which compose an imaginative work—all of these are expression of a cultural sharing, upon which literature inevitably depends. This is communication in its most communal and organic sense. Then, more broadly still, there spreads a yet larger body of com- munications—of editors, publishers, directors and producers; of books, magazines, theatres and other media; of bookstalls and booksellers; of readers, theatregoers and television-viewers.[1] We may think of this web of communications serving him and letting him act effectively; that, in the past, is how it usually has been seen, as the process of literature's reaching outward, providing a more or less invisible system which puts the writer in touch with his reader on his audience. Or we may think of the writer existing to serve it; and today it is perhaps more relevant to see the instrument as logically prior, a high capital investment consisting of serial spaces that must be filled with writing, a medium that *is*—rather than one that *contains*—the message, into which the writer is invited to fit.

Now these two views are, in effect, two very different views of culture. The first takes culture as an active, living force, a community of sensibility and value that shapes and invigorates literature. The second sees literature phenomenologically, as a manifestation, structured by certain established means, of social interaction. The first has to do with culture felt from the inside, and with communication seen as a common, selective scrutiny of

[1] Or to use the phrasing of Robert Escarpit, in *Sociology of Literature*, trans. Ernest Pick (Painesville, Ohio, 1965): 'Each and every literary fact presupposes a writer, a book and a reader; or, in general terms, an author, a product and a public. By way of an extremely complex transmitting mechanism, a circuit of interrelationships is constituted. It combines art, technology and business, uniting well-defined individuals in a more or less anonymous though limited community.' (It is relevant to my argument here following to note that Escarpit's sociological and apparently objective language in fact depends on a metaphor: art is *metamorphosed into* technology and business.)

experience. It is in effect a conscious achievement—the achievement of certain selective individuals of accomplishment interacting with the potential of the society at large. The second has to do with culture seen objectively, as a body of shared practices, operating according to certain structures and logics. The first view, involved, selective, internalized, is closer to the literary view of culture; the second, detached and more inclusive, is closer to the sociological view of culture. I shall be returning in a later chapter to this crucial distinction—for modern society itself, in response to the kinds of change that have taken place in it, tends increasingly to see culture less in the first way and more in the second.[1] In an age depersonalized and relativistic, the word *culture* has itself become a difficult one;[2] and the literary definition normally diverges quite radically not only from the sociological but from the popular view. This definition normally emphasizes culture as a conscious social achievement—the achievement both of a society at large and of certain individuals of particular accomplishment within it, a cultural élite. But while, often, the definition extends to include, as T. S. Eliot observes in his *Notes Towards the Definition of Culture* (1948), the 'whole way of life of a people', that 'whole way of life' is itself usually regarded more positively as a living, creative fabric of values, morals and manners than is the case in the sociological definition. For the sociological definition is inevitably more objective and neutral; it recognizes culture as, in effect, the total body of practices, behaviour and beliefs, the total body of what is learned and shared, in the society you happen to be studying,

[1] See below, Chapter XI.

[2] For a fascinating and extended discussion of the changing meanings of the word, see Raymond Williams, *Culture and Society: 1780–1950* (London, 1958) —with its powerful implication that the very destiny of the word in our society has profound significance. Williams points out that the early meanings of the word comprise the idea of a 'separate body of moral and intellectual activities' which afford a court of human appeal. He says that this idea has changed to include the idea of a whole way of life as well, and so becomes a mode of interpreting and humanizing all our common experience. My disagreement would be that as all experience is included it becomes impossible effectively to value it; so culture increasingly means not the humanization of all life, but the objective analysis and documentation of it as phenomenon.

seen, relativistically, in relation to all the other forms of social culture you happen to know about.[1] Moreover, by the literary definition there is a degree of implied participation, culture being of a species of awareness, the humanistic standpoint from which we observe what we see; while in sociology it is *what* we see, a subject-matter. The writer, obviously, is in fact engaged with, and interacts with, culture in both of these two senses—the positivistic one, which means a commitment to certain intellectual and moral priorities in which the arts stand near to the centre; and the more general one, the 'totality of what is learned and shared by individuals as members of a given society'. But we should remember that the writer, especially if he has some form of humanistic conception of himself, as our serious writers commonly have had, is likely to find the cultural sources of his art quite as much among that self-consciously narrower cultural community, the literary elite, the body of the educated, the public that is an active participant in the values creative to art, as in the broader social community. However, over the last century this conscious community of good writers and good readers has clearly weakened; and this has been one of the sources of strain upon modern art. The difficult problem for the analyst is to show how; and that is my subject in this chapter.

Clearly, the writer is crucially an independent agent (and literary criticism often chooses to regard him entirely as that). He is the essential producer of literary art, and no committee or computer will ever make an effective substitute. But he produces his art within a culture, in both our senses—in a world of values, assumptions, traditions and communicative institutions. And, we might add, that culture and context can effectively favour or disfavour the literary enterprise. Any culture is a complex web of myths and meanings, of stylizations and social

---

[1] The often-quoted sociological definition is that in A. L. Kroeber and Clyde Kluckhohn, *Culture: A Critical Review of Concepts and Definitions* (Salem, Mass., 1952): 'Culture consists of patterns, explicit and implicit, of and for behaviour acquired and transmitted by symbols, constituting the distinctive achievements of human groups, including their embodiments in artifacts; the essential core of culture consists of traditional (i.e. historically derived and selected) ideas and especially their attached values. . . .'

inheritances, and it is a living ecology for the writer. But, in these terms, it can be more, or less, 'dense'. The distinction implies preferences which sociologists (though they may be aware of them) can hardly emphasize without compromising their neutrality; and it is indeed part of that difference between our two views of culture that literature and criticism *have*, persistently, asserted and emphasized it.[1] And in terms of comparative cultural analysis, the distinction does have meaning. We can recognize, for instance, that the Elizabethan period in England was a culture particularly invigorating to imaginative literature— whereas the early republic in the United States, though it sought and found a literature, was not notably so. Likewise, there can be little doubt that in our own highly rationalistic and egalitarian society, with little concern for ritual practices, little sense of the numinous or the power of inherited myths and meanings, with a not notably vigorous language and a want of strong cultural and aesthetic convictions, there is a certain kind of cultural 'nudity'— of which literature can make and has made us aware. In this situation both the eminence and influence of the literary imagination— the capacity, that is, not just of writers but of others in the culture to see through particularly literary ways of knowing, feeling and ordering—and the very commitment of society to its conscious and articulate culture seem reduced. There is no clear way of seeing the consequences of this, since one thing the study of the cultures of the past and their effect on literature shows us is that the contexts of creativity are various indeed. But what is clear is that literary culture in our society has been under social and historical pressure from various sources—from the degree to which other forms of knowledge of a more rationalistic, scientific and neutral kind have power with us; from the lessening influence of those communities in the society for whom a literary view of life has some fundamental value; and from the rise to dominance of much more homogenized, and less personal and élitist, forms

[1] See, for instance, F. R. Leavis's stress (in his essay 'Sociology and Literature', *The Common Pursuit* (London, 1952)) on the need to raise 'questions as to the conditions of a vigorous and spiritually vital culture, the relations between the sophisticated and the popular, and the criteria by which one might attempt to judge the different phases of a national civilization'.

of cultural expression which carry many of the functions of art without being so—which is to say mass-culture.[1]

Today, literary culture has much less of the force of the entire culture behind it, and so the analysis of the artistic sector in the society and its general values and meanings become very much more difficult. For example, it is clear that if we wish to analyse the characteristic expressive culture of modern and modernized society, we would have to turn our attention to mass culture. There may be a considerable number of people who are not in fact exposed to it directly; and there are certainly many other important forms of cultural expression containing much more significant 'content'. But mass culture is a fundamental form of interaction in massified society, and the lives and experience even of those who are not directly exposed to it are profoundly affected. The very fact that it is less individualized and less dependent on personal response, that its effects are very generalized, makes it a ready instance of large-scale forms of value-transmission and value-interaction. It is, indeed, itself a much more sociological form of culture, with an inbuilt statistical reference; and in a sense it represents our contemporary tendency to view culture as a happening or manifestation, to see it less positively and much more from the standpoint of a sociological *laissez-faire* attitude. Indeed, a growing dislike of the conscious element, because it is the élitist element, in the notion of culture seems to have marked modern democratic development. And since we live in a society that, both in its commercial and its democratic aspects, tends to measure attitudes, influence and success rationalistically and statistically, we find it not only difficult to validate the importance of more serious forms of cultural expression but even to chart their social influence. Yet in the past, of course, with a different and a narrower base of social power and more hierarchical forms of value-transmission, high culture could

1 The historical and social developments have, of course, been supported by expressed assaults on the 'literary imagination' or on the idea of 'culture' in what I have been calling its literary sense. See for instance C. P. Snow's famous assertion of the claims of the scientific over the 'backward' claims of the literary imagination in *The Two Cultures and the Scientific Revolution* (London and New York, 1959).

perform functions like those of mass-culture, unifying socially influential audiences, and bearing—as one sociologist has put it—'fundamental symbols and values which give cohesion to social groups, ranging from nations and epochs to special social sub-groups and points of time'.[1] That is to say, the standards for appreciation of high literature and art were sufficiently closely associated with the standards of those who were in a social élite in other ways, and who held social prestige, for cultural hierarchies to be almost as clearly marked as social hierarchies. No culture can exist without a social base; but in the modern world what we call 'high culture' has found difficulties in finding that social base—in being a culture at all. In this pattern, the high cultural segment has shifted to specialized minorities, to the intelligentsia, who are largely responsible for maintaining the cultural dialogue, the process of selecting and validating works, creating the climate of demanding ideas, and debating aesthetic issues and questions of standards and values. It is this dialogue, publicly pursued, through which today the significance and reputations of particular writers emerge, and also through which a context of articulate culture is created. The dialogue extends from classrooms to the serious newspapers and magazines, and is an important aspect of the educational and intellectual dimensions of the society. In a democratic society it is normally heterodox in nature, expressing many different attitudes and interests while at the same time finding certain grounds for aesthetic and cultural agreement. Many of its assents and judgments reach only a narrow audience—though some go much further, giving a kind of agreed classic status to certain writers, certain aesthetic assumptions, in the society at large. The participants in this debate of course include many who do not speak in it but attend to it and accept its validity. It is the totality of these that make the cultural élite—an élite because they are a self-selected audience which in turn has some influence in forming the taste of society. The standards and distinctions shared by this audience can be part of complex schemes of social preference and life-style, part of a notion of taste, accomplishment or refine-

---

[1] Leo Lowenthal, 'Introduction' to *Literature, Popular Culture and Society* (Englewood Cliffs, N.J., 1961).

ment. Or they may be institutionalized and validated in a rather more abstract way—as when literature becomes an educational 'subject' and acquires a certain classical subject-matter and lore. Or they may be derived from more casual groupings in society; at different times we as individuals all participate in different cultural audiences, watching television for entertainment now but engrossing ourselves in a particular aspect of literature with much greater depth, concern and expertise. The important point is that the existence of the serious writer inevitably depends in some degree on the living value attached to serious and complex art, and hence on certain radical distinctions of taste that are alive in the culture.

The significance of such an audience is not then statistical, and it depends on stratifications of taste that function in highly complex ways. Nor will it do to see the literary 'audience' as simply a passive one, a body of respectful recipients; it is one that functions creatively both in relation to the society and the arts themselves. 'Where, then,' asked F. R. Leavis, trying to suggest the function of his review *Scrutiny* in its last issue in 1953, 'shall we look for the effective centres of that indispensable public, the informed and disinterested key-public without which the appeal to mature standards cannot be made, or remains a more offensive breach of manners on the part of the critic?' Leavis's point was, in fact, part of a long-lived recognition that literary activity depends in some sense on a 'saving remnant', a cultural élite of some sort in whom its best standards or interests thrive. He also assumes that this élite will be focused in the magazines, and will consist of an audience actively participant in the climate of literary culture. The problem that faces any discussion of modern literature, the literature of an increasingly egalitarian world, is to get at the idea of, and the nature of, the stratified audience and the creative interaction writers have with it: at the ways by which writers have found not only readers but an active context of literary values and a formative constituency.[1] This

---

[1] For an important attempt to discuss the notion of the writer and the responsive audience as a bound and creative community, see Q. D. Leavis, *Fiction and the Reading Public* (London, 1932). Behind that, the classic statement is, of course, Matthew Arnold's essay 'The Function of Criticism at the Present Time', in *Essays in Criticism: First Series* (London, 1865).

is far from easy to do. In studying mass culture we can presume
some relationship between the large audiences they pursue and
the values of those audiences. But with high culture the tactics
of reading and relationship are much more difficult, the form of
art more complex, the audience mysteriously self-selected.[1]
None the less, it is a crucial aspect of our understanding of the
workings of serious culture in society.

II

There is, in fact, one fairly useful way of doing this, and that is
by looking at the fortunes of the literary periodical. This is
because the periodical is one of the most immediate contexts
for literature, in that it normally provides a fairly close communicating medium between the writers who contribute to it and the
the readers who take it. Periodicals of a literary kind thus often
have fairly clear manifestations of the reciprocal relationship
between writers and readers—while of course being on their
own account one of the 'media' and hence in some sense standing
apart from both. Periodicals are also more broadly typed than
the work of a particular writer—they are 'institutional' at least
to the extent of having continuity, a distinct character, a feeling
of cultural focus and an awareness of a likely audience reflected
in the format and editorial selection. Unlike books, they appear
serially, and therefore adapt to situations fed back into them;
they mediate writers to readers and readers to writers; they
also often maintain a running discussion of their aesthetic aims
and priorities. To a large extent they are responsible, through
these things, for maintaining the cultural dialogue of which I
have spoken, for giving a public currency to ideas and discussion.

[1] On the difficulties of analysing literary audiences, and on the dangers of
assuming that the audience *shares* the values of works they read, see Lennox
Gray, 'The Literary Audience', in *Contemporary Literary Scholarship*, ed. Lewis
Leary (New York, 1958). This point applies both to the serious and the
popular audience, in different ways. For instance, in matters of mass culture,
'what the public wants' often turns out not to be what the public does, actually,
want.

They are, therefore, very much a context for writing as well as an assemblage of it; they select works, direct taste, review and judge, and influence both parties in literary communication. A good editor is, indeed, a central cultural mediator, and the good magazine a stock of essential issues and a basic body of judgments. From the readership figures, from the reputations supported and the movements espoused, from the running dialogues and the very sense of audience maintained in such journals, we can often make quite effective surmises towards a sociology of literary taste.

The periodical is also a useful touchstone because its origins in England were heavily literary. In other words, the early English periodicals are, many of them, worthy objects of study in their own right as examples of serious and intelligent minds employing literary skills and commitments. Both in the eighteenth and nineteenth centuries, many of the major writers had associated with them and regarded writing for them as an important branch of letters. But during the nineteenth century, with the rapid expansion of the reading audience and of the periodical form, they began to run into obvious difficulties as quality and circulation began to seem less and less compatible. Many critics have presented the story as one of a serious cultural degeneration—as the earlier periodicals which represented the interests of a relatively intelligent, literate and homogeneous audience were dispersed or crowded out by other periodical forms which produced a lowering of standards. Obviously a certain caution is necessary here, since the contacts between writers and readers can take place through various media—of which the periodical is just one (though a peculiarly effective one from a literary point of view). Still, there is some justice in this view, though the change can be seen only as part of a much larger social process which changed the dispositions of power in society, the relative status of the classes, and the values and consciousness of men, and hence produced a large-scale cultural repatterning. But certainly they do reveal a process of fragmentation in the cultural audience and a change in the function of the literary word and the literary imagination in society. The heyday of the periodical coincided wih a rise in literacy and cultural aspiration; hence its strongly literary associations. Today the periodical is distinctly a species of journalism, and it certainly does little to define its readers in terms of their *literary* taste. Of course there still are literary periodicals in existence, but they are specializedly literary, appeal to limited, and often by implication dissident, sectors in the community, and make only the most insecure assumptions about the standards of taste and value among their readership. This marks a radical change in the cultural constituency, and it is worth briefly following it through.

The serious periodical, the periodical as a form of cultural communication, grew up in the eighteenth century in response to a new technology and a new readership.[1] The important papers of the eighteenth century—the notable example is of course Addison and Steele's *Spectator*—consisted chiefly of essays of general character, though with a strong literary basis of attitude and style. They appealed to a general audience in the middle classes and thus, as Richard Altick says, 'enlarged the specifically literary interest of the middle-class public'. Their circulations were fairly large in relation to the total literate community; *The Spectator* printed some 3–4,000 copies of a single issue, but it was taken and read in coffee-houses, so that Addison's own estimate of twenty readers to a copy could be fair. The taste for the periodical, in its various forms (weekly, monthly, quarterly), underwent even greater expansion in the early nineteenth century, when it became a medium for numerous forms of expression, a striking intellectual forum in which a variety of realms of debate emerged. The early nineteenth century was the great period of the Great Reviews—*The Edinburgh*, *The Quarterly*, and so on—which were general papers of a literary bias, oscillating, as De Quincey said, 'pretty equally between human life on the one hand and literature on the other'. Many were quarterlies, with a reflective and reviewing character, and they associated politics, general ideas, commentary, humour and letters. They undoubtedly achieved close contact with a large,

[1] For fuller details, see W. S. Graham, *English Literary Periodicals* (New York, 1930).

intelligent and general cultivated audience—Denys Thompson has said that they drew life from 'an educated, responsible and homogeneous public' and that 'at least one reader in two hundred read a first-rate review, of a quality now unapproached'[1]—and their circulations were indeed remarkably high (the *Edinburgh* had in 1814 a circulation of 13,000; the *Quarterly* had between 12–14,000 in 1817–18; *Blackwood's* sold 10,000 copies of a single issue). But as competition in the market increased and the literate constituency extended, they themselves quickly ran into problems of the 'many' and the 'few', and the problems of whether they could lead or only reflect the public taste. And what happened during the Victorian period was that the homogeneous audience of common readers with uncommon interests began to splinter, as a much more socially varied reading public developed. The periodical remained importantly at the centre of cultural communications in the Victorian period (indeed it has been called *the* age of the periodical); the great arguments and currents of national debate are there and in many cases the great writing too. But there was a growing departmentalization of interest, along class and cultural lines. The 'reviewing' function, the function of containing the impulses and tendencies of thought in the culture, also became more difficult to sustain, though it survived well into this century and to a point survives in the few weekend reviews we have left. But towards the end of the century the pattern was changing radically, and literature was fading as a point of consensus, a base for cultural positivism. In our century, the typical literary periodical has not been a wide-circulation review with a strong literary character, and the general serious audience has lost its social distinctiveness. On the other hand, specialized serious literary periodicals have grown up within the mass-journalism pattern of modern written

[1] Denys Thompson, 'A Hundred Years of the Higher Journalism', *Scrutiny*, IV, i (June 1935), 25–34. And R. G. Cox, in the same journal, comments that they 'played a major part in creating for the writers of the age that informed, intelligent and critical public without which no literature can survive for very long, and which is so conspicuously lacking today'. R. G. Cox, 'The Great Reviews', *Scrutiny*, VI, 1 & 2 (June & September 1937). Circulation figures from R. D. Altick, *The English Common Reader*.

communications. They have obviously found new types of audi-
ence-groups, which themselves have changed quite considerably
in the course of the century.

   One decisive element in this cultural repatterning was the
rise of the 'little' magazine; and in this century there have been
thousands of these, many short-lived and often subsidized. They
have printed many of our most important writers, and they have
been aimed at various audiences—the intelligent general reader,
the intelligentsia, the fashionably smart public. But with the
decline in the central middle-class audience as a cohesive
grouping they all deserve the name of 'little'. Some have
emphasized their *avant-garde* tendencies and their links with
progressive movements like feminism or Marxism; some with
movements in the other arts, like painting (*Blast, Rhythm*, etc.),
or with broad intellectual tendencies like 'classicism' (*The
Criterion*) or agrarian socialism (*The Adelphi*). Others, particularly
more recently, have been directed at specific intellectual sectors
—teachers of English in schools or universities (*Critical Quarterly,
Essays in Criticism*) or the dissident underground. Up to the end
of the war there were a good number of journals appealing to the
cultivated and normally middle-class general reader (*The London
Mercury, Art and Letters*) but few of these survive, though their
functions are vestigially there in the weekend review sections of
the Sunday newspapers and in the weekly journals. A decisive
element in this change was the rise, in the later nineteenth
century, of a number of magazines, like the Pre-Raphaelite *Germ*
of the 1850s and the *Yellow Book* of the 1890s, which were self-
consciously and entirely literary and artistic, small-circulation
ventures appealing to minority audiences. When Ford Madox
Ford began his *English Review*, an important venture of which I
have already spoken, in 1908 he said: 'to imagine that a magazine
devoted to imaginative literature and technical criticism alone
would find more than a hundred readers was a delusion I in no
way had'. Ford took the path of making his review a mixture of
the old reviewing pattern and a semi-*avant-garde* magazine, and
when he lost control of it in 1910 it moved further in the former
direction. Other papers, faced with the same situation, made

themselves self-consciously 'little'. These, the true little magazines, have had enormous importance—first printing many of the
writers of the early part of the century that we now regard as
important, and containing most of the cultural-aesthetic debate.
They sharply reflected the conviction that the serious literary
audience had narrowed; and their function was often rather to
select, print and critically promote rather than to *circulate* their
writers. They were in fact the product of a sense of sharp
cultural stratification, but at the same time they created the
possibility of cultural acceptance of writers and tendencies
among a small group of peers and so the possibility of a broader
acceptance in the longer term.[1]

The heyday of little magazines in England was between about
1910 and 1920, when new movements were proliferating and a
new literary generation was emerging in circumstances different
from those of its predecessors. They were concerned to promote
not only themselves but a new aesthetic attitude, and this meant,
as Ezra Pound stressed, the creation of a critical environment,
pursued through debate and polemic. Most of these magazines
—*Rhythm* and *The Egoist* are important examples—were dependent on subsidies and on the voluntary activity of those who
worked for them. They themselves became intellectual foci and
centres of patronage, trying to pay their writers wherever
possible. Their modest circulations are an indication of their
specialism but not, of course, of their influence—for the names
they particularly promoted often gradually acquired, over
following decades, enormous prestige. A significant instance is
the path taken by *The Egoist*, a small fortnightly which began as a
feminist paper with the sponsorship of Harriet Shaw Weaver. It
allowed Ezra Pound to take over the literary section, and from
1914 on he used it to get into print important work of a non-
popular kind by T. S. Eliot, James Joyce and a number of
important experimental poets, English and American. Its audience
was always very small and when it ended in 1919 it had, according to Pound (who may have exaggerated the lowness of the

---

[1] For a further exploration of their importance, see J. Isaacs, *An Assessment of
Twentieth-Century Literature* (London, 1951).

figure), a readership of 90. But it had appealed to a predominantly advanced and intellectual audience and this laid the foundation for a future spread of influence; many of the writers who appeared there are now regarded as major figures. A number of other papers—like *Blast* and *Art and Letters*—acquired rather more fashionable success. But most of the considerable number of such ventures that appeared between 1910 and 1920 were irregular in publication and appeared for only a few issues, fading away for lack of funds, loss of interest, or because the progenitors had passed on to something new.

By the 1920s, the little-magazine pattern was well established, and we can see at work an attempt to bring in, side by side with it, a version of the twentieth-century literary review. Though these sometimes resembled the great reviews of the nineteenth century, most of which had by now disappeared, they were based on a different economy and a different audience. The three most important were *The Criterion*, which ran from 1922 to 1939 and was edited by T. S. Eliot; *The Adelphi*, edited by John Middleton Murry and existing from 1923 to 1955 (in its later days with other editors and interests); and *The Calendar of Modern Letters*, which ran from 1925 to 1927 under the editorship of Edgell Rickword and others. All three were in various ways sponsored periodicals, and ran into periods of financial difficulty; all three were at various times quarterlies and monthlies. They published —in various combinations—stories, poetry, reviews and literary criticism, and deliberately sought to create a climate of up-to-date critical debate, a literary context. The audience they sought was one that was a generally educated one, rather than *avant garde*; but they did a great deal to develop the reputations of writers who had earlier published in the little magazines, to extend the aesthetic debate of those magazines, and to promote new writers. In this they represented a conscious stratum in the literary scene, and as we shall see they can be markedly distinguished from other ventures of a more middlebrow kind. *The Criterion*, the most substantial and influential, printed most of the major authors of the decades, including not only Eliot, Pound and other important figures of his generation but also Auden and his contemporaries, many important European writers, and a number of important critics. It had a circulation of 800 (most of it abroad) which dropped to 600 at the end; it hence combined considerable literary influence and prestige with a very low readership. Its demise in 1939 brought from Eliot the comment that: 'For the immediate future, perhaps for a long way ahead, the continuity of culture may have to be maintained by a very small number of people indeed. . . . It will not be the large organs of opinion, or the old periodicals, it must be the small and obscure papers and reviews, those which are hardly ready by anyone but their own contributors, that will keep critical thought alive, and encourage authors of original talent.' Murry's *Adelphi* was a conscious opposite to *The Criterion*, defining its commitment as 'romantic' in opposition to Eliot's 'classicism', and it too printed many important authors and much semi-philosophical literary debate. Cheaper than *The Criterion*, it had, in its early years as a shilling monthly, a circulation of 4,200. When in 1927 it became, for a time, a half-crown quarterly this dropped to 1,700, reverting towards the original figure when it reassumed monthly appearance. *The Calendar of Modern Letters* was more specifically literary-critical in character, and was indeed a forerunner of *Scrutiny*. Beginning as a shilling monthly, it had the (high) circulation of 7–8,000, but this gradually slipped down to 2–3,000 and then, when it became a half-crown quarterly, to 1,000.

These were (especially in the light of the expansion of the national population and extended literary) very different circumstances from those of the great nineteenth-century reviews, and they meant that the papers were consciously minority ventures appealing to minority tastes and standards. They were 'institutional' ventures in that, unlike the earlier little magazines, they sought permanence and attempted to act as magisterial cultural institutions. They clearly did a great deal to define taste and assert standards of judgment, and to keep intellectual thought and evaluation alive around a literary centre. Just as, if we want to see how the literary reputations of some of our most important writers began, and in what sort of climate they were made, we

P

have to turn to these earlier little magazines, so if we want to
understand how modern critical attitudes emerged, how modern
thought about literature developed, we must turn to these
reviews. They were in their different ways self-consciously
élitist and, though the nature of their audiences must be a matter
for surmise, we may assume that it was that of a well-educated
intelligentsia, probably largely metropolitan, or possibly rooted
in schools and universities and hence likely to influence the
tastes of others. The theme of many of these journals was the
debasement of cultural standards. Their cultural preferences
were a mixture of the radical and the preservative, and they therefore felt compelled to speak out—often from very different
perspectives—on socio-cultural matters. In the 1930s, their
enterprise was notably extended by *Scrutiny*, which ran from
1932 to 1953 and was particularly remarkable among minority
journals in that it paid its way and held a considerable circulation.
Edited by F. R. Leavis and others, it was a conscious attempt to
appeal to and sustain minority literary standards by devoting
itself to literary-critical matters alone. Its audience was fairly
clearly defined; essentially among university and school teachers.
It maintained a persistent debate on the cultural issue, attacking
the destruction of literary standards and the domination in the
literary scene of a metropolitan 'socio-literary élite'.

What, perhaps, it most crucially represents is the attempt to
forge a conscious alliance between literary creation and the
teaching of it, in a period when the study of literature was
expanding and changing. It saw the health of a literary-critical
environment as closely linked with the health of society itself;
it centralized a cultural vision drawn from the arts; and it urged,
in a way that had not been so strongly urged since the nineteenth
century, the liberal function of artistic activity in society as a
function of absolute human value, a moral force. *Scrutiny* was
more concerned with creating an environment than with sponsoring writers directly. But it undoubtedly had a considerable effect
on English writing. It helped to enfranchise a much more provincial audience for literature (while it is fairly apparent that
most of the other journals mentioned more or less assumed a

metropolitan clientèle) and had a very strong educational dimension. By the postwar period, it had created a climate, a mood of provincial 'rebellion', in which many new writers grew up. So, indirectly, it *did* sponsor writing (though it is a testament to the paper's commitment to standards that these new writers obviously failed to satisfy *Scrutiny*'s critics and reviewers!).

There were in the 1930s a number of important magazines sponsoring new writers and movements—notably Geoffrey Grigson's *New Verse*, John Lehmann's *New Writing* and *Contemporary Poetry and Prose*. Because the battle for a new literature had been more or less won, they were not 'little' in quite the ways of the earlier small reviews. They introduced a generation of writers distinct from the previous one; but these were usually less innovative technically and were, furthermore, obvious inheritors of many features of the climate created by their predecessors. The cultural despair of Eliot, the unease of Pound or Lawrence with contemporary commercial civilization, the sense of participating in the advanced European intellectual tradition that marked Bloomsbury—these elements survived into the Auden-Isherwood-Greene generation but were mixed with a much more predominantly left-wing bias. Their very specific social involvement tended to make them less arcane, and they never acquired the aura of difficulty associated with the works of writers like Joyce or Eliot. And since too they attempted to use neo-popular forms—from ballad and the detective story to reportage—they were structurally less remote from their potential audience. None the less the circulation of these reviews, often of pro-proletarian or surrealist bias, remained small until the war, when there was a remarkable expansion in their readership. For instance, John Lehmann's monthly *Penguin New Writing*, an extension of *New Writing* but with the resources and cheap costing of Penguin paperbacks behind it, is said to have reached a circulation as high as 50,000, dropping off in the post-war period. Cyril Connolly's monthly literary magazine *Horizon*, an attractive and well-produced paper that started around the outbreak of war in 1939, printed both appreciative essays and also plenty of good writing and criticism, and kept well abreast of prevailing literary tendencies, also had a good war, and still held a circulation of 7,500 when it ended in 1949. There were quite a number of other very effective papers over this period, and Eliot's gloom must at this time have seemed premature. After the war, however, came a simultaneous drop in readership and rise in printing costs by which many small-circulation ventures were hit. This caused large-scale casualties, and over these next years *Scrutiny*, *Horizon*, *Penguin New Writing*, *The Adelphi* and *Life and Letters Today* all went. The number of movements also declined, and the interest of the general intelligentsia in literature seemed to decline. This was generally a bleak period in literature, though one or two important ventures—particularly John Lehmann's *London Magazine* (never quite as successful as his earlier ventures) and Irving Kristol and Stephen Spender's *Encounter* (less a literary than a general intellectual review)—did emerge, usually with heavy backing. The academic audience had the *Critical Quarterly* (which published much good poetry) and *Essays in Criticism*; but so obvious was the lack of good reviews that American journals like *Partisan Review*, *Kenyon Review* and *Hudson Review* were circulated in England to fill the gap. Though some of the newer writers appeared in good small ventures like *Listen*, *Mandrake*, *Nine*, *Stand*, and *Transatlantic Review*, there were few effective literary centres. That situation has continued until recently. The state of the scene today is hard to determine, since there has been a revival of *avant-gardism* and quite a number of small-circulation ventures have pushed through. But they are too scattered to present anything like an active literary scene, they have not shown any direct concern with the creation of literary standards, and the level of self-consciously literary action is not remarkably high. Not for a very long time indeed—and this applies to the entire postwar period—has the literary scene, as represented and activated by periodicals, been so thin.

In addition, it takes more than serious reviews or *avant-garde* magazines to sustain a literary climate. Beneath them there has long been another level of literary action—the middlebrow papers, concerned with reviewing, or with gossip and more popular, perhaps even more amateur, writing. These show an even more striking history of postwar decline. There are many examples, but a famous one is the *London Mercury*, a popular literary paper started in 1919 by J. C. Squire, with a circulation around 10,000, in due course rising to double that. It was not always very serious, though it had its serious moments, taking up with Auden, Spender and Isherwood in the 1930s, for example. In 1935 it linked up with another similar paper, *The Bookman*, which had been in existence since 1891. By 1939 it was itself incorporated, into the (rather better) *Life and Letters Today*, which had begun in 1928. Three important literary periodicals therefore disappeared when the entire venture collapsed in 1950. At a slightly lower and more gossipy level still was *John O'London's*, a weekly paper of literary comment, which lapsed in the 1950s, to recover a vestigial existence later as part of *Time and Tide*. If one turns to the weekend reviews, the story is similar: a declining number, often involving the consolidation of several papers into one, and a similar reduction in the social dialogue. In these cases there has also been a marked shift away from literary discussion in the survivors (*The New Statesman*, *The Spectator*), with the last vestiges of a once-active scene in literary journalism crowded into reviewing-pages that make more and more space for television and popular music. The same story can be traced in the newspapers; and even the emergence of large magazine sections in Sunday newspapers like the *Observer*, the *Sunday Times* and the *Sunday Telegraph* has not really compensated for the variety, range, level of interest and general fascination once held by books and writers. Nor can it really be said that the literary dialogue in society has moved to other media, like radio and television. It is there to a point, but only to a point. The fact of the matter is that it has, on the one hand, consolidated into a few ventures and, on the other, diminished in range and in the space given to it. The blackest period of all has been the period since the war.[1]

Looking back over the last two centuries in the fortunes of

---

[1] A similar argument could be made about the theatre. In 1900 there were about 400 theatres and music-halls in the country; now there are about 200, and the opening of new ones does not check the loss of old. As with literature, it could be argued that the cultural activities are shifting into television. Drama is a more obvious case than the other literary arts; the fact remains that there is a tendency for the arts to lose their identity *as* arts.

the literary periodical, then, we can make a few deductions. The first is that, while it has long tended to reveal stratification in the reading audience, that stratification has very much increased in this century. At the same time, however, this new periodical complex, developing around the turn of the century, brought about a lively and vigorous literary scene. The pattern was largely one in which small magazines became the voices of new movements in literature and criticism (around World War I, when they represented the new waves of writers; in the twenties, when they represented a new critical attitude; and in the thirties, when they promoted writers of advanced literary and political tendencies). But the issues and reputations that grew up there frequently penetrated less self-consciously artistic journals, and general literary and intellectual debate. Even when they did not, the more middlebrow journals maintained an active literary interest, selling books, reviewing, providing literary gossip and news for audiences of fair size. In addition, the pattern included a number of small-circulation reviews (like *The Criterion*) which linked literature with a variety of other intellectual interests, and so maintained a lively dialogue about life and society from a predominantly literary perspective.[1] Though many of these magazines existed precariously, they existed in variety and numbers. But at various points there were periods of marked collapse, sometimes but not always compensated for by the rise of new ventures tapping lively new sectors in the cultural scene. However, the overall effect has been one of an increasing diminution, starting in the 1930s and particularly marked in the 1950s, when inflation and socio-cultural change combined to weaken the whole structure. The phenomenon that began with the increased fragmentation of the literary-cultural audience ended with its virtual disappearance. Partly what has gone, of course, is a whole middlebrow set of functions— providing relief and dream, engaging people's interests in characters and in the personalities of writers—which have often, in

---

[1] Not of course that the highbrow-middlebrow stratification seemed a happy cultural pattern at the time: see Q. D. Leavis, *Fiction and the Reading Public*.

fact, been taken up by other media. But with that has also gone a specifically literary contribution to the ongoing intellectual debate in society, a large number of important outlets for serious writers, a social community for writers, and finally, and perhaps most important, an audience formed and shaped for the writer to sense and to appeal to. In addition to economic factors, which are crucially important in the situation, a few other reasons for this fading can be suggested. One is that the reviews and magazines from the beginning of the century into the 1930s took their momentum from the modern movement in literature and then, gradually, from the task of reconciling it with more traditional cultural attitudes; by the 1950s the traditions both of the new and the old were declining. Writing as a topic for interested discussion and criticism was drifting out of society and into the academy, the intelligent common reader giving way to the literary specialist: reviewers and audiences gave way to teachers and students. The 'professionalization' of reading is one factor; but it still fails to explain why an increasingly educated and literate society should become so remarkable lacking in literary journals. A further reason is surely a shift of intelligent discussion in society should become so remarkably lacking in literary journals. in sociology, in politics, in economics. In short, the pattern seems to indicate a realignment in the character of intelligent debate in society.

Does this mean that literary activity itself has diminished? Hardly: in these days we are in no sense short of literary production, though it has shifted from periodicals to other places. One is to the book; another is to the mass-media. The writer today is not excluded; his opportunities for success are, as we have seen earlier, quite good. Indeed it may be that precisely because success today is more immediate, especially for writers who are novel or outrageous, that the slower process of making one's way through small magazines is less necessary. What has weakened is the literary *context*—the way writing put its roots down in society. The periodicals had two main functions. One was to make writing coherent, to create a critical, evaluative environment, a professional dialogue; there are few signs of this in

England just now. The other was to maintain a self-conscious dialogue with readers; and today the contemporary reading-public is not really exposed to, or responsive to, an effective debate about literature and literary views of life. There is little evidence of a value-consensus around literature; and the writer competes for attention with all the other happenings of our society, from news to politics. Today writers and audiences probably have less grounds for community of interest and values, less homogeneity of viewpoint, than ever—which is, precisely, one reason why there is no traditional and engrained hostility to new work. With the slipping away of an environment of a certain cultural stability formed by the magazines and reviews in their plurality (the reviews themselves were often short-lived, but the broad continuity of the serious forum for debate and discussion tended until lately to transcend the losses), with the waning of the atmosphere of literary belief, value and concern which T. S. Eliot in 1939 was calling 'the continuity of culture', the writer has lost a coherent literary community to appeal to, test himself against, draw his sense of standards from. Today his problems have changed; they are not problems of gaining access but of gaining authority, of claiming any real significance for his work, of formulating his aims, purposes and creative career, of finding an environment in which his best work can be valued. In other words, writing tends now to become part of the bland overall environment of the mass-culture situation itself—even when its final appeal is that it be *not* assessed in those terms. The new environment and the new relationships of literature are a good deal more fluid and evanescent, less open to the impact of the individual creative identity. The consequences are not quantitative, affecting the *amount* of writing; they are qualitative, affecting the *excellence* of writing. Writers are uncertain about their values, their audience and their chances of survival as remembered artists; and literary art now tends to become either a version of history or documentary or a fictive game. There is an environment for the arts, in the expansion of leisure and books discussed in the next chapter. But it is a much more impersonal environment than before. And in its impersonality it is not the discriminating environment that writers have long regarded as something necessary to put them in relation to common experience, to stimulate their sense of value, and to encourage their best work.

III

My basic theme in this chapter has been with one aspect—but a very important one—of the makings of a culture: the forming and repatterning of the literary community in society as its own cultural environment. The topic reaches into many areas—into the ways writers form and reform groups, make relationships both personal and professional among themselves, and acquire a sense of community.[1] But the periodical is a particularly interesting index, since it shows the relationships between literary groupings and audiences; and it is, in the end, in meaningful relationships with audiences that such 'communities' are best conceived as existing. But at different times the audience may come to be seen as an encouragement to art or as a threat to it— just as the important need may seem to be to change the nature of the literary community or to stabilize it. Modern literature has normally oscillated considerably between both views. Looking back over the last hundred years of English literature, we can see both of these efforts being made, and in rough historical sequence.

By 1870, the general impetus was towards creating change in the literary community and towards severing many established links between writers and audience. This impulse goes back well beyond 1870 and is there in the Romantics, concerned as they were about the way in which literature had a double audience:

---

[1] There has been surprisingly little study of the character of modern literary communities, though one good example is J. K. Johnstone's *The Bloomsbury Group* (London, 1954). Of course there are innumerable memoirs, autobiographies and biographies, and some interesting fictional treatments (Aldous Huxley's early novels, for example).

of the 'few', and the 'many'. The 'many' were a danger both to the standards of established art and the making of new: 'The public taste hangs like a millstone around the neck of all original genius that does not conform to established and exclusive models', complained William Hazlitt in his *Lectures on the English Poets* (1818). But by about 1870 this cultural concern had identified in the audience not two strata but three: a tiny precious few, a large body of middlebrow taste and a vulgarized general taste. The Foolish Audience was essentially the middle rank, who constituted the dominant weight of taste. The attacks of writers like Pound and Yeats on the traditional bad taste of the nation are less concerned with vulgarity than its engrained morality and traditionalism, its incapacity to take art seriously as art.[1] In the face of what Arnold Bennett called the 'gigantic temperamental dullness' of the British public, courting any form of popularity could seem an obvious danger, a potential source of contamination. And the cultural need was for criticism—what Henry James called 'discrimination on other than infantile lines'— which would invigorate the environment of writers and change the general taste as well. 'Time is ripe for the forging of a weapon of criticism, and for the emphatic assertion of literary standards,' said Harold Monro in an editorial comment to the first number of his *Poetry Review* in January, 1912. But the true source of such criticism could only be writers themselves: 'It is certain,' said Ezra Pound, 'that the present chaos will endure until the Art of poetry has been preached down the amateur gullet . . .'[2] In fact, of course, a vigorous artistic environment did spring up; the appropriate revaluations were made and circulated, the new aesthetic effectively promoted. By the 1920s and 1930s a large-scale change in intellectual taste had obviously occurred, while, with the spread of magazines and of English as a university subject, criticism itself had become something like a growth industry. The task now was one of consolidation, to find a place

[1] For details of these attacks, see Chaps. 1 and 2 of C. K. Stead, *The New Poetic: Yeats to Eliot* (London, 1964).

[2] Ezra Pound, 'A Retrospect,' in *Literary Essays of Ezra Pound*, ed. T. S. Eliot (London, 1954).

for the new art in the broad stream of civilization; it was also one of education, to reach an audience and change its sensibility.

What now became apparent was that the audience for literature was itself diminishing and taking on a different stratification. For, with the centralization and democratization of communications, the significant sector in the cultural audience was becoming not High as opposed to Middle and Low, but High as opposed to Mass. The critical environment of literature now seemed to be the one effective alternative to a completely unselective cultural situation in which standards were not so much different as absent. The urgencies of cultural humanism therefore seemed to become very much greater in the inter-war years (though, when the real massification of English culture occurred in the postwar period, it became extremely hard to assert). And to some extent this produced a divergence of function, between humanist critics and writers who might or might not sympathize with the issues they raised. By the 1950s, this situation had developed further. The critical function had now largely passed to specialist literary critics. The writer was in effect caught between the professionally specialist literary-cultural audience focused in and around education and universities, and an increasingly unseamed and indeterminate general audience of ill-defined tastes and preferences. It is possible that today we are at the beginning of a new oscillation, one in which the public funds of high culture are themselves grown exhausted, and in which writers may have to find the force for their activity within or around the world of mass-culture. And since it is undoubtedly true that mass-culture enshrines many remnants from the older patterns of cultural stratification, this is possible. What does seem clear is that the strong sense of cultural stratification that ran through the cultural debate a few years back has tended to fade, partly for political reasons; equality is more fashionable than excellence. But with it has also tended to fade many benefits for the writer. However bad the stratification was, it did involve a sense of standards and hierarchy; it involved bodies of internal communicants, and it involved a sense of a cultural order in which standards and serious literature were formed at the top and percolated down to the bottom. The model was too simple,[1] but it did enable writers to localize a particular audience or constituency, to feel the standards by which they might be judged, in a way that is a way that is diminishingly possible.

[1] And, as Raymond Williams points out in his fascinating analysis *Communications* (London, revised edition 1968), to which I shall refer more fully later, such communication models tend to create and reinforce the situation they seem to describe.

CHAPTER X

The Institutions of Literary Culture:
The Book and the Media

I

The literary periodical can reveal a great deal to us about the particular communities, small or large, in which literature has part of its social existence. But it is not of course the most central form of literary expression and communication in our society. That place is held by the book. Writing may be communicated to us in a number of forms, from privately circulated manuscript to public reading or theatrical performance. But since the seventeenth century most important works of literature—even those for periodical publication or stage performance—have sought and been given the status of printed book form. They have become part of the Gutenberg Galaxy, and so have acquired a form of permanence and long-term survival, a form which has allowed the past to persist into the present and for our creative inheritance to be stored. With the book goes the signed, personal style; with it also goes the library; and with it too goes those subtleties of reading and response we call appreciation or literary criticism—a whole body of humanistic activities. For several centuries, then, the book has been *the* central literary medium; and though today it has been seriously challenged in various of its functions by other media—in its function of communication by radio, film and television; in its function as a form of copying and repetition of existence by new processes like Xerox and microfilm—it remains, at least for the moment, the main agency of literary presentation. It has, of course, been argued that we are now in a stage in history when the 'book' sequence is coming to an end, and man is moving beyond his commitment to linear print; he desires a more visual immersion in experience and art.[1] But, although a number of the subsidiary functions of the book have been challenged or taken over, it seems doubtful whether it can be totally superseded. It is hard to think of an object more easily carried and stored, as easily retrieved for further consultation or study, and with the same elements of permanence, that can have the same subtlety of content. Equally in literary terms there are few media as much open to the presence of the writer's individual mind, art and signature, capable of such refinement and sophistication, and equally open to the reader's own time, place, pace and intensity of consumption. Certainly it still holds an enormous place in our culture, its use is now vastly increasing, and it does not seem too much to say that serious literary art in its familiar sense is completely and profoundly bound up with its fortunes.

Even so, the book itself is open to many uses in society, and these uses keep changing. At one time it was a selective form of communication, in an era in which literacy was a limited and precious possession; today in our society we are all ostensibly literate, though it does not mean that we all read, much less buy, books. The conventions associated with it change; once largely assumed to be a moralistic instrument, it is now largely thought to be an instrument of instruction or entertainment. In more minor ways norms shift: in the last century novels were of great length, whereas now the familiar convention is that they are about 75,000 words long. Similar changes have taken place in the production-appearance of books, as in the current shift towards a predominance of paperbacks, with their implications of short-term survival in use as opposed to the hardback's association of long-term, possibly elegant, survival in libraries. Above all, of course, the larger number of books are not in fact literary. The literary sector is a very important aspect of the book considered as a medium or as an institution; but it is a very variable part of the total book-market. Once it was possible

---

[1] The most famous version of this not entirely new argument is of course by Marshall McLuhan, in *The Gutenberg Galaxy* (Toronto and London, 1962) and *Understanding Media: The Extensions of Man* (New York and London, 1964).

to produce books in large quantities at reasonably low prices, the book also became a commodity—an object of trade, merchandized in particular ways to the end of bringing profits, in the long or the short run, to a publisher and (sometimes) to a writer as well. The idea of the book has increasingly come to involve the idea of a publisher, who selects what he prints, sells it as best he can, and functions as an editorial and an economic middleman, in an intricate operation that requires a written work at one end of its activity, a reading public at the other and a whole convention of communication in the middle. As we have seen, the conventions involve matters of tone, language, style and communal experience, which is to say culture; and they also involve various institutions (bookshops, schools and universities, libraries public and private, and the simple fact of literacy itself). To this complex, a writer must relate; and, however original he may feel himself to be, his actual possibilities for radically changing or transforming it in the large scale are relatively slight—even though the growth of literature has much to do with the smaller changes in culture and context that are available to him. In the period with which we are dealing, the whole nature of the book as an institution of communication *has* been transformed quite considerably—partly by writers exploring relationships among new means and new audiences, but also, of course, by many conditions quite outside their particular control. The comments that follow have all kinds of implications for the fortunes of writers, and the nature of the works they write —but I have deliberately kept them general, so that the wider context can become visible.[1]

[1] My comments about the book as a convention or institution can be further illuminated by looking at Robert Escarpit, *The Book Revolution* (London, 1966). Escarpit distinguishes three sorts of book: the book as thing to be consumed, the functional book, and the literary book, and gives an interesting international account of their different formats and economics in the present era of increasing industrialization in publishing. (See also Richard Hoggart's interesting comments on it in 'The New Battle of the Books', *New Society* (August 11, 1966).)

II

I have already suggested that the change in the texture and nature of literature in the late nineteenth century coincided with, and in many ways was deeply connected with, changes in the pattern of the book-market itself, changes which were changes in the entire pattern of social communication. They set writers a whole new climate, and a whole new set of difficulties, to explore; and in exploring these they evolved styles, tones and assumptions which cut deep into the quality and flavour of the words they wrote. In the late-nineteenth-century climate there began patterns of authorial financing, book-merchandizing, lines of taste and modes of approach to the reader which have, many of them, continued until today. But beyond these, still, lay changes in the reading public that were not simply the result of changes in ways of writing books or of publishing them. They came from much deeper changes in social organization and economics, from profound shifts in social behaviour and in the growth and urbanization of the population of England, from alterations in the level of education and awareness in the public which brought about new kinds of dialogue and communication, and of *stratification*, in society. One of the striking features in all this is the proliferation of uses which, in this situation, the book acquired. It became a form of use of growing leisure; it offered a means to alleviate the commuting railway journeys of the new suburban classes; it served as a means of escape from a limiting environment; it afforded a way to education and self-improvement. With the coming of a wider range of media in the 1930s and 1950s, some of this range of use has become less visible; but we might take the change in the book, along with that in journalism, as the significant media explosion of the last century.

The beginning of the nineteenth century saw the beginning of the book-market that was fully independent of patronage, the writer moving at this point into the environment of the book-trade. Publishing at this time was an important and expanding industry, and many of the patterns evolving then were to become fixed as the normal pattern of publishing practice into the second half of the century. Partly because of taxes and partly because of the style of the profession, the book at this time was a high-priced object, and the normal outlet for it was the circulating library of a fairly expensive kind. The tradition of cheap pamphlet publishing persisted, but on the whole literary expression was directed towards a reasonably coherent and socially central audience. The main forms of literary publication were the three-decker novel costing a guinea-and-a-half and the guinea volume of poems. What was apparent was that there was a possibility of spilling over beyond this audience, as writers like Scott and others saw. And as paper grew cheaper, machine-runs grew faster, and the steam-press became available, the movement towards cheaper books took on force. Many had sought it, for commercial, educational and broader social reasons. But around and after the middle of the century a period of innovation and acceleration in publishing brought about a whole new group of uses and meanings for the printed book. Part of this innovation—one aspect of which was a more direct appeal to the audience, the embracing of a larger responsive community—was sought by the schemes of writers themselves: Dickens, Thackeray and George Henry Lewes are particularly notable examples of men who at once extended the scope of their own work and that of publication practice generally in this way. But of course many of the changes occurred within the structure of publishing, book-borrowing and buying, and the publics themselves. Though the book in this period is particularly associated with a dominantly middle-class audience, we must not overlook the range of its use. Mechanics' Institutes and Bible Classes alike were dependent on books, and the literacy which enabled men to read the Bible and religious works provided the means for reading many other things as well.

It was, however, in the second half of the century that the most remarkable expansion occurred. The number of books rose remarkably: the annual number of titles in 1850 was 2,600 and in 1901 6,044. The kinds of book published became enormously more varied. In 1870 religious works still, as in the past, formed the largest class of books published. One of the main

Q

beneficiaries was the novel, particularly the entertainment novel. In 1870 there were only 381 new novels; by 1886 969 novels appeared, exceeding religious works; and in 1899 1,825 novels came out in the course of the year. This was accompanied by, and partly created by, a steep decline in the price of books. Publishing was becoming more centralized and efficient in distribution; the spread of bookselling outlets, notably in railway stations and news agencies, encouraged cheap large reprints; the spread of education and leisure alike encouraged inexpensive light reading and also classics and 'student' editions. Altogether the reading public was undergoing a considerable expansion in numerical and in class terms, under opportunities deriving from rising income, increasing leisure and a growing literacy.[1] The situation encouraged a much greater competition within the book-trade itself, especially as it saw the implications of that new constituency which did not simply borrow books but bought them. The books most affected were reprints and new editions of existing works, especially those which were free of copyright; these could be run off in large numbers as an overspill from the original pattern of publishing. But more and more that original pattern was forced to change. The three-decker novel, the guinea volume of poems, the library edition all came under pressure from cheaper publishing. One special point of pressure was the 'yellow-back' railway novel, which developed in the 1840s and 1850s and consisted predominantly of popular reprints, selling for 1s. or 1s. 6d. This radical division between the cost of a new work and a reprint (not uncommonly a reprint pirated from American authors without copyright protection) was an obvious danger to new writers and to new literature, though it took to the end of the century to conclude the reign of the library three-decker. But the older, more expensive circulating libraries were themselves under pressure, from new cheaper ventures ranging from Mudie's in 1843 to Boots' Book-Lovers

[1] Richard Altick (*The English Common Reader* (Chicago and London, 1957)) shows that male literacy rose from 63.3% of the population in 1841 to 92.2% in 1900. The rise was fairly steady, and the Education Act of 1870 did not, as is often supposed, step up the rate of growth remarkably.

Library founded in 1900. The Public Library system grew from 1850 onward.[1] And cheap books competed with the libraries themselves. From the late 1860s the 6d. paperbacked reprint and the 2s. 6d. or 3s. 6d. bound reprint, of major classics and popular novels alike, became standard; and in the price-wars of the 1870s and 1880s these prices got lower.[2] Non-copyright works got down as low as 3d.; and in 1896 Newnes started their famous Penny Library; Dickens's works were even given away with tea. The cheap book was now a staple of the market.

Behind these changes lay, of course, a variety of new uses for the book and reading in a changing society, in which various forms of imaginative literature were serving an increasing entertainment function. The new patterns had the effect of driving a wedge between good literature and bad on a price basis, so hardening the levels of taste. In addition, the sheer bulk of popular reading increasingly posed the threat of a collapse of selective taste, as Edmund Gosse said:

One danger which I have long foreseen from the spread of democratic sentiment, is that of the tradition of literary taste, the canons of literature, being reversed by a popular vote. Up to the present time the mass of educated or semi-educated persons, who form the vast majority of readers, though they cannot and do not appreciate the classics of their race, have been content to acknowledge their traditional supremacy.[3]

This had been a growing worry throughout the century (and indeed before), but it acquired an increased importance as the best-sellers, largely popular sensationalism remote from any literary merit, dominated the market. One way of preventing this sharp separation of taste seemed to be that of breaking the dominance of the libraries over new literature, which kept up prices and created highly selective audiences. Even the better cheap books were normally reprints of classics out of copyright,

[1] Though the levy for public libraries was first permitted in 1850, by 1896 only 334 districts had levied a library rate.

[2] One interesting feature of the change in presentational techniques at the end of the nineteenth century is that the new cloth-bound editions could, through cheap colour-printing techniques, have highly illustrated covers (e.g. to editions of Henty and Ballantyne), often bearing little relation to the content.

[3] Edmund Gosse, 'What Is a Great Poet?' in *Questions at Issue* (London, 1889).

or of works well past the date of their original publication. Hence they did little to finance contemporary writers. Indeed some writers who wished to reach wider audiences found themselves compelled to sacrifice royalties in order to do so. One of the consequences of this was that the reading of contemporary serious writing remained in the hands of a minority who shaped this particular area of taste, while the more general taste was formed on the basis of large-scale commercial success. And this was of course encouraged by the growing secularity of the broader reading public, the lower middle classes, for instance, who were now markedly less concerned with literature in its dominantly moral or improving aspects. That certainly, was one of the reasons for the expanding fascination of imaginative literature, and especially in the growth of a large subliterature of the lush best-selling kind. The cultivated middle classes may have dominated taste in terms of better writing, but they were only one constituency among several, each of which seemed to be acquiring its own brand of writing. They may have dominated literature; they did not dominate books. By the 1890s cheap publishing had broken through to command the market and, as Richard Altick comments, 'the common reader in the last days of Victoria was more amply supplied with books than ever before'. But the variety and stratification of the books was striking, with a marked gap between serious and popular imaginative writing and a declining commercial basis for the former. In fact the serious writer found it difficult to make a living; the conditions of George Gissing's *New Grub Street* had come to prevail. The dominant basis of writing was commercial, supplying a popular commodity at a popular price. The serious writer, though, now found his following small; and it was hard for him to acquire a publisher, earn a living, or discover an environment in which he could preserve his best gifts. More than ever before, his work had become minority work.[1]

In the early years of this century, the price of books levelled

---

[1] Data throughout this section drawn largely from Altick, *The English Common Reader*; Q. D. Leavis, *Fiction and the Reading Public*; and Raymond Williams, *The Long Revolution*. All should be consulted to extend this brief sketch—especially as their work contains interesting differences of interpretation.

and the writer's situation improved somewhat. If one checks the advertising endpapers of books of this period, one can see prices were still very low. The staple of the expanding market in new hardbound fiction was the six-shilling novel, though it was still sold largely to libraries. There were shilling bound volumes of *belles lettres*; and in 1907, to the consternation of the book-trade, Nelson and Collins introduced 7d. clothbound editions of *copyright* works, reprinting fiction like Wells's and Bennett's. Bennett complained that the hardbound novel at 6s. was still over-priced, and needed to be reduced to extend the market in new work.[1] Ford Madox Hueffer, on the other hand, pointed out that novelists were much underpaid; that cheap books encouraged publishers to stick to their safe and popular authors; that the sale of an average novel could be as low as 1,000 copies; and that the effect of price-reduction was to work against the system whereby publishers sponsored the better, low-selling books which were the staple of literature from the profits of best-sellers—the Henry Jameses that compensated for the Marie Corellis, the poetry that balanced the documentary novel. 'The world, in fact, is too much with us,' Hueffer said. 'It is with us to such an extent that non-commercial writing is almost an impos-sibility to-day.'[2] It was undoubtedly this situation which en-couraged the confessed self-limitation, the specialized commit-ment to art, of the *avant-gardists*. Yet the new situation un-doubtedly released many new literary energies. The reign of the expensive library-novel—the three-decker—had ended in the 1890s, largely as a result of attacks by writers (like George Moore, in *Literature at Nurse* (1885)) complaining not only about the price but the censorious principles of selection. This broke the gap between old and new writing; and not only the novel's circulation but its content expanded. It was more than the ending of a mere form of publication. 'Actually,' said Holbrook Jackson,[3]

---

[1] Arnold Bennett, 'The Sevenpennies', in *Books and Persons* (London, 1917).

[2] Ford Madox Hueffer, 'The Two Shilling Novel' and 'English Literature of To-day' in *The Critical Attitude* (London, 1911).

[3] Holbrook Jackson, *The Eighteen Nineties* (London, 1913). He quotes Rudyard Kipling's verses called 'The Three Decker':
'We asked no social questions—we pumped no hidden shame—
We never talked obstetrics when the Little Stranger came . . .'

'it was the capitulation of a type of novel: the old sentimental
lending-library novel of polite romantic atmosphere and crudely
happy endings; the novel which was guaranteed to tax no brain
by thought and to vex no code of morals by revolutionary suggestions . . .' The consequence was not only cheaper fiction; it was
the coming of new *types* of fiction which introduced radical
themes, and took newly realistic or experimental forms, 'with
the ultimate result,' said Jackson, 'of increasing the number of
novel readers beyond all bounds.' There was certainly a large
expansion in the book market in the following decade: by 1913
the annual number of titles had doubled since 1901, to 12,379.
This was not only the result of the growth of the novel; social and
political reading expanded too. As Holbrook Jackson also points
out, the 1890s had seen the expansion of two different types of
culture, that of the Yellow Press and that of the *Yellow Book*. The
former went in the direction of realism and muckraking, the
latter of sensibility and aestheticism; both, however, shared in
common a sensationalist, excitable, exploratory mood. But
whereas the former tended to move away from literature and
towards a popular appeal, the latter tended towards a coterie audience. And in publishing the former impulse relied increasingly
on the cheap book, while the latter tended towards small-press
elegance, fine printing and illustrated editions. The market
happily bore both, apparently: small publishing houses like
those of John Lane and Elkin Matthews throve in the period, as
did the small-circulation little magazine ventures and bookshops like Harold Monro's famous Poetry Bookshop, with its
associated publishing enterprises. As Hueffer points out in his
essays in *The Critical Attitude*, the market was precariously
balanced between the literary and the commercial situation.[1]

And just as the market was, so was the writer. The apparently
expanding audience gave him the possibility of courts of appeal
beyond conventional middle-class taste, reaching below it into
lower middle-class improving sensibility, or into the 'cultured'
audience moving onward with the more startling writers: 'In
those days, as in these,' said Frank Swinnerton, writing in 1935 in

[1] Hueffer, op. cit.

The Georgian Literary Scene, 'the play and the novel were the chief recreations of those who considered themselves cultured. At the beginning of the Georgian age it was the correct thing to see or read Shaw's plays or to read Wells's books.'[1] And writers like Wells obviously delighted in the situation: 'The last decade of the nineteenth century was an extraordinarily favourable time for new writers and my individual good luck was set in the luck of a whole generation of aspirants,' he wrote, '. . . New books were being demanded and fresh authors were in request. Below and above alike there was opportunity. More public, more publicity, more publishers and more patronage.'[2] If the economic pressures were considerable, it was, as we have already seen, a period remarkably productive of writers and forms of expression. The centre of the audience, and the mainstream of publishing, was still focused around or upon middle-class taste. 'The crowd I see in [bookshops] is the prosperous crowd, the crowd which grumbles at income tax and pays it,' said Arnold Bennett, remarking, too, that these 'top million' in society were the determinants of, and an encumbrance upon, literary taste.[3] But if indeed the audience was 'mediocre', it was obviously possible for the writer to extend beyond many of its assumptions, and to find support among readers and publishers for doing so, as Bennett's and Wells's own success shows. In that undertaking, he may on the one hand risk his artistic standards by moving in the direction of journalism, or risk his audience by moving in the direction of art. But the literary ferment of the time clearly

---

[1] Frank Swinnerton, *The Georgian Literary Scene* (London, 1935).

[2] H. G. Wells, *Experiment in Autobiography* (2 vols., London, 1934).

[3] Arnold Bennett, *Books and Persons*. Bennett constantly deplored this audience for its 'mediocrity' and 'blindness to beauty', and also because it exerted obvious moral restriction over literature:

'As sure as ever a novelist endeavours to paint a complete picture of life in this honest, hypocritical country of bad restaurants and good women; as sure as he ever hints that all is not for the best in the best of all possible islands, some witling is bound to come forward and point out with wise finger that life is not all black.'

The moral issue was perhaps one of the main reasons for literary unease about the power of the middle-class audience and middle-class critics, especially after Hardy's difficulties with *Jude the Obscure*.

derives from a sense of the possibility of appealing outside the conventional centre of taste; and it was in this environment that the new modern literature dealt with in the earlier part of this book developed.

By the inter-war years, the situation had changed somewhat, though not markedly. After levelling off earlier in the century, the price of books was beginning to rise slightly again. The cost of a novel went up somewhat, from 6s. to 7s. 6d., increasing somewhat the already existing stratification between the formative, cultured audience who bought books and those who bought reprints or cheap editions. Some of the reprints themselves had gone up in price, especially to the self-improving audience (Nelson's Classics went up from 7d. to 1s. 6d.); and the cheaper substitutes that came in—like the Reader's Library, sold by outlets like Woolworth's—tended to produce somewhat coarse fare, ranging from classics to books of the film, at 6d. The situation was very much improved by the emergence, in 1935, of Penguin Books, which cost sixpence and were remarkable, not because paperback books were new, but because the format was simple and more easily merchandizable and the level of taste was high, the titles being selected from impressive contemporary works. As Robert Escarpit says, they were particularly successful in taking to a very much broader audience books which had previously been part of the 'cultured circuit'—the literary community, so crucial to writing, of specialized bookshops selling their books to specialized audiences and creating a centre in taste.[1] In some ways, the stratification of the audience seemed to be decreasing, certainly. For example, the Public Library system had now come fully into its own, especially since the emergence of County Libraries after the Public Libraries Act of 1919. The service was now much more widely used by borrowers, and by 1926 it was available to 96.3% of the population. However, the circulating libraries charging a fee or subscription were still successfully continuing, the important ones at the centre of the trade being Boots and the backstreet small-shop ventures who

---

[1] Robert Escarpit, *The Sociology of Literature*, trans. E. Pick (Painesville, Ohio, 1965).

charged modest fees for the borrowing of their staples, usually Zane Grey, Edgar Wallace and P. C. Wrenn. In addition the Book Club method of publishing, borrowed from the U.S.A., and preselecting books for readers 'too busy to do it for themselves', had come into the market, with considerable influence on taste. After a falling back during the First World War, the annual number of titles went on increasing. By 1937 it was up to 17,137, including 6,347 reprints, the number of novels now having reached well over 2,000. As before, a high degree of commercialism existed in what seemed like a constant-growth industry; and despite the advent of radio and film the popularity of the book seemed to be maintained. This growing commercialism, however, tended to increase the stratification in taste, less clearly now by class than by inclination. The centre of the book-market was a well-established middlebrow (and largely middle-class) audience, with a minority intellectual audience and a lowbrow audience for sensational, shocking and cheap writing, now available in new forms, including imports from America.

According to Q. D. Leavis, what was happening over this period was a general intensification and organization of capricious and fashionable middlebrow taste, with less variety and flexibility in the market than ever before. Booksellers stocked only easily saleable books; well-reviewed books in the general middlebrow press did well, the others doing very badly; the Book Clubs formalized the situation much further, exercising powerful influence on the market and on publishers, and purveying easy, generally assimilable commodities with expert techniques of salesmanship; and the notion was growing that writing was a matter of satisfying easily recognizable demands by formula. Now this general tendency was not of course new: the changing factor was the degree of organization and formalization of the situation through commercial interests like Book Clubs, and the way in which this had reached the centre of literary taste (as opposed to existing only at its lowest levels). It was because of this that one could hardly avoid concluding, says Mrs Leavis, that 'for the first time in the history of our literature the living forms of the novel have been sidetracked in favour of the *faux-bon*';

and that the novelists who serve the taste were now identical with their publics in background of taste and environment—both sharing an emotional code 'actually inferior to the traditional code of the illiterate'. This concern with the growing standardization of taste is very much a topic of the thirties, and the 'worsening' of the situation may well have been exaggerated. But the assessment partly results from the increasingly effective usages of the producers of mass media generally. The seamless, undemanding and above all standardized quality of this writing, designed to appeal to a wide spectrum of people at the lowest common denominator of interest, and tricked out with sensational and gaudy appeals both of packaging and content, showed that the book was being drawn even more into the expanding universe of the mass media. And in the presence of this broad pattern of development, it became extremely difficult to conceive of the idea of 'literature' at all. It seemed a minority function on the edge of taste both lowbrow and middlebrow; for these two tended to cohere, leaving the serious author and a minority of critical readers isolated from the large mass. Mrs Leavis traces the difficulties of good novelists in gaining recognition and support. Poetry, simultaneously, was declining in quantity; the theatre was dominated by a commercial middlebrow taste as well; and the extension of the audience, in which Bennett had placed such hope, simply enlarged the constituency of mediocrity.[1] In some ways the audience was much more stratified in tastes and values, so that it was no longer possible for a great author to take a total and commanding view of it. On the other hand, there was a level of literary production, represented by the formula bestseller, which could have not only vast national but vast inter-

[1] Q. D. Leavis, *Fiction and the Reading Public*, cited above. It is the organization of taste as its most undistinguished centre by those responsible in the market, and the uncritical acceptance of what is offered by the reading public, that are the main points of her attack. For another useful comment, see Dwight Macdonald, 'A Theory of Mass Culture', where he defines the bland uncritical centre as Midcult. (In *Mass Culture*, ed. Bernard Rosenberg and David Manning White (Glencoe, Ill., 1957).) The other convenient word is *kitsch* (Clement Greenberg, 'Avant Garde and Kitsch', in the same collection), which he defines as a machine-made derivation of *avant-garde* culture, popularized to such an extent as to have a global appeal.

national appeal. All this was in many ways a logical enough extension of a tendency toward homogenization of a superficial, bland taste in reading which had been developing from the beginning of the nineteenth century, now further aided by an expanding reading public, an increase in leisure and literacy, a general growth in the amount of interest in entertainment, and a certain social prestige attached to the idea of book-possession. It developed rather than changed the existing pattern—unlike the post-Second World War period, when we can see another era of change in the general use and nature of the book.

The war had a marked effect on reading, and it increased in amount and diversity. People bought hardback books, sold at controlled austerity prices, or borrowed them in large quantities from libraries like Boot's. The literary part of the market seemed invigorated, and there were considerable hopes of a marked change and improvement in public taste. But by the 1950s this began to be disappointed; private book-reading and book-buying now seemed to be on the decline, partly as a result of the remarkable rise in book-prices that took place with the postwar rise in printing costs. In the early part of the century book-prices had remained relatively stable, rising gently; but between 1955 and 1967 the average price of a book more than doubled, from 15s. 6d. to 37s., according to the *Bookseller* index.[1] This extraordinary growth was, of course, part of a generally inflationary climate which radically affected social stratification and culture. In many ways this did no direct harm to books. Indeed the market went through a very striking expansion, as we can see from the remarkably rapid increase in British publishing turnover (about £10 million in 1939; about £142 million now), and from the rapid rise in the number of titles that are published annually. In 1850 2,600 titles had appeared; a hundred years later, in 1950, the figure had reached 17,072 (including 5,334 reprints). And, in the twenty years since then, the figure has about doubled: it was

---

[1] There is an excellent analysis of these developments—it argues that the effect of such large price-increases is a real decline in volume sales—in Clive Bingley, 'Why do book prices go on rising?', *Library Association Record*, LXXI, 3 (March 1969), pp. 70-4.

23,783 in 1960, 26,023 in 1963, and by 1968 it topped the thirty-thousand mark for the first time, with 31,420 different titles in the year. British publishers, therefore, put on to the market about 90 titles a day. Publishing has been in a continuous state of expansion since Caxton; but this constitutes a remarkable period of expansion, vaster in scale than that at the end of the nineteenth century. It shows an enormous increase in book-reading and book-buying. Yet the question is: who buys what, for whom to read, and where? For what it means is an enormous shift in the character, nature, function and purchase of books. Behind these figures lie enormous changes in the market. For instance, Britain publishes more titles than any other country in the world; but the situation reflects Britain's increasing role as a publisher *for* the world. 44.3% of the publishing output is exported, with a turnover of £59 million.[1] Or, to give the figures in a different form, there are estimates that some 300 million books are issued annually in Britain, half of them for export. Then again the largest part of this expansion has been in educational, scientific and technical publishing. This means, too, that there has been an enormous shift in the nature of book-purchase, in the balance between private purchase and institutional buying by libraries, etc. Of that £86 million spent within England on books, about £28 million is bought by institutions and another £21 million accounted for by educational purposes, leaving about £25 million spent in bookshops. (That is why the expansion can be accompanied by a decline in book outlets.) Publishing increasingly becomes a trading activity between one institutional group called publishers and another institutional group called libraries, and many books undoubtedly by-pass not only the purchaser but the reader, being stored for storing's sake. All these factors—the export-market; the scientific and technical expansion; the role of the book in the international education explosion; and the

---

[1] Julian Critchley, 'Hope of greater rewards in the world of publishing', *The Times*, November 20, 1969. See also Eric Roll, 'The Writer in the Export Market', *Times Literary Supplement*, 3517 (July 24, 1969), which points out that 'writing as an export is now "big business"' but that authors' royalties and copyrights are threatened by the 1967 Stockholm Copyright Agreement. On the general evolution of English publishing in this century, see R. J. L. Kingsford, *The Publishers Association: 1896–1946* (London and New York, 1970).

institutional purchaser—have changed books and publishing. It has become a vastly capitalized activity with an enormous scope for operations in new kinds of book. 'What has changed in British publishing is the disappearance of the "gentleman publisher with his list of general books". Firms have amalgamated; or because of his need for capital the once independent publisher has been obliged to cede control to groups.'[1] In English publishing, then, there has been a vast concentration of outlets; a much greater impersonality in the system; and the enormous expansion of areas of trade having little to do with individual writers and readers. The complex of inflation and concentration, in addition to affecting taste and behaviour, has had large structural consequences for the 'literary' book, especially the new book as opposed to the well-established classic in the educational-reprint market.

'Very few people . . . publish poetry with the primary hope of making a profit,' commented a director of the publishing house (Faber) with probably the best poetry list in England. He comments that he receives about 500-600 manuscripts a year but 'we take on a new poet only about once every two or three years'. The first printing of a first volume of verse is about or under 1,000 copies, resulting in high prices. The result is, in effect, that the poets printed must be the potential classics with a continuing sale.[2] But poetry has long been a declining part of the market; what of the novel? In the 1950s the number of new novels rose, but in the 1960s it actually fell back and was not markedly higher than the figure for 1937—2,375 new novels appeared in 1963, compared with the 1937 figure of 2,153.[3] And not only in numbers of titles but in actual circulation the novel has been showing signs of decline—so much so that several houses now are reducing their lists of novelists. The print order for a new novel today has dropped to about 3,000 copies, sold at a vastly higher price than in the 1930s, and hence almost entirely purchased by libraries.[4]

---

[1] Ibid.

[2] Charles Monteith, 'The cost of publishing poetry', The Guardian, June 5, 1964.

[3] The total figure for 1963 was—including reprints—4,315.

[4] A sample report on what is happening with novels is given in Michael Dempsey's comments in The Writer in the Market Place, ed. Raymond Astbury

According to Michael Sissons, the literary agent: 'Authors who were selling six or seven thousand copies of each new book ten years ago, may now sell around four or five thousand copies. The gap is widening between the totally unprofitable and extremely profitable novel.'[1] Indeed, the publishing of fiction has, in the climate of rising prices and publishing concentration, become a highly speculative business for the publisher and a disappointing one for the author. Part of the reason for this is a technical one: as faster letterpress machines and offset-litho systems dominate printing, as the cost of keeping type standing or storing printed sheets has soared, short-run printing, or printing small runs with a possiblity of reprinting if the book does well, become much less possible.[2] All this is reflected in the startling rise in the cost of a hardback novel. As we have seen, it was usually 6s. in 1910 and 7s. 6d. in 1939. Today it becomes, according to figures given by James Price, almost an absolute commercial necessity that a novel with a 3,000 print order must cost about 32s. 6d.[3] It need hardly be added that this reflects the costs of running a publishing or printing business, and that (as we have already seen) the benefits do *not* go to the author, who in fact loses on this pattern. Indeed the novel appears now to be caught in a vicious circle where the break-even point on a print run rises but the sales, because of increasing cost, decrease. And above all the literary book becomes of increasingly less significance to publishers. For the essential circle of contact in which it exists—the writer reaching a private reader—is dissolving. The entire pattern of book-outlets has now changed. Rising costs of property and stock have radically cut back the number of bookshops and—since the bookshop is

(London, 1969): a first novel of 1967 which had remarkable reviews and was chosen as book of the month by the *Guardian* sold only 2,243 copies. Of these 2,050 went to libraries. This fits in with a memorandum by A. P. Herbert to the Society of Authors in support of Public Lending Right; he says that if a first novel is printed in 3,000 copies then over 80% of home sales go to libraries.

[1] Quoted in Richard Findlater, 'The Writer Considered as Wage-Earner', *Times Literary Supplement*, 3517 (July 24, 1969).

[2] James Price, 'How publishers are leaving the 1950s behind', in ibid.

[3] Ibid. Price demonstrates how a rise of 6d. in printing costs means that the publisher must add 2s. 6d. to keep his percentage gross margin. It is reported that printing costs over the last three years have risen by 40%.

a diminishing part of the trade anyway—publishers are hardly interested in supporting or founding them.[1] In addition, the circulating libraries, which were always a significant outlet for fiction, have begun to disappear. Mudie's went in 1937; and more recently many small news-agency libraries and, even more significantly, Boot's have now gone. On the other hand, the Public Libraries (much better financed in the Welfare State of institutional provision) have increased vastly in use; and their issues rose from 76 million in 1924 to 441 million in 1960-61 and about 500 million a year now. In fact they constitute, as we have seen, the main outlet for the new hardback book, which, under the net book agreement, they actually acquire at a 10% discount. A force in maintaining the circulation of the book, they are also a force in keeping its costs high and limiting its sales: a paradoxical situation that explains the current campaign among authors for a levy through a Public Lending Right. Evidence suggests that most of those who borrow books from libraries never (or very rarely) buy books, just as members of Book Clubs very rarely buy books in the open market.[2] For the largest part of the reading public, the book is now a 'free' provision of the society. At all points in the circuit—to note one consequence— the pattern has become very much more impersonal, abstract and institutional.[3]

All this means that the figures of publishing growth are not a good guide to an enlargement of the literary reading public. It is often assumed that we live in a period of cultural explosion in which reading has vastly increased, has greatly broadened in its social spread, and in which the writer faces better prospects for success and wealth than he has for a long time. For example,

[1] For some interesting figures on the scale of bookshop closure, see Richard Findlater, *What Are Writers Worth?* (London, 1963)   [2] Julian Critchley, op. cit.

[3] One interesting sidelight on this is a letter from Doris Lessing in *The Author*, LXXX, 2 (Summer 1969) commenting on the loss of the personal relationship between writer and publisher. Houses change hands without consultation with authors: 'There is no value to us in the "old" or "gentlemanly" or "traditional" (what you will) kind of publishing without that continuing personal relationship with one person. That was the whole point of it, and now it has gone. What one has now is dozens of charming acquaintances everywhere in publishing, all of whom have been one's publisher for a few months.'

Raymond Williams, in *The Long Revolution*, argues that in the 1950s we probably had for the first time a *majority* reading public for books, spread right across the population—just as we had this for Sunday newspapers by about 1910 and for daily newspapers soon after 1918.[1] But this depends very much on what one takes a book to be, and also to what extent the large book-circulation of today is socially spread. The book is perhaps less the sole preserve of the middle classes now than it ever was—though there can be no doubt that this sector still constitutes a very large part of the audience. But perhaps the most marked shift of use probably is not so much a matter of class as of age and social mobility. For it is the vastly expanded social sector involved in education that seems to play a significant part in the market; more young people are exposed to more books than ever before, though it is often notably the case that reading diminishes once the appropriate educational qualifications have been gained. Moreover, in the vastly expanded service classes of our society it is increasing as a matter of professional use. In short, the spread of the reading habit is undoubtedly accounted for in part by the spread in the numbers of those who, for educational or professional purposes, *have* to read. A further point is that the book expansion also indicates a very large increase in book *storage*: the institutional buying of public, school, university and industrial or scientific libraries is by no means all buying for use. As I have said, the signs all are that individual buying of hardback books has actually declined. In a pilot study done with a small sample by the Opinion Research Centre in 1967, it emerged that only 15% of the adult population ever buy a hardback book; only 12% could remember buying a book in the last year; and much of this buying was not 'literary' but was of non-fiction, normally taking the form of travel, reference, technical or children's books. And purchasing was almost entirely within the 21–35-year age group.[2] If, then, our

[1] Raymond Williams, *The Long Revolution* (London, 1961), Part 2, Chap. II ('The Growth of the Reading Public').
[2] Cited in Michael Roberts, 'Tracking the Real Best-sellers', *Sunday Times*, August 13, 1967.

national reading is supposed to amount to 15 books per head per annum, a good deal of this must be in the form of paperback purchase or free borrowing from libraries. The importance of the paperback in the democratization of books I shall return to in a minute; but the same survey already quoted shows that sales of these are more limited in range than one might expect. About 25 % of the population bought paperbacks, but these bought them fairly regularly. A more recent survey by Peter H. Mann confirms the total impression by indicating that 20 % of the population buys books. Another 20 % reads them without buying—mainly of course by borrowing them from a public library.[1] (Hence, of course, the already mentioned concern of writers over the Public Lending Right issue—deriving from the fact that a very large part of their readership consists of multiple borrowings of the same copy of their book, for which they receive royalty once only.) It is difficult to acquire evidence about the social range of readership, and whether it is markedly stratified in taste—whether working-class readers read different things from middle-class readers[2]—and this in spite of the fact that a considerable proportion of readers are now brought within the purview of one agency—the public library system.

The overall impression one has is that the real change in publishing since the war is not so much in the texture and flavour of the audience or the techniques of the writer, but in the commercial base of the industry. This is particularly evident in the most radical development of all—that of what we like to call the 'paperback revolution'. The paperback itself is not, of course, revolutionary; as we have seen, it reaches well back into the last century, and many effective paperback series existed before the postwar period. Nor is the revolution one of remarkable reduction

---

[1] Peter H. Mann and Jacqueline L. Burgoyne, *Books and Reading* (London, 1969), offers an extensive if in fact highly contradictory survey of statistical details about reading in the form of a progress report.

[2] One survey, by Luckham and others, suggested that the bulk of borrowers came from white-collar workers, and managerial and professional sectors; and Peter Worsley, 'Libraries and Mass Culture', *Library Association Record*, LXIX, 8 (August 1967), suggests that libraries set up a 'culture barrier', because they link a service with a quasi-educational function.

R

in the price of books. The average price of a Penguin book—
which was 6d. in the 1930s, and which even then did not represent a new 'low' figure in publishing—is now 5s.; and a great
many paperbacks, particularly scientific or academic ones, are
no cheaper than many hardback books. In many respects the
paperback market has simply shifted many of the activities of the
old book-market into a new format, allowing the hardback book
to price itself off the public market and serve largely institutional
uses, as a form of library edition. In short, the situation is in some
ways a reversion to that of the last century, when the libraries
(in that case the circulating libraries) carried the main weight of
circulating new books and financing authors, while there was a vast
secondary market in reprints. From the writer's point of view,
this is very much the case with paperbacks. Paperback publication
is normally a form of secondary publication rather than a direct
dealing with an audience. His work normally appears in hardback
first, though a certain proportion of paperbacks are originals, and
it is normally on hardback publication that success or failure depends. While the fact that he succeeds in selling the paperback
rights of his book does provide him with a second court of appeal to
readers, and while it of course increases the total circulation of his
book, it by no means necessarily increases his profits (as compared
with a situation where *only* hardback books are on the market). His
royalties from a paperback are low; they are normally divided with
the original publisher of the book, whose share will be between
25% and 50%; and the appearance of the paperback can cut into
the sale of the hardback and may even prevent or replace the traditional *hardback* reprint.[1] The radical features of paperbacks lie else-

[1] Julian Critchley, op. cit, gives some of the relevant figures from the
authors' point of view. On a hardcover novel published at 21s. (nowadays a
too low figure) with a print order of 3,000 the author will receive about
£315. All further profits he will divide with the hard-cover publisher. He
could receive a paperback advance of £350, which he divides. On a print
order of 20,000 at a royalty of $7\frac{1}{2}$% of a selling price of 3s. 6d., he will receive
£262 10s., also divided. Hence his total profits from the paperback may not
amount to the total of the paperback advance. It should also be noted that sale
of subsidiary rights to films, etc., equally benefits the original hardback publisher, possibly as much as the author in some cases, and plays a significant part
in the economics of hardcover publishing.

where: basically in the technical and commercial processes which affect the size, scale and manner of paperback production and distribution, in the relative mixture of levels and tastes to which they appeal, and in their very expendability, which makes them often appear more like magazines than books.

There can be no doubt that the paperback has vastly expanded the book market in a period in which purchase and bookshops were shrinking. Paperbacks now represent in England something like a third of the total book-market in terms of annual sales. In 1968 something of the order of 60 million were sold. They are necessarily large-circulation ventures, for their profits are only partly derived from their apparently cheap format (cheaper paper and paper covers). Rather it is derived from the larger print-run (normally between 20,000 and 40,000 copies); the method of marketing; and from the plurality of titles. There are also some benefits derived from the fact that it is a form of back-list publishing, with a considerable number of titles gained out of copyright or at a low rate of royalty: some paperback houses have recently run into trouble by paying huge advances out of proportion to the potential royalty earnings of the book. All this implies a total different pattern of distribution, a high density of circulation. The paperback normally uses, in effect, the methods of magazine distribution to reach a wide audience. Its outlets reach far beyond the normal bookshops, which are responsible for no more than half its sales. It is also sold through news-agencies, bookstalls, tobacconists, laundrettes and vending-machines. It sells a very large number of titles, which are constantly changed. In 1960 there were 5,886 titles in *Whitaker's Paperbacks in Print*; by 1968 the figure had risen sixfold.[1] It mixes most of its titles in a seamless web of sales, confusing the familiar stratifications of the audience—which otherwise today might well be hardened by the expensiveness of hardcover books. It is this cultural mix of the paperback that constitutes an important part of its novelty. It reaches a very wide mixture of audiences—sometimes by seeking to differentiate them by distinguishing better paperbacks from worse ones, often by price, but sometimes by the established

[1] Julian Critchley, op. cit.

association of a particular imprint (Penguin books differing in popular association from Corgis); sometimes lumping them together, for instance by putting lurid packaging on what is in fact a specialized title. And it reaches them with a very wide mixture of books. Lately, though the number of titles and companies has increased, the total sales have not been rising greatly, and it has become apparent that one of the great staples of the market is an excellent backlist such as Penguin have. This has led to some shrinkage in titles and outlets, and to a movement towards linking the publication of hard- and soft-cover editions (so that the same type or sheets can be used). As a 'revolution', paperbacks have undoubtedly maintained the social existence of the book, and extended it. By their apparent cheapness they have doubtless increased book-buying among those disposed to purchase anyway; and they have reached young people who constitute in an expanding educational climate a crucial part of the audience. But they, too, have made the literary book a small portion of their activities. In the case of Penguin the strength has been non-fiction; in the case of other series it has been in sub-fiction. And finally they have been a very derivative form of publishing, largely drawing on existing books and hardening the success and failure pattern of the books already in print.

The paperback is undoubtedly an important agent in the further democratization of the book as such, vastly extending its sale as a commodity in a time of affluence when cultural goods can be brought to new markets. It is, therefore, the most obvious evidence we have of a new cultural abundance in a time when similar phenomena are apparent in gramophone records and in filmgoing. It has done a good deal to change the mix of the market, though, in fact, it lacks, because of its large print-runs, the flexibility and variety of the old market; the subtler variations of taste and innovation finally belong with the hardback. What is more, evidence about the new spread in degree and kind is remarkably unclear. Peter Drucker has claimed of the even vaster and more continuous paperback revolution in the United States that it is a sign of the status-hunger of an expanding white-collar class, and the presence of cultural variety in its offerings calls for some such explanation. Yet, though the paperback market includes many different kinds and levels of publishing within itself, we cannot really be very clear just whom these books do reach. As we have seen from the Opinion Research Survey already quoted, about 25% of the population, mostly young, buy paperbacks. But the same survey indicates that the categories most bought were those right in the 'yellow-back' tradition—romance novels, spy and crime stories, books with a strong sex interest. The classic best-sellers may include *The Odyssey*, which has sold nearly 2 million in Penguin; they also include James Bond (Fleming's books have been selling in paper at 4 million a year) and Agatha Christie, a global best-seller. Though the range contains many titles of quality, it is not clear how far they penetrate; there is certainly some real extension at this level for which paperbacks (and particularly Penguin, the biggest firm in the market) are responsible. Poetry seems to have benefited significantly, for instance. But among the many quality titles are many which have sales analogous to hardbacks and are priced accordingly; nor must we forget that the paperback audience is not additional to the hardback audience, but includes many buyers who would formerly have bought a hardbound edition. The general pattern in fact suggests that the paperback has enlarged audiences somewhat, but has also captured most of the old hardback purchasers as well; it has become the new book-market. If this is so, the new pattern represents an interesting mixture of change and conservation; it has produced a certain expansion and restratification of the audience, changing its mix somewhat while containing many of the old stratifications and reading habits. One can read in the situation genuine signs of expanded interests in books, and of extended reading, especially among young people; one can find in it greater use of the classics and of new authors who acquire prestige or popularity. But one can also find a large growth of disposable reading of undifferentiated quality, an increase in sensational reading, and a general coarsening of the pattern of the market, partly derived from the fact that paperbacks block out in larger scale the extant patterns of the hardback market. Most writers, after all, still write 'hardback' books and assume traditional modes of publishing. And this perhaps partly explains why it is that there has been a relatively small amount of literary exploitation and innovation in the modern artistic situation among serious writers; it has not had the same remarkable creative stimulus that the change in the pattern of the book had between 1880 and 1920.

The changes in the book-trade over the last hundred years, then, have been considerable and from the point of view of literature highly significant. They have, of course, changed the writer's entire view of his audience and his framework of relationships in it. The constant expansion of the audience has reshaped the trade and the place of literature in it. Many more readers have been enfranchised, though that process has meant the disenfranchisement of many for whom the book had special and distinctive meaning. Many of the clear stratifications of the market have either disappeared or become submerged in the enormous scale of publishing activity; today, less than ever, does it seem clear what the social bases of readers are, what kind of cultural assumptions and standards unite them, and what part literature plays in their lives. Amid the apparent homogeneity of the paperback audience and the institutional voids of the libraries, a lot of old definitions have disappeared. That 'top million' which was so distinct to Arnold Bennett at the beginning of the century has become an indistinct and much bigger community amassed around the book. This of course reflects that gradual equalization of British society as a function of taste. But what kind and quality of taste? The fear in the past has been of a levelling *down* of taste; the dream, especially in educational circles, has been of a levelling *up*. But what seems to have happened is a levelling *out*, a flattening away of cultural distinctions and differentiations. The idea of an improving standard has certain evidence to support it— the greater provision of books at all levels, increased borrowing from libraries, the growing range and variation of titles, the greater spread of educational and serious non-fiction reading. But sensational, popular and routine reading has also grown. Perhaps a more accurate portrait is of a growing flexibility of taste: an increased crossing of the lines among some readers, especially young ones, in both directions. In terms of the fortunes of literature, this seems to have caused a certain displacement: indeed the evidence is clear that the centrality of imaginative literature—that is, in other than its most popular forms—has declined, becoming just one factor in the vastly growing output of communications, rather than representing a central association of the very idea of the book.

The postwar period was, of course, the first period in which the book-trade had to compete with other media—particularly television—on equal footing for a share of attention and interest. There were fears, when this situation was realized, that the reading habit would decline. Of course it has not. In some sections of the community, for some of its functions, it has increased a great deal—especially for educational, specialist and professional purposes. What is apparent is that the book now exists in a vastly expanded totality of cultural provision. Overall, there *has* been an enormous explosion of expression in our society. But it has been spread across the various forms of art and expression, and above all across all the technicalities of expression: the media. And so the book has become one medium among many in an age in which leisure, affluence and the amount of education have all spread further through the population, and in which the amount of secondary service provisions—from cars, transistors, record-players and washing machines to records and books—have been one of the most significant areas of modern commercial expansion. But, like other media which expand their audiences when the high capital cost of plant needed to sustain them increases, the book-trade has become concentrated, institutional and commercially democratic. It has had to feel its way towards the majorities and lose many of its marked hierarchies of taste; it has also had to sustain its variety in taste. The stratifications of value of the past have had to fade, but this is not to say that there is no stratification; it is simply sketched vertically rather than horizontally. It has the characteristic multiplicity of any of the media of mass-culture, to which in situation and style it now approximates. For many writers, of textbooks and handbooks, works of reference and of social history or commentary, the situation is one of enormous possibilities. It is in imaginative literature that we may see a marked contrast between the remarkable imaginative expansion encouraged by the changes of 100 years ago and the relatively less vigorous ones today.

III

Of course the book, as I have said, has always been a 'medium'— a technology of communication—as well as a form of literature; many of its deepest literary associations may almost be conceived of as happy accidents. But, while it has always expanded itself technologically (through new methods of typesetting, better machinery, larger print-runs, greater distribution), it has normally tended to present itself, so to speak, on a pre-technological model—as a species of relatively intimate communication, as a source of values and community, and for that matter as an object of elegance. It has profoundly distilled associations in our society. With its growth and development, with the social change it has brought, there has been linked a long artistic evolution, and clustered about it are a body of forms, genres and conventions, from the novel to the lyric poem (many of them transferred from the even greater intimacy of manuscript publication). But with assumed universal literacy, literature lost some of its privacy. And with the growth first of journalism and then in this century of other instrumentalities of communication, it was made increasingly 'relative' as a communications form. Some of its specialism was restored, but in other ways it was influenced by the techniques and audiences of the new media. Most of these new media emerged largely as a result of technical developments of a sophisticated kind and they accelerated to majority use very quickly. Radio went through a 'protected' period under the brilliant control of Lord Reith; but television, with its need for much higher capital investment, underwent expansion rather more quickly. The book differs from these media in that they take their character and expansion of means and technique as much from technical research as from the contribution of artists.

For instance, though we often speak of the 'modernism' of the film—its use of quick-cutting, flashback and the like—and compare it with modern literature, these are often as much improvements in the technical instrumentalities as considered artistic interpretations. That is why film and television have a large element of ephemerality and obsolescence, and why they are hard to subject to conventional critical estimation. The species of permanence conferred by the book is sometimes illusory, but it is apparent; so, too, is the fact that it is the centre of an inheritance of forms and practices which *are* subject to critical evaluation. The book contains much of the institution of literature.

To a point, it still does so. Though it has been very heavily centralized in the last few years, publishing still retains some of its older commitments to literature as such. It has not completely lost, though it is losing, some of the traditional intimacy between writer and publisher; it also still retains a kind of immediacy between writer and audience. Unlike other media, which tend to dichotomize form and content, and in which the frame or means of presentation tends to dominate any particular artistic event within it, the book itself seems to contain a certain inherent personality, to radiate a certain individuality, and helps to preserve the idea of the writer. If the amount of imaginative writing has not held its place in the total market, it is still an active part of it, and to many publishers still a part to be preserved. It is not outstandingly difficult for a writer of promise to acquire publication and recognition, and a number of publishers actively encourage new writers, even through such specific series as Hutchinsons New Authors or the Penguin Modern Poets. On the other hand, the book has shifted much further towards the character of a 'medium'—a form of broad communications provision which is less specifically committed to literature as such. At the start of the century, when writers were asserting their commitment to 'serious' art, this was partly derived from their need to distinguish between ordinary communication and the literary uses of language, the intensities of art. Those intensities we are perhaps losing. As we have seen, there has been a progressive weakening in our society of the cultural centrality, even

of the communal ideal of education, out of which such convictions can derive. Now literature is produced by writers of many
more varied types for readers of many more varied types; and
it has become, on both sides, less an exploration of cultural or
humane values. As that happens, the relation between writer and
reader tends to become more formal, remote and more competitive in relation to other writers. And so the writer tends to
see himself part of a pattern of established relations between a
variety of media at a variety of levels, to which pattern he may
attach himself. Dealing with a much more impersonal cultural
situation, his gift is more of professional efficiency than personal
distinction. He attaches himself to forms and media which have
already charted the market, in the hope of extending them further.
Amid the abundance and variety of modern provision, his own
imaginative acts become dwarfed.

It is this sort of situation that has shaped and affected modern
writing, especially since the war. And it is partly the consequence
of our vast proliferation of social communications—one of the
most important and familiar marks of a modernizing society.
Such a proliferation—developing throughout the century—is
closely linked with high industrial and technological sophistication, with urbanization, with literacy, affluence and leisure, and
a high degree of response to innovation. It expresses, up to a
point, the increased need for impersonal social contacts and
awareness, for the distribution and information of knowledge,
for a sense of participation in the action of the world. It is part
of our social rationalization; so that today ours is a post-village
age in which both total literacy (we are all assumed to be able to
read *No parking* signs and the labels on cans) and a high degree of
exposure to changing custom, rule and law is expected. All this
depends on a vastly spread communications sytem, through
which the circulation and transmission of ideas, attitudes and
images is maintained. But of course communications not only
increase our awareness and involvement; they also change the
sorts of awareness, the kind of impressions and realities, we
possess. That is why it is possible for a social analyst like Marshall
McLuhan to see the great revolutions of the modern world as

being revolutions in the form of the communications processes themselves: as he says, they are extensions of man, and changing uses of his work. In a very real sense, such large changes as the book has gone through in our century are substantial changes in the forms and relationships of internal dialogue. And in their transforming and expanding nature itself they manifest what is happening; they not only treat but *are* our complex environment, in all its relativism and pluralism. And they grow not only for us but within themselves, usually through technological advance or increasing capitalization, which means that they expand in scale and take in constantly larger audiences with more sophisticatedly structured appeals. This in turn increases their impersonality, their de-localized quality, their multiplicity of content and of level. What is also clear is that communications, both written and visual, are more and more used *for* communication, in a direct and factual sense. We live in an age of news and of knowledge. Events, on a global scale, have more power with us than they used to: events, of course, being those things which happen twice, one because they happen and once because they are reported, filmed and published. Today, then, we live in a world in which communications are not selective; they do not pass through chains of command, but are transmitted to all receivers; they do not easily form into coteries or social sectors; they do not easily inhere values other than documentary or impersonal or, as they say, impartial ones. All this is the world of mass-communications, and most of us are direct members of it. By 1959 television viewing in Britain had reached an average daily level of $2\frac{1}{2}$ hours per person, showing a degree of exposure outside the family and the immediate community to the large world of communications such as to make it a form of intrinsic national contact. The book cannot aspire to such command, but it exists within the context of it. The writer today faces an audience enfranchised by communications, exposed to more scenes, more events, more information, more knowledge and more changeability than ever before. This limits his imaginative power: the world itself becomes sensational literature. But, in the plethora of all that is communicated, his book, his individual interpretation, becomes no more than that: it is one more thing in the universe of phenomena. Not only, then, does the modern situation in communications weaken those features of a communal culture in which art was traditionally created and consumed; it also competes persistently with the artist for a view of reality. But the problems here raised are the problems of literature in a mass-society, the problems of imagination and of selective culture: and I will examine them further in my next chapter.

PART FIVE

The Culture

CHAPTER XI

High and Mass Culture

I

I said at the beginning that this book was about culture, and the different ways in which we can see it. By now it should be clear how very differently it *can* be seen, and what varieties of experience and activity are capable of being embodied in any such notion. Indeed one of the difficulties of the present situation is to secure it *as* a notion. For not only does the word have many different associations depending upon whether one is sociologist, literary critic, historian or writer. It also has a kind of plural applicability, so that we think of and speak of *many* cultures: folk culture, working-class culture, high culture, mass culture, youth culture. The destiny of the word is profoundly involved with the destiny of the thing; and both thing and word have been appropriated in many different quarters. Perhaps the best we can do, in evoking the topic, is to go back to some of the simpler and more familiar meanings.

Probably the most familiar usage of the word still is when we talk of culture as an accomplishment of particular people. When we think of someone as being 'cultured,' we mean to recognize that he has achieved certain refinements and resources of character by effort, devotion and education. Something in him has been brought out, by himself and others—brought out in such a way as to put him into active relationship with, on the other hand, certain socially inherited and valued skills, manners and forms of knowledge, and, on the other, with the present-day and changing world (he reads the newspapers, is *au courant*). In the novels of Jane Austen there is a vivid, critical evocation of culture in the first sense. Her books are very much about the selection and refinement of culture in a community, to the point where, it seems, only the good couple who marry at the end of the novel seem to possess it in any adequately moral and internal way. But culture depends on a relation between moral-*cum*-social involvement and a critical selectivity, and the attributes are a mixture of both dimensions: accomplishments in reading and music, but also critical self-awareness; social poise, but also gentleness; affection and compassion, but also the submission of fancy or feeling to understanding; and so on. In the second sense, culture is perhaps closer to Gumbril's ideal second self in Aldous Huxley's *Antic Hay* (1903):

> . . . He explored the horrors of Roman society; visited Athens and Seville. To Unamuno and Papini he conversed familiarly in their own tongues. He understood perfectly and without effort the quantum theory. To his friend Shearwater he gave half a million for physiological research. He visited Schoenberg and persuaded him to write better music. He exhibited to the politicians the full extent of their stupidity and their wickedness; he set them working for the salvation, not the destruction of humanity. . . . He found it easy now to come to terms with everyone he met, to understand all points of view, to identify himself with even the most unfamiliar spirit.

But in either or both senses, those who are 'cultured' are felt to be in touch with a wider world, to possess more sensitive awareness, to live out their human relations more delicately and interestingly, than most of us. They are a manifest culture within the culture; they are the humanistic best self of the human creature. In practice, of course, such refinement is not always found very likable, especially by those who do not possess it. Hence the unfortunate connotations that a few years ago were apt to cluster round the word 'Bloomsbury,' as used to define a more or less distinct species, selected out by accent, manners and style, and assimilating certain national cultural functions very much into themselves. Not only are the cultured often associated with a snobbery of cultural possession, but also with the female rather than the male role in society. In Virginia Woolf's *To the Lighthouse* the evaluative principle of the book depends very much on this sexual distinction. The men, who 'negotiated treaties, ruled India, controlled finance,' might have culture, but it is the women, above all Mrs Ramsay, who possess the imaginative, artistic and sensitive responses that really cohere families and societies into cultures.

As a culture within a culture, the cultured are of course open to attack from those not of their party—not only for their own sweetness and light but their desire to enjoin it on others. In particular, they are likely to be assaulted by a kind of disenfranchised or populist imagination which wishes partly to enter but partly to destroy. Two classic instances—in no direct way linked—are the deflationary sentiments of Jim Dixon in Kingsley Amis's *Lucky Jim*, and those of Herman Goering, in his famous phrase, 'When I hear the word culture I reach for my gun.' But of course these accomplishments, though they can become petty or decayed, have intrinsic human value at best, and they constitute an essential feature both of our sense of human worth and of national community— things often invisible unless actively threatened, but then often socially important again (Cyril Connolly commented on a familiar wartime response to Nazism and Goering: 'When I hear the word gun I reach for my culture'). But in this general usage of the word, culture obviously means something more than, say, reading books, listening to music or visiting cathedrals. While it is an aspect of individual character, and in some ways an ultimate manifestation or refinement of it, something deeply to do with our particular achievement as people in the course of our own personal lifetime, it obviously has a great deal to do with society—with the way we are in society, the way we are aware of particular strata in it, the way we feel it changing around us and in us. It reaches into our capacity to take in thoughts, ideas, beliefs and mannerisms; it is expressed in styles, conversational tones, modes of personal inter course—in the way we eat what with what, and when, and what we call what we have eaten.[1] It is at once a conscious achievement *of*

[1] I am thinking here of the U and non-U controversy; see Nancy Mitford and others, *Noblesse Oblige* (London, 1956). But for a very good discussion of the way fiction embodies this world of manners as a world of morals, see Lionel Trilling, 'Manners, Morals and the Novel', in *The Liberal Imagination* (New York and London, 1950).

S

society, and in another sense a selection *out* of society; a process of perpetuating, enshrining and valuing certain features of it. This can, from the point of view of the populist imagination, be called a kind of 'privatization' or appropriation; it can be viewed more positively as a disinterested and critical filtering of the best parts of the tradition and the contemporary situation in order to hold these as the recognized part of human and social enrichment and fulfilment. This is culture in its aspect as taste or criticism.

What is clear, then, is that though culture may be a personal matter, an individual accomplishment, it in fact transcends the single individual. It depends upon the forms and practices of society, on what Henry James called 'forms' or 'density'. In his study *Hawthorne* (1879), he observed that it took a great deal of civilization to set a writer in motion, and remarked on the relative 'denudation' of the America in which Hawthorne began to write. That 'forms' in the social sense had something to do with form in the artistic sense he had no doubt; the density of cultural creation in Europe was related to the density of its institutions and its social order, and to the presence of cultural and artistic roles through which cultural creation was encouraged. James also recognized that it was still possible for a society to lack a regard for cultural accomplishment and still have artists; that was, he said, the American 'joke'. But clearly there are marked variations in the capacity of societies to stimulate individual or communal creativity and selectivity, and to encourage the growth of a high art. As De Tocqueville observed in *Democracy in America* (1835: 1840), the democratic society in which there was little stratification by wealth and accomplishment offered less support for high artistic accomplishment, even though it might produce a literature of sorts in very large quantities; similarly it tended to validate artistic production in useful rather than ornamental or critical terms. In a society where all was as good as all else, it was hard to provide a social validation for literary activity *per se*, or for any active pursuit of the arts of life. To some extent, leisure, wealth and the right to conceive of own's own growth humanistically were necessary features of a high degree of personal cultural accomplishment. Now in fact all societies enshrine, codify and transmit their wisdom, best experience and most valued activities in some way, through priesthoods and castes. In our world such wisdom is not characteristically fixed or codified; and its transmission is through loose castes or élites, who are less and less members of any one class or sector in society, but rather of various social origins and viewpoints. But the tendency is for these castes to be loosely attached to society and to lack definition of association, so that the social or communal roots of the culture are tapped less deep, encouraging an eclectic assimilation of values, experiences and art-forms. But even in these terms culture remains partial or selective: and it is precisely this feature which makes it significant.

For it is in fact only when culture *is* partial—when it is consciously pursued, and represents an effort and achievement— that it is interesting and creative. It is precisely in this sense that the arts are enlarging and significant. As sociologists and anthropologists say, and as is now well known: we are *all* cultured, as part of the human condition, in that we live in communal environments with a shared language and so something like a shared reality. But we are so by various degrees of self-consciousness and effort. At times in society it becomes the case that the achievement and accomplishment involved in the idea of being 'cultured' gets narrowed down to a highly selected group of powers which can be possessed by a very few people. At other times (like ours) the definition spreads in the other direction, so that virtually everything is included. In situations of the first type, being responsive to classical music may be cultured but being responsive to football matches not. In those of the second type, not only may both be cultured, but it may be impossible to see any qualitative difference between them (so, as Bentham said, pushpin becomes as good as poetry; so, from the other point of view, bad money drives out good through a cultural Gresham's Law). All such things are aspects of culture, in being aspects of individually and socially enlisted involvements in the reality of the world. But another, essential aspect of culture is precisely that it embodies systems of preference and selectivity that enable us, or have enabled us, to think of certain activities as *more* cultured or *less* cultured. In short, they have enabled us to think of a hierarchy of culture and a factor of criticism and discrimination at the heart of its functioning.

And so culture involves us in some notion of an élite. For if such preferences are to have meaning, they have to be validated socially. People must be able to promote them and win prestige for doing so. In societies of the past, this kind of culture was an aspect of enshrined wisdom and magic and was transmitted by a caste; or it was an aspect of the behaviour of certain leading classes and was transmitted as a responsibility. In our kind of society it is a flexible body of selective preferences, mediated more and more by a shifting, free-floating, up-to-date, non-class group called an intelligentsia. Between these two extremes there are more intermediate situations, in which the intelligentsia does not hold all the prerogatives of and responsibilities for culture. In the nineteenth century, for instance, when the very idea of a cultural cohesion as a substitute for the religious cohesion of society was canvassed in depth, a persistent ideal was that of a 'saving remnant' of a 'clerisy' or a body of 'guardians' who were the lay clergy of culture, culture being the onward movement of the best and most selectively critical thoughts and feelings of society, that which stood between a religiously centred society and a purely material, rationalistic and self-seeking one. Culture was the essential mitigating force in the community; and it was hence not only a species of individual moral demand which held men responsible for being responsible —for being civilized, gentle, educated, unselfish—but was expressed in institutions: the classics, poetry and art, places of learning, museums and art-galleries, as in the onward, historical flow of thought itself. The 'desire' for culture was a response to the fact that written communication and artistic communication was becoming more important at all levels of society. And, as it became more important, it became more stratified— stratified not only among the classes but between the various functions of those responsible for administering different sectors of society: men of religion, men of science, men of business. To

Matthew Arnold, the classic spokesman of the humanistic cultural ideal, the problem was to find the means of institutionalizing culture as an aspect of total social coherence, rather than as a private possession of the few. He saw three main ways of doing this. One was through the spread of education; a second was through the existence of an active cultural dialogue running through all the communications (magazines, newspapers, reviews and books) of the society; the third was through the emergence of a disinterested or non-sectarian group of aliens, responsible for cultural transmission and for the maintenance of its standards. This élite must necessarily be in a position somewhat independent of society, an intelligentsia attempting to mediate disinterestedly and variously. But it also involved the acceptance of a common stock of civilization and a validation of its value, the recognition of art and ideas as moral forces. To that end, it involved the idea of the cultural élite as that part of society which had internalized the best and most living experiences valid for all men. By these various means, then, culture could transform the material of society into a meaning, overcoming a utilitarian view of man and society, transcending the stratifications of class, the partisanships of politics, or the divisions of a religion split between established and nonconformist churches. *Its* spirit would come from the onward flow of progressive and humanistic thought in the age, the *Zeitgeist*. In fact culture was to be a kind of secular church, its ministry the educated disinterested élite, its lay orders making their devotions through education and aspiration, its message being the self-critical and most human values the society could embody and conceive. It was linked with social mobility itself; it could be transmitted through education and acquired through cultivation. But the problem is that as the attempt to convey the ideas of culture in this sense penetrates through an ever wider segment of society, it can risk attenuation; the ideals themselves can become modified, denuded or lost. Moreover, the structure of the society, and indeed its very processes of communication, can militate against it, for if culture is put to the test of the open market its success is inevitably in question.

Increasingly, in a modern society of ceaseless internal communication, deriving from a plurality of kinds of relationship,
such ideas of cultural cohesion become both more easy and more
difficult. The idea of cultural 'growth' in the humanistic sense
obviously does play a large part in modern society, and forms of
cultural prestige still exist there. Education, which in modern
democratic societies is financed on an enormous scale of provision, is the obvious case in point. But even here certain cultural
paradoxes abound. Education can cover an enormous range of
activities. Its very activities itself can be resented, either in part
or whole, by the louts in the back row. But it can also come into
question in more profound ways—even, indeed, in those sophisticated and selective cultural clearing-houses called universities,
where, today, the climate is itself one of cultural uncertainty and
division.[1] For this there are various reasons, having to do with
uncertainty about the status of ideas and values in the society. The
very plurality of modern culture draws out sharp differences
between the 'various' cultures of arts and science; the commitment to scepticism encourages not a healing but a revolutionary
view of society; the competition for cultural possession among
different groups, class, ethnic or generational—all tend to
disintegrate the 'disinterested' ideal. Perhaps also, because of the
very expansion of education and its association with social
mobility, the élites responsible for the standards of culture have
lost in social prestige. But perhaps the most significant factor of
all is that education itself has become more than ever a relative
rather than an absolute end of society. It competes for attention
with innumerable other forms of social interaction and communication—especially those forms that come under the general

[1] Even among those apostolic figures called dons. 'My students can teach me
more than I can teach them' has become a familiar cry. This involves a curious
view of education and culture; it assumes that the primary force of instruction,
in a changing world, is to be as newly born as possible. The idea of instant
culture, derived not from the internal motivations of individuals or the humanistic
inheritance, but from the historical process and the determinants of the age,
has however gained increasing ground; and I have tried in the course of this
book to suggest some reasons why. In addition, there is a tendency for the
culturally disillusioned to pin their faith in proletariat groups who manifest
not culture but cultural discontent.

heading of mass-culture and carry a much more ready appeal. Presumably we conceive that this too is our wisdom: this transmitted hail of images, this endless web of experience that makes a hole in the living-room and lets the plurality of the world in. In this sense it is much easier for people to acquire the instant culture of the day or the hour, but much harder for them to find environments in which this largely unmitigated and unassessed experience can be assessed and ordered. Education has aspirations towards doing that, but has no means of asserting any particular priority; it is simply one more form of the prevalence of expression. Here, we might say, are two distinct strata in the culture, two contrasting or contradictory functions drawing on two different constituencies. In fact, of course, it is much more feasible to see the first encapsulated or subsumed within the manifold expressive environment of the second.

What, then, seems apparent is that in the modern world the amount of cultural provision enormously increases. There are more books than ever before, and more different kinds of book. Their range is socially, historically and spatially broad. We live in an age in which techniques of mass reproduction of books, pictures and music make the funds of culture more available than ever before, to people with more money to purchase them and more leisure to attend to them. As André Malraux puts it, we live in a vast 'imaginary museum without walls'.[1] All the forms and styles of the past and the world become simultaneously available. Necessarily, then, the notion of culture as a stable body of accomplishments must decline; it is a plural fund and an ever-changing one. Likewise those élites who administer it tend in their very exposure to range and novelty to be forced to extend and explore rather than stabilize and confirm. The tendency is therefore for culture itself to be in some sense proletarianized, acquiring an objective, unlocalized and unassimilable character. It tends to become a phenomenon, to be witnessed without being internalized, assessed or related to human value. If, as I have said, culture has the double meaning of referring to individual and group accomplishments in those who achieve and possess it, and

[1] André Malraux, *The Voices of Silence* (London, 1954).

to a general and impersonal provision of society, to be taken or left alone, then culture today tends much more to the second rather than the first condition. It becomes less humanistic.

This is to say that it tends towards the character of modern communications themselves—but, paradoxically, the extension of communications is not necessarily an extention of culture. We live, of course, in an age of massive communications, centralized, concentrated, expensive, created by professionals at one end and consumed by audiences of a widely diffuse kind at the other. Such communications are basically an urban activity, created largely by people whose training is in the management of the media themselves and not in selective values. Within the large-scale welter of communication many forms of more selective communication can take place; these do have more the character of culture, but they take place as an aspect of a larger provision. Within mass-communications there are many cultures, but they are structured within abstract, distanced situations in which the providers are markedly other than the receivers, and whose special competence is in objective technological and professional skills. Mass communications may contain minority culture, but it creates its own supra-culture in offering to us all the detached, serial, bland nature of its existence as a totality. It does not necessarily deny accomplishment or creativity, or the seriousness of the arts or the ends of education; it does not necessarily attack the localized or the regional or the personal; it simply puts all these in a context which is the context of massification itself.[1] In that sort of situation, cultural stratification can be said to get broken down; provision is broadspread, and any can participate. But any intensity of participation is impossible, any individual intervention minimal; the composite culture is a montage, a vast scenario of expression against which modern man leads his life. As such, it

[1] In this, of course, there are significant distinctions to be made between media-systems primarily commercial in emphasis and those 'democratically responsible in emphasis' (e.g. American corporation television and the BBC). But such differences can be over- as well as under-estimated (Raymond Williams puts an interesting but too emphatic stress on them in *Communications* (London, 1968)). For the media have characteristic needs which produce marked similarities and global uniformities whatever the system.

ceases to embody the principles of its own selectivity, despite the fact that it may be selective within itself. Its standards of success and effectiveness become related to objective factors, like size of audience, or admiration from critics, rather than to the critical structure of the society itself. It becomes, also, much less individualistic; the frame of reference for any given communicative act is all the many others the media produce. In all these ways culture becomes much less humanistic. Indeed culture becomes much less what it actually is; it is not the meeting place of values and preferences, but the thinning out of those things to the point of suggesting that we have none. Today, when we speak of culture, we increasingly come to mean the communications processes themselves, rather than the meanings and preferences they embody: which is one reason why the word itself becomes, in modern society, problematical.

II

In the changes of the last two hundred years in society, then, our models of culture—and with those our cultural ideals—have considerably changed. At the beginning of the nineteenth century, it was reasonable to assume that the nature both of cultural stratification and cultural transmission in society was rather like a pyramid, divided into three hierarchies corresponding roughly to the three main strata in society. Culture had three levels, high, middle and low—not precisely identified with the classes, but resembling them. There were the high and serious arts, which tended to be associated with leisured and educated ideals of society, were marked with appropriate finesse and elegance, tended to represent the heroic aspect in art and were produced by and for an élite. There were the general arts of the many, conceived more for entertainment than preservation, expressing less elevated images, and marked by less refinement and finesse; and there were the folk or popular arts, which had demotic vigour but were communally funded and essentially 'low'. Such

stratifications can never be clearcut, of course; there was large
leakage movement of readers and writers through the categories;
there was percolation downward and a certain filtration upward
in the interests of novelty (as in Wordsworth's poetry)—so that
creative energy frequently derived from the interaction of the
three. Compared, though, with this 'aristocratic' model, there
was another—offered for instance by Alexis de Tocqueville in his
Democracy in America. Tocqueville visited the United States in the
early 1830s, for nine months, though his book is less a description of America than an exercise in the making of a sociological
model for a democracy. And his postulate was that in a democracy
without superfluous wealth the types and levels of art would be
much less clearly defined; that refinements of practice appealing
especially to the educated would not have high regard; that and
the arts would increase in quantity, but 'opulent and fastidious
consumers will become more scarce'. Its writers did not write for
coteries, but tested their wares in the general market; they
forwent claims to specialized powers, and rested their claim to
prestige on their general professionalism; their work was not
marked by refinement of signature and individuality of expression, but shared rather a general level of common competence.
An important aspect of the society was journalism; the book had
more limited and less extensive functions. In all this, De Tocqueville was writing about agrarian rather than modern industrial
democracy; but he saw the industrial potential in the situation,
and above all its tendency towards seriality of production. In
short, he was offering an early version of a new kind of cultural
stratification: that between an elite, but an isolated one, and a
mass culture.

   All such typifications, of course, contain a danger; in practical
experience, whether we are writers or consumers of art, we do
not know where we fall, or our works fall, within such schemes.
Indeed any single work of art may be used in many different ways
to many different ends—just as any individual may be interested
in art at various levels, or may be ignorant in some central
areas as he is specialized in others. None the less, there are
ways in which these types are telling, describing large-scale

relationships in society. Over the past 150 years, the relationships between those works of art and those accomplishments
accredited as of high value and those designated as incidental or
inferior has undergone a marked change. To some extent we have
reachieved, for things once regarded as inferior, a significant
meaning; the *kitsch* of the past, preserved, becomes art for the
present . . . as can, indeed, the *kitsch* of the present, depending
on the spirit in which it is cultivated. None the less, over these
150 years—and I have tried to suggest something of the general
texture of this movement, and its high moments (the expansion of
the press at the end of the last century, and the waves of technological innovation in communications—gramophone, radio, film,
television, which have been the main instruments of its extension) in previous pages—there has been a general drift from
something roughly like the first model to something like the
second. In other words, from a social order in which there was a
marked cultural stratification and a marked élitism at work in it,
that élitism having a great deal to do with the validation of an
humanistic art, we have moved towards a social order in which
there is a new form of cultural stratification. In this new form
high or serious literature persists, but has something of the
character of a survival from the past, or an energetic context of
specialized innovation whose forms and insights then percolate
into the larger communications of society. The expansion of the
field of communications by steady progression has brought more
and more parts of the society within the scope of its provision.
Often the new communications media tend to begin as a form of a
localized culture in the society and then to spread. So television
in England began with a predominantly middle-class audience in
the 1930s, but extended with increasing affluence to lower-
middle-class and then working-class audiences, in that process
achieving not only new species of value and reference but also
something like a logical extension of its tendency towards scale,
towards monopolizing cultural space. Like the book, then, it has
tended not to become a form of the folk or low arts, though it
possesses many of their qualities: lack of permanence, want of
individual signature, low definition, an elimination of the highs

and the lows. It is not simply, then, an extension of the old 'middle' or 'low' arts; it has become a total environment subsuming almost all the aspects of our culture, and producing as well novel and instantaneous artefacts of its own. As high culture has changed in form and nature in the modern century, so has that which we once thought lay beneath but in fact lies around and in it: mass or technological communication. As Tocqueville so early suggested, it is a cultural order founded on a quite different model.

The use of the word 'mass' to define this kind of communications and the kind of society it both expresses and in many respects *is* has been resisted by many who have written on the subject. In his book *Communications*, Raymond Williams appropriately suggests that masses are always people other than ourselves— and that the notion often involves a refusal to look selectively and qualitatively at the content and nature of mass-communications and mass-audiences. This is fair warning; indeed, as I have suggested it is the cultural complexity and inclusiveness of range of the media that constitutes an essential part of their interest and significance. In what is called popular music there are infinite qualitative distinctions to be made, and markedly different groups enfranchised; in modern cinema, where the pattern of competition *among* media has produced an erosion of audience, there is a marked drift towards its taking the form of a new species of minority art. The 'mass' media do embody many artistic aspirations on the part of their creators, especially when they are not conducted at full economic stretch; and they satisfy many selective criteria on the part of their consumers. It is the responsibility of the analyst to follow up such matters—for instance, the kind of comment made by one critic, Raymond Durgnat:

I would suggest that the key process of the century's second half will be the clash, the mutual enrichment, and partial merger of three traditions: the informality of folk oral culture (and many of its assumptions), pop idioms, and high culture complexity.[1]

[1] Raymond Durgnat, 'The Mass Media—A Highbrow Illiteracy?', *Views*, 4 (Spring 1964), pp. 49–59.

None the less, it is also true that overemphasis on the content of the media can create illusions about its true nature. It is important to recognize that it is part of social, cultural and intellectual history and tradition; it is also important to recognize the peculiar relations between form and content that prevail in it, as a result of the fact that the media are very much technological systems in themselves. 'What emerges from such industrial or semi-industrial production is obviously very different from the "works of art" of the traditional handmade type and cannot be judged in the same way,' an anonymous critic wrote in *The Times Literary Supplement* a few years ago, 'There may still be identifiable "works" of a revolutionary type, but capable of being judged in the old way, like major films; though it is not clear that this is the best way to judge them.' And he noted that what is important is not the fact that they contain qualitatively good productions, which are survivals into this industrial-technological culture,[1] but the sequence of *bad* stories, films and television episodes which create its most characteristic materials and mythologies, its atmosphere of ceaseless juxtaposition and simultaneous multiplicity, by-passing the techniques of art and proceeding directly to a heightened stylization of life.[2] As the French critic Edgar Morin has stressed, the mass communications have their own ways of image-making, their own peculiar types of myth, their own languages and codes, their own species of approach and relationship to audience and environment, their own modes of fantasizing, their own species of polymorphous culture.[3]

One startling tendency of mass-culture is its tendency to 'modernize' men by drawing them into its fantastic and relatively

---

[1] The critics who have most valuably raised questions about the quality of the mass-arts and the possibilities of startling variation within it are Richard Hoggart, *The Uses of Literacy* (London, 1957) and *Speaking to Each Other* (2 vols.) (London, 1970), and Stuart Hall and Paddy Whannel, *The Popular Arts* (London, 1964).

[2] (Anon.), 'Pop Goes the Artist', *Times Literary Supplement*, 3277 (December 17, 1964).

[3] Edgar Morin, *New Trends in the Study of Mass Communications* (Birmingham, 1968).

standardless world.[1] It is an urban, industrial and also an inclusive kind of art, forcing itself on attention whether we want it or not, present in hotel bedrooms and lounges, reaching into innumerable corners of our environment. Its urbanism shows as a kind of perpetual sophistication and fashion-consciousness which forms our general views of society and history. Its industrialism shows in the fact that it develops essentially by technological momentum, of which any artistic consequences are simply a by-product. Its advances lie in new systems of transmission, tending to increase coverage, amount of presentation and its global range; and new arts of presentation which increasingly acquire the capacity to replace traditional personal creation in the way that the photograph replaced and isolated painting.[2] They are an expanding technology, requiring an optimum and rationalistic use of the plant, to the maximum productivity of their resources. They expand into as much time as possible, and fill as much social space as possible. (One of the startling discoveries resulting from the onset of commercial television in Britain was that there was nothing to stop its existence. Many people predicted that the writers, producers and artists necessary could never be found to operate its structure, duplicate to that of the BBC: they were found at once.) In this they are like the modern factory, their nature being serial; they consist of spaces that must be filled— whether there is anything to fill them or not. The newspaper must appear every day, whether there is significant news or not; so 'news' becomes that which fills newspapers. The hours of television are an expensive appropriation of airtime, whether

[1] On this see Harold L. Wilensky's important paper, 'High Culture and Mass Culture', *New Society* (May 14, 1964), which points out that there is an inherent tendency in the media to draw almost everyone within its purview, so that active discouragement is created towards developing more selective or highbrow tastes, even among those portions of the population who possess the traditions, education or intelligence to do so. These findings have been disputed, but mainly on the grounds that the cultural stratification is too precise.

[2] The article 'Pop Goes the Artist', cited above, notes this and also the tendency towards dissolving individual production into collectives, dominated by a director or manager, breaking up the creative process into specialized segments.

there is worthwhile material to present or not.[1] The technology exists prior to its content, and influences independently of its content. The media are bureaucratic because they are essentially institutions, developing in ways appropriate to such (whether they be the law or a Hollywood studio, the church, a university or a television system). Their instinct is to expand and, in expanding, to proliferate administration, rationalize accounting, replace any smaller competing institutions, thrive on conglomerate technology, and obtain a larger social existence than that of the community of those who produce it. No one is responsible for them; they bureaucratize their own participants. They are centralized and concentrated, therefore; the press, for instance, provides less range for more readers, reducing the variety of 'cultures', and it tends, like most of the media, to use the capital city as the filter through which all the experience of the nation must pass. In all these ways, the media tend to provide deep-seated encouragement to the patterns of modern social change: towards conglomeration, centralization and concentration, towards a lack of social variety. They do so not simply by reporting it but enacting it; they are not simply communicators of what is already there, but are creators of what is there. They are our eyes and ears providing the world we see, hear and take as real; and the world they manifest is that of modern industrial democracy itself.

It is, of course, on technological democracy that they depend; as sociologists have noted, the primary conditions of their existence are those of a free, industrial, centralized society, where the media can develop technically, approach the public on their own terms, and acquire large audiences which are of sufficiently heterogeneous composition to permit consensus, and which are capable of acquiring the character of 'a collectivity unique to modern society'—in that they consist of independent persons in no way in contact with one another 'engaging in an identical form

[1] For some interesting illumination of this, see Daniel Boorstin, *The Image* (New York and London, 1961). And H. G. Wells has some fascinating comments on the use of the banner headline in the First World War, whether the news warranted it or not, in *Mr. Britling Sees It Through* (1916).

of behaviour, and open to activation towards common ends'.[1] In addition they also tend to depend on the 'instantaneousness' of a modern society, its concern with itself at the immediate historical instant, its willingness to yield to fashion and mood. In short, the mass media are a cultural expression in, and a cultural influence upon, a certain kind of society, which is mass-society. They can, then, be represented as an achievement of a new type of community through communications: 'There are, within mass society,' says Edward Shils, 'more of a sense of attachment to society as a whole, more sense of affinity with one's fellows, more openness to understanding and more reaching out of understanding among men than in any earlier society of our Western history . . . The mass society has gone further in the creation of a common culture than any previous society.'[2] Such a society can evoke a high degree of intellectual involvement and integration.[3] On the other hand, it can be represented as the opposite: a form of *ersatz* community, with *ersatz* expression, in which no one accepts responsibility for values, and in which genuine cultural bonds are weakened progressively while nothing worthy and binding is put in their place.[4] By the first version, culture is something that everyone participates in, adding to the total contribution in the common fund; the forms of mass culture are an available means. By the second, existence only constitutes membership of culture, and hence we have hardly a culture at all—rather a non-culture of which mass communications are the expression. (There is a third, usually Marxist, version which argues that the common culture is the as yet unachieved dream to come in some happy post-historical situation.) The truth lies somewhere between these extremes as far as mass-culture itself—our expression, and our

[1] Denis McQuail, *Towards a Sociology of Mass Communications* (London, 1969). See also Charles R. Wright, *Mass Communication: A Sociological Perspective* (New York, 1959).

[2] Edward Shils, 'The Theory of Mass Society', reprinted in *America as a Mass Society*, ed. Philip Olson (Glencoe, Ill., and London, 1963).

[3] Such as is shown by T. R. Fyvel's reports in *Intellectuals Today* (London, 1968).

[4] Philip Selznick, 'Institutional Vulnerability in Mass Society', reprinted in *America as a Mass Society*, cited above.

insidious environment—is concerned. We do need to analyse its content, its inner complexities, its capacities for significant or shoddy expression, its capacity to innovate or explore significant values and standards, its instinct towards art; we need to recognize the way it is subject to our control. In England, for instance, it represents many aspects of that cohesiveness of the nation that surprises many foreigners, giving it a human dimension. But we also need to see that in many respects it is a medium that is the message, a prototypical technology which, whatever the proportion of serious programmes and high cultural content, remains both bland in character and deeply influential in force, not by its particular penetration but by the generalized environment it provides.

At the start of this book I looked at the nature of modernization, and the kind of world and the kind of men it created; it now remains to say that in a deep sense it is these mass arts, which have been developing over the century towards a greater concentration, distillation and power, that represent the most direct and significant 'art' and 'culture' of the modern world. To understand the character of the modern arts, we need to recognize behind them that vast expansion of expressive resources which has taken place in the wider society over the period dealt with in this book. We have to reckon with what it has meant that, between 1850 and 1900, with the 'Northcliffe Revolution,' the number of adult newspaper readers rose from one in eighty of the population to one in five or six; that by 1939 the cinema audience in Britain was nineteen million people a week, and more than half as much again by the end of the war; that between 1936 and the present, the number of homes possessing television rose from a tiny few to, in the 1950s, more than 90% of the population, watching television about 2½ hours every day. We have to reckon, likewise, with what it means when television becomes accepted as a normal and necessary feature of everyone's environment. This expansion of cultural expression and interaction through the media, which has given modern man new points of reference, new courts of appeal, new views of his closeness to and distance from the social centres, new measures of purpose, new types of

T

consciousness, has gone on steadily during the century, but a special distillation occurs with print in the late nineteenth century and with other media in the 1950s, when affluence broadly spread made possible general expenditure on the technology of radio, record-players and television sets which permitted the bulk penetration of these forms of cultural expression into people's personal lives.[1] Behind the growth of the 'popular arts' has been a wealth of social and economic energy which has in effect displaced the traditional arts. As Raymond Williams has said, the new arts are in some sense a human expansion and we may suppose that their world will remain in part a human world.[2] But, precisely because they are not entirely a human world, they are also less than arts. It is the selectivity, the complexity, the fineness of definition, the personalization of genuine art that carries the essentially human aspect of culture. In part the theme of the serious arts has been the internal erosion of that essentially human aspect; and the internal crisis to its own nature has been one reason for their strained complexity. But another has been the surrounding presence of the profuse popular arts, penetrating and changing not only the conditions of art but the content too. The social context of modern writing has been the struggle of the serious arts not simply for form and insight into modern experience, but for meaningful existence; and with that struggle the selective and creative aspects of culture, as a personal and as a social matter, seem to be tightly bound.

[1] In this respect, English social change for once clearly moved faster than did the American; the same revolution in the United States, the home of the mass media and a profound source of its styles, took place over a longer span, beginning in the 1920s, when for the first time America seems to become a 'media-oriented' society.

[2] Raymond Williams, *Communications*, cited above.

Conclusion

I began this book by talking about some of the similarities between literary and sociological study. In the course of it, I have said something about the divergences between them. I want to conclude by discussing some of the differences. It is obvious that these differences derive from an activity which has always been considered a part of literary criticism but not of most subjects with a scientific bent: evaluation. Inevitably enough, this is the most contentious area of critical activity. T. S. Eliot once proposed an ideal of criticism as 'the common pursuit of true judgment', though he doubted whether it could ever be attained. Yet it is one persistently there: in the selection of texts for study; in the feeling of relevance and representativeness which makes certain bodies of work, certain traditions of writers, seem essential; in our general tests of success and failure. And in making evaluative judgments we reach out into large-scale cultural preferences; for if we are to read literature sympathetically, to be engaged with the central forces of creativity and persuasion in it, then we will tend to acquire a view of human need, a sense of relevance in human experience, which is particularly literary. Partly this comes from the individuality, the concern with lived life, the responsiveness to experience and the intense creation of experience, which is an attribute of any particular literary work: poem, novel or play. And partly it has to do with the way the tradition of literature tends to accrete to itself certain broader values, forms of belief and of knowledge, which encourage us to see the literary intelligence as in some ways a distinct, special and illuminating intelligence.

In this book I have said enough about the difficulties of literature in the modern and the modernizing world to make the uninformed reader wonder whether it is possible that we should have had a modern literature at all. Yet, if we look back over the last hundred years of the English literary tradition from our present vantage point, we will find behind us what I think to be a great age of literature, amazingly rich and expressive, exercising the profoundest resources of artistic form and self-consciousness, cutting deep into experience, and engaging our deepest sympathies and involvements. Many of its figures are major on any scale—one might name Lawrence, Yeats, Joyce, Conrad, Forster, Eliot and Beckett, and perhaps a little less confidently Virginia Woolf, H. G. Wells, W. H. Auden, Evelyn Waugh and George Orwell—and many more are writers of great qualitative significance (to list them would be long and boring). What is more, as I have been arguing, it has been a remarkably plural and various literature, deriving from many different cultural sources, embodying many different kinds of vision, conceiving of the very nature of art in different ways. It is not easy to find a consistent pattern of themes and perspectives in it, and I am conscious that—despite having resisted the temptation considerably—I have been decidedly too neat in labelling styles and forming groups. Its achievement is the more curious and ambiguous because it has been, as I have said, a literature that has deeply embodied its own uncertainty as literature, frequently structuring itself self-critically and sceptically, expanding but at the same time decreasing its own form. Frank Kermode has spoken of this as an aspect of literature's 'clerkly scepticism',[1] and the phrase is illuminating, because it carries the implication that, while literature operates under certain contextual and historical necessities, and falls into certain stylistic and mythological communities, it contains within itself, and interests us by, the perpetual possibilities that the writer has, in making his work, to assert his own freedom. Literature may be historical; but there is nothing in literature that is, in an absolute sense, historically necessary. If we as readers think so, we think so after the event—after the writer has closed off one aspect of his freedom by closing off his book.

Yet major and various as it is (and the more major for being so

[1] Frank Kermode, *The Sense of an Ending*, cited above.

various), modern literature does contain certain features that
mark it as something like a consecutive literary perspective on
modern experience. I am not now talking about its stylistic
community, which has already been dealt with, but something
else. For, as I have implied throughout, one of the things that
has marked the great works of our literature is that they embody
a vision of their culture. In a deep, realized way, culture is very
much what they are about—or the state of the nation, or the
quality of prevailing life. And if there is a 'modern' view of
culture in the English literary tradition, we will need to reach
it by going beyond the arguments about it—T. S. Eliot's *Notes
Toward the Definition of Culture*, F. R. Leavis's *The Common Pursuit*
or *Education and the University*, Raymond Williams's *Culture and
Society*, say—and into the imaginative works that lie behind them.
For works like Hardy's *Jude the Obscure*, Forster's *Howards End*,
Lawrence's *The Rainbow*, Joyce's *Ulysses*, Eliot's 'The Waste Land',
Pound's 'Hugh Selwyn Mauberley', the bulk of Auden's 1930s
poetry, George Orwell's *Keep the Aspidistra Flying*, Angus Wilson's
Late Call, or Nigel Dennis's *Cards of Identity*—all these are works
about the state of the nation, the feel of society, the texture of
human order, and the place of the individual; they have society
as their theme, as a moral theme, and they concern themselves
as participants with the scale of modern history. But of course
they do so in the light of possibilities determined by a creative
and artistic preference—which is to say that they are more than
an individual's subjective response, but are a creative response.
They are not histories but fictions, and acquire their special
quality from what a fiction is. Today writers are constantly urged
towards commitment, which usually means direct identification
with some prevailing political ideological system, more often than
not on the left. Such systems are often the selfish vulgate myths—
more and more in our time myths enacted in violence—of
sectors in the society who, seeing the historical process as the
only thing that matters, seek in the long or short run to monopolize it. In short, they have little to do with the free run of ideas;
indeed it becomes the case that you monopolize history through
ideas, by selectively describing it. Now in two senses literature

seems to me a different and an alternative language. The first
is that in literature ideas are no longer quite ideas; they become
a part of a differently realized world of experience, in which
ideas are related to linguistic enactments and to speakers, and in
which the force of language is never wholly rational—as Yeats
suggested, when he asked to be guarded from 'those thoughts
Men think in the mind alone'.[1] The second is the part played in
literature by that 'clerkly scepticism' Kermode speaks of—
which is the power of individual artists to personalize, reinterpret or create myth. Lionel Trilling speaks about another aspect
of the same thing when he notes the importance in much of our
modern literature of a 'moral realism'—which is a sense of the
contradictions, paradoxes and dangers of living the assertive
moral life.[2] In modern literature, in fact, there has been an
important ideal of the artist's experiencing the range of the culture and embodying its contradictions as a form of internal
'tension' or 'ambiguity'. And it is precisely this double ambiguity
of literature that seems to me to constitute an essential feature
of literature's openness and hence in a sense its a-historicism.

Another way of saying this is to say that the only real commitment that good art can have finally is to art itself. Writers, of
course, may commit themselves politically; but their literary
motivation must, if they are serious writers, finally predominate
over their political one when it comes to a declaration of interest.
This, to come back to Matthew Arnold's word, is 'disinterestedness', and it is perhaps partly a conditioned aspect of a kind of
artistic independence only possible after the disappearance of
the patron and the appearance of a cultural dialogue independently
placed in society. But the major art of the past 150 years undoubtedly comes out of this spirit; and it is likely, to say the least, that
writers and critics will have some sort of vested interest in it.
The view that writers take of society—and it would appear to be
highly probable that by virtue of being writers they should take a

[1] There is an excellent discussion of the ways in which literature can be said
to embody ideas in Lionel Trilling's essay 'The Meaning of a Literary Idea', in
The Liberal Imagination (New York and London, 1950).
[2] Lionel Trilling, 'Manners, Morals, and the Novel', in ibid.

view—seems to me, then, one that is likely to come not primarily from political judgments or sociological judgments, but from judgments having to do with art and the kind of values of felt independence and individuality it embodies. It embodies these by feeling across the range and variety of the culture, but also through its relation to a whole tradition of such experiences built up in the art of the past. This means that it has its own ways of measuring the standards of human worth, and they are in no sense fixed ways or totally consistent in all writers; but they do involve at best a way of knowing particularly well placed to speak to questions about the quality of life. Now the view that art stands against politics or history, and that its sympathies and priorities do constitute a fund to measure society against, seems to have got displaced lately, in a world in which the liberal and humane virtues close to much art, if not to all, have become not only socially but intellectually at risk. And that in itself is a form of cultural attenuation such as, in my view, modern literature has been persistently aware of, critical of, and shaken by.

At any rate, if we are to assess the significance of the complex pattern of relationship and dissent that exists between modernity in society and in literature, we need to reckon with it not just as a series of responses to conditions literary or social, nor as a retreat from reality into an ivory tower of art, but as a cultural vision. For anyone who thinks of himself as a writer is bound, as part of his own capacity and competence to write, to have a view of the possibilities and limitations of his culture. I have tried here to suggest some of the practical dimensions of that exploration, and suggest some of the literary forms it takes; but one has only to turn back to these writers and their books to see it more liberally, as its own fullest self-illumination and its own best account of modern 'reality'. To do that is to begin being a critic and writer oneself again, and out of those commitments and sympathies to feel all the qualitative doubts and uncertainties about one's times and culture that seem to me a part of seeing experience through a literary perspective.

Now if it is true that the literary perspective is a good deal less sure than it used to be, then one of the temptations for the modern reader is to distance literary creation by placing it within a frame—one which objectifies it, sociologizes it. It is indeed a likely consequence of the sceptical, rational and secular spirit of 'modernity' as I have described it that it should doubt the competence of any artistic fiction to contain or encompass 'reality', while at the same time also distrusting the hermetic privacy of the work of art, its claim to be completely and unconditionally itself. These challenges have, as I have been arguing, been felt by modern artists—and indeed have been embodied within much of modern art to the point of representing an element of auto-destruction in it. My aim in this book has been to consider the ecology of modern writing in England, and to explore it, at various levels and in various dimensions, as a difficult and a challenging environment, potentially a threatening environment. And to a considerable extent the conditions about which I have been talking will inevitably shape all cultural action. But they will not, ultimately, confine or imprison it; nor will an account such as the present one serve as a total or thorough-going explanation of what that action is in its most creative aspects. In a book like the present one, then, it is right that I should end by suggesting as briefly as possible the relationship that I see existing between any contextual awareness we may bring to literature and the active internal existence of works of art, which gives them their force, value and asethetic dimension. This is the ultimate crux in any attempt at a sociology of literature, and one that in my view will not be solved if we think of a sociological definition—a definition derived primarily from perceiving society first and man in it second—as an ultimate or total version of men and what they create. It is right, then, that, with whatever awareness we have accrued from looking at the literary ecology, we should pass into another form of criticism and analysis, much more internal, much more dense, much more precise about the creative embodiment of the single text. In doing that, we pass over a boundary into other emphases and other forms of knowledge, into a world in which the essential terms are laid down by the creativity of writers themselves. That will, I hope, take the present reader back into the literary texts; and the present writer into other books than this one.

Select Bibliography

(NOTE: In view of the fact that this book is concerned with a high productive period of English literature (1870 to the present) and touches on several disciplines, a bibliography, to be useful, must necessarily be selective. This bibliography has been sectionalized to suggest different lines of approach; and it is intended to be a guide to further reading in the areas covered by the book. Detailed bibliographies on particular aspects of discussion have been provided *passim* as footnotes to the text, and can be traced from the index.)

I. LITERATURE AND SOCIETY

On the general topic of the RELATIONSHIP BETWEEN LITERATURE, LITERARY STUDY AND SOCIETY, see F. R. Leavis, 'Literature and Society' and 'Sociology and Literature' in *The Common Pursuit* (London, 1952); Richard Hoggart, 'Literature and Society' and other essays in *Speaking to Each Other* (London, 2 vols., 1970); Rene Wellek and Austin Warren, *The Theory of Literature* (New York, 1949; London, 1963); and Malcolm Bradbury, 'Literature and Sociology', *Essays and Studies: 1970*, ed. A. R. Humphreys (London, 1970). For more theoretical approaches, see Alan Shuttleworth, *Two Working Papers in Cultural Studies* (Birmingham, 1966); Roland Escarpit, *Sociology of Literature* (Painesville, Ohio, 1965); and the essays in *The International Social Science Journal*, XIX, 4 (1967), especially those by Jacques Leenhardt, 'The Sociology of Literature: Some Stages in Its History' and Lucien Goldmann, 'The Sociology of Literature: Status and Problems of Method'. Works of literary criticism with a sociological emphasis include Ian Watt, *The Rise of the Novel* (London, 1947); Diana

Spearman, *The Novel and Society* (London 1966); Harry Levin, *The Gates of Horn: A Study of Five French Realists* (New York/ London, 1963); L. C. Knights, *Drama and Society in the Age of Jonson* (London, 1937); and Georg Lukacs, *The Historical Novel* (London, 1962) and other works. Many works of literary history— for instance, Richard D. Altick, *The English Common Reader: A Social History of the Mass Reading Public, 1800–1900* (Chicago, 1957)—draw on sociological method and insight. On the specific relationship between MODERN LITERATURE (AND/OR MODERN ART) AND MODERN SOCIETY, see Roland Barthes, *Writing Degree Zero* (London, 1967); Raymond Williams, *The Long Revolution* (London, 1961); Herbert Read, *Collected Essays in Literary Criticism* (London, 1951) (American title: *The Nature of Literature* (New York, 1956)); Edwin Muir, *The Present Age from 1914* (London, 1939); Martin Turnell, *Poetry and Crisis* (London, 1938); Christopher Caudwell, *Illusion and Reality* (London, 1937); G. S. Fraser, *The Modern Writer and His World* (London, 1953); Lucien Goldmann, *The Hidden God* (London, 1964); Arnold Hauser, *The Social History of Art* (New York, 4 vols., 1951; new ed., London, 1963); Ernest Fischer, *The Necessity of Art* (London, 1963); etc.

Important WORKS OF SOCIOLOGY WITH A LITERARY OR A 'CULTURAL' EMPHASIS include Leo Lowenthal, *Literature and the Image of Man* (Boston, Mass., 1957); Karl Mannheim, *Essays on the Sociology of Culture* (London, 1956); Robert N. Wilson, *The Arts in Society* (Englewood Cliffs, N.J., 1964); and Cesar Grana, *Bohemian Versus Bourgeois: French Society and the French Man of Letters in the 19th Century* (New York/London, 1964). Also see F. Znaniecki, *The Social Role of the Man of Knowledge* (New York, 1940); Karl Mannheim, *Ideology and Utopia* (London, 1936); Peter Berger and G. Luckman, *The Social Construction of Reality* (London, 1967); Erving Goffman, *The Presentation of Self in Everyday Life* (New York, 1959; London, 1969); and *The Intellectuals; A Controversial Portrait*, ed. G. B. de Huszar (Glencoe, Ill., 1960).

On CULTURE, works with literary-cum-sociological per- spectives include Leo Lowenthal, *Literature, Popular Culture, and*

Society (Englewood Cliffs, N.J., 1961); T. S. Eliot, *Notes Towards the Definition of Culture* (London, 1948); and Raymond Williams, *Culture and Society: 1780–1950* (London, 1958). On MASS-CULTURE, POPULAR CULTURE, and FOLK-CULTURE, see *Mass Culture: The Popular Arts in America*, ed. David Manning White and Bernard Rosenberg (Glencoe, Ill., 1957); *Mass Leisure*, ed. Eric Larrabee and Rolf Meyersohn (Glencoe, Ill., 1960); Stuart Hall and Paddy Whannell, *The Popular Arts* (London, 1954); Jeff Nuttall, *Bomb Culture* (London, 1968); George Melly, *Revolt Into Style* (London, 1970); Charles R. Wright, *Mass Communication: A Sociological Perspective* (New York, 1959); Denis McQuail, *Towards a Sociology of Mass Communications* (London, 1969); Marshall McLuhan, *Understanding Media: The Extensions of Man* (New York/London, 1964); Harold L. Wilensky, 'High Culture and Mass Culture', *New Society* (14 May 1964); Robert Warshow, *The Immediate Experience: Movies, Comics, Theatres and Other Aspects of Popular Culture* (New York, 1964); Joseph T. Klapper, *The Effects of Mass Media* (New York, 1950); etc.

2. MODERN SOCIAL CHANGE,
THE PSYCHOLOGY OF MODERN MAN

The sociological literature on SOCIAL CHANGE is enormous; the reader is referred to the bibliography in R. M. McIver and Charles H. Page, *Society: An Introductory Analysis* (London, 1950), for one convenient but dated listing; and to Wilbert E. Moore, *Social Change* (Englewood Cliffs, N.J., 1963), for a brief survey. For further perspectives see P. A. Sorokin, *Social Philosophies in an Age of Crisis* (Boston, 1950); *Social Change: Sources, Patterns, Consequences*, ed. E. and A. Etzioni (New York, 1964); and B. Hoselitz and W. E. Moore, *Industrialization and Society* (Paris, 1963). On the impact of SCIENCE AND SECULARIZATION, see A. N. Whitehead, *Science and the Modern World* (Cambridge, 1926); Bertrand Russell, *The Scientific Outlook* (London, 1931); Will Herberg, *Protestant, Catholic, Jew* (New York, 1955); B. R. Wilson, *Religion in Secular Society* (London, 1966), and

Alasdair MacIntyre, *Secularization and Moral Change* (Oxford, 1967). On MECHANIZATION in the modern world, see especially Siegfried Giedion, *Mechanization Takes Command* (New York, 1948); Elting E. Morison, *Men, Machines and Modern Times* (Cambridge, Mass., 1966); *Technological Innovation and Society*, ed. D. Morse and A. W. Warner (New York, 1966); Jacques Ellul, *The Technological Society* (New York, 1967); and Lewis Mumford, *The Myth of the Machine: Technics and Human Development* (New York, 1968). On URBANIZATION, see especially Lewis Mumford, *The City in History* (New York/London, 1961); Asa Briggs, *Victorian Cities* (London, 1963); Louis Wirth, 'Urbanism as a Way of Life', in *American Journal of Sociology*, 44 (1938), pp. 1–24, reprinted in Wirth, *On Cities and Social Life*, ed. A. J. Reiss (Chicago, 1964); and R. E. Pahl, *Patterns of Urban Life* (London, 1970). On INNOVATION generally, see Homer G. Barnett, *Innovation: The Basis of Cultural Change* (New York, 1953).

On THE PSYCHOLOGY OF MODERN MAN, classic works include Sigmund Freud, *Civilization and Its Discontents* (London, 1930; New York, 1948), etc.; C. G. Jung, *Modern Man in Search of a Soul* (London, 1933); and Albert Camus, *The Rebel: An Essay on Man in Revolt* (New York, 1958; London, 1960). Norman O. Brown, *Life Against Death* (Middletown, Conn./London, 1959) and Herbert Marcuse, *One-Dimensional Man: Studies in the Ideology of Advanced Industrial Society* (Boston/London, 1964) offer fashionable modern versions. Also see Philip Rieff, *The Triumph of the Therapeutic* (New York/London, 1966); William Barrett, *Irrational Man: A Study in Existential Philosophy* (New York, 1958; London, 1961) and *Identity and Anxiety: Survival of the Person in Modern Society*, ed. M. R. Stein, A. J. Vidich and D. M. White (Glencoe, Ill., 1960).

3. MODERNITY AND MODERN STYLE IN LITERATURE

On MODERN CONSCIOUSNESS IN LITERATURE, there is an excellent anthology of primary texts, *The Modern Tradition: Backgrounds of Modern Literature*, ed. Richard Ellmann and Charles Fiedelson, Jr. (New York/London, 1965) and one of critical commentaries on modern literature, *The Idea of the Modern in Literature and the Arts*, ed. Irving Howe (New York, 1967) (paperback ed.; *Literary Modernism* (Greenwich, Conn., 1967)). The best discussions of modernism in literature and other arts occur in Ortega y Gasset, *The Dehumanization of Art and Other Writings* (New York, 1956); Harold Rosenberg, *The Tradition of the New* (New York, 1959); Lionel Trilling, *Beyond Culture: Essays on Literature and Learning* (New York/London, 1966); Harry Levin, *Refractions: Essays in Comparative Literature* (New York/London, 1966); Frank Kermode, *Continuities* (London/New York, 1969) and *The Sense of an Ending* (New York/London, 1967); *Innovations: Essays on Art and Ideas*, ed. Bernard Bergonzi (London, 1968); Wylie Sypher, *Rococo to Cubism in Art and Literature* (New York, 1960); Stephen Spender, *The Struggle of the Modern* (London, 1963); Northrop Frye, *The Modern Century* (Toronto, 1967); and Louis Kampf, *On Modernism: The Prospects for Literature and Freedom* (Boston, Mass., 1967).

4. MODERN SOCIAL CHANGE IN BRITAIN

For different aspects of the response to MODERNIZATION, see Asa Briggs, *Victorian Cities* (London, 1964); K. S. Inglis, *Churches and Working Class in Victorian England* (London, 1963); E. J. Hobsbawm, *Industry and Empire* (London, 1968); D. C. Marsh, *The Changing Social Structure of England and Wales: 1871–1951* (London, 1958); T. G. Williams, *The Main Currents of Social and Industrial Change: 1870–1924* (London, 1925); Henry Pelling, *The Origins of the Labour Party* (London, 1954); G. Kitson Clark, *The Making of Victorian England* (London, 1962); Peter Mathias, *The First Industrial Nation* (London, 1969); and Arthur Marwick, *Britain in the Century of Total War* (London, 1970). Also see Josephine Klein, *Samples of English Culture* (London, 1965), and Reyner Banham, *Theory and Design in the First Machine Age* (London, 1959). On the intellectual texture of the turn-of-the-century period, see G. F. Dangerfield, *The Strange Death of Liberal England* (London, 1936); Noel Annan, *The Strange Strength of Positivism in English Political Thought* (Oxford, 1959); Samuel

Hynes, *The Edwardian Turn of Mind* (Princeton/London, 1968); and Wallace Martin, *The New Age Under Orage: Chapters in English Cultural History* (Manchester/New York, 1967). For contemporary documents of this period, see amongst others 'George Bourne', *Change in the Village* (London, 1912); C. F. Masterman, *The Condition of England* (London, 1909); Beatrice Webb, *My Apprenticeship* (London, 1926); Hilaire Belloc, *The Servile State* (London, 1912) and L. T. Hobhouse, *Liberalism* (London, 1911; New York, Galaxy Books, 1964)—all of which can be read suggestively against some of the literature especially conscious of the tendencies toward urbanization, rationalization and secularization (e.g. Samuel Butler, *Erewhon* (1872), George Gissing, *Demos* (1886); Thomas Hardy, *Tess of the D'Urbervilles* (1891); G. B. Shaw, *Man and Superman* (1903); H. G. Wells, *Tono-Bungay* (1909); Joseph Conrad, *The Secret Agent* (1907); and E. M. Forster, *Howards End* (1910)).

For the impact of THE WAR, see Robert Graves, *Goodbye to All That* (London, 1930); Siegfried Sassoon, *Memoirs of an Infantry Officer* (London, 1930); and E. Wingfield-Stratford, *The Harvest of Victory: 1918–1926* (London, 1935). On THE INTERWAR PERIOD, see Robert Graves and Alan Hodges, *The Long Weekend: A Social History of Great Britain, 1918–1939* (London, 1940); Lionel Robbins, *The Great Depression* (London, 1934); C. L. Mowat, *Britain Between the Wars* (London, 1956); J. L. Hammond, *The Growth of Common Enjoyment* (London, 1933); F. R. Leavis and Denys Thompson, *Culture and Environment* (London, 1933); and Malcolm Muggeridge, *The Thirties* (London, rev. ed., 1967). On THE POSTWAR PERIOD, R. Titmuss, *Essays on the Welfare State* (London, 1958); Kenneth Allsopp, *The Angry Decade* (London, 1958); and *Declaration*, ed. Tom Maschler (London, 1957) are evocative works. Among important memoirs are George Orwell, *The Road to Wigan Pier* (London, 1937); Stephen Spender, *World Within World* (London, 1951); Richard Hoggart, *The Uses of Literacy* (London, 1957); and John Wain, *Sprightly Running* (London, 1962).

5. MODEN ENGLISH LITERATURE

The following GENERAL SURVEYS of modern English literature are especially worth noting: G. S. Fraser, *The Modern Writer and His World* (London, 1953); William York Tindall, *Forces in Modern British Literature: 1885–1946* (New York, 1947); H. V. Routh, *English Literature and Ideas in the Twentieth Century* (London, 1946); Graham Hough, *Image and Experience* (London, 1960); and J. Isaacs, *An Assessment of Twentieth Century Literature* (London, 1951). On particular genres, see David Daiches, *Poetry and the Modern World: A Study of Poetry in England, 1900–39* (Chicago, 1940); F. R. Leavis, *New Bearings in English Poetry* (London, rev. ed., 1950); Louis MacNeice, *Modern Poetry: A Personal Essay* (Oxford, 1938); and V. de Sola Pinto, *Crisis in English Poetry* (London, 1951). David Daiches, *The Novel and the Modern World* (Cambridge, rev. ed., 1960); Frederick J. Karl and Marvin Magalaner, *A Reader's Guide to Great Twentieth Century English Novels* (New York, 1959; London, 1968); Frederick J. Karl, *A Reader's Guide to the Contemporary English Novel* (New York, 1959; London, 1963); Walter Allen, *The English Novel* (London, 1954) and *Tradition and Dream: The English Novel from the Twenties* (London, 1964); Leon Edel, *The Psychological Novel: 1900–1950* (New York/London, 1955); Alex Comfort, *The Novel and Our Times* (London, 1948); F. R. Leavis, *The Great Tradition* (London, 1948); Raymond Williams, *The English Novel from Dickens to Lawrence* (London, 1970); Alan J. Friedman, *The Turn of the Novel* (New York/London, 1966). Raymond Williams, *Drama from Ibsen to Brecht* (London, 1968); Denis Donaghue, *The Third Voice: Modern British and American Verse Drama* (Princeton, 1958); and *Modern British Dramatists*, ed. John Russell Brown (Englewood Cliffs, N.J., 1968). For more contemporary developments, see especially John Russell Taylor, *Anger and After* (London, 1963); Rubin Rubinovitz, *The Reaction Against Experiment in the English Novel: 1950–1960* (New York/London, 1967); and *On Contemporary Literature*, ed. R. Kostelanetz (New York, 1964).

For supplementary BIBLIOGRAPHICAL LISTINGS, consult the

large bibliographical section in *The Pelican Guide to English Literature: Vol VI (Dickens to Hardy)* (London, 1959) and *Vol. VII (The Modern Age)* (London, 1961), both ed. Boris Ford; that in E. Batho and B. Dobree, *The Victorians and After: 1830–1914* (London, rev. ed., 1969); and the recurrent bibliographies in *English Literature in Transition, Twentieth Century Literature, PMLA* and *The Year's Work in English Studies.*

Index

U